REACHING
THE VOTER

This is Volume 20 in a series of studies commissioned as part of the research program of the Royal Commission on Electoral Reform and Party Financing

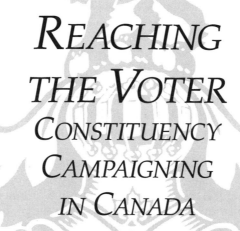

REACHING THE VOTER
CONSTITUENCY CAMPAIGNING IN CANADA

~

David V.J. Bell
Frederick J. Fletcher
Editors

Volume 20 of the Research Studies

ROYAL COMMISSION ON ELECTORAL REFORM
AND PARTY FINANCING
AND CANADA COMMUNICATION GROUP –
PUBLISHING, SUPPLY AND SERVICES CANADA

DUNDURN PRESS
TORONTO AND OXFORD

© Minister of Supply and Services Canada, 1991
Printed and bound in Canada
ISBN 1-55002-116-8
ISSN 1188-2743
Catalogue No. Z1-1989/2-41-20E

Published by Dundurn Press Limited in cooperation with the Royal
Commission on Electoral Reform and Party Financing and Canada
Communication Group – Publishing, Supply and Services Canada.

Canadian Cataloguing in Publication Data

Main entry under title:
Reaching the voter

(Research studies ; 20)
Issued also in French under title: La Communication avec l'électeur.
ISBN 1-55002-116-8

  1. Campaign management – Canada. 2. Communication in politics –
Canada. 3. Political psychology. 4. Electioneering – Canada. 5. Election
districts – Canada. I. Bell, David V.J., 1944 – . II. Fletcher, Frederick J.
III. Canada. Royal Commission on Electoral Reform and Party Financing.
IV. Series: Research studies (Canada. Royal Commission on Electoral Reform
and Party Financing) ; 20.

JL193.R42 1991   324.7'0971   C91-090532-0

Dundurn Press Limited
2181 Queen Street East
Suite 301
Toronto, Canada
M4E 1E5

Dundurn Distribution
73 Lime Walk
Headington
Oxford, England
OX3 7AD

CONTENTS

FIGURES

TABLES

3. THE CAMPAIGN–MEDIA INTERFACE IN LOCAL CONSTITUENCIES: TWO ALBERTA CASE STUDIES FROM THE 1988 FEDERAL ELECTION CAMPAIGN

4. THE MASS MEDIA AND FEDERAL ELECTION CAMPAIGNING AT THE LOCAL LEVEL: A CASE STUDY OF TWO ONTARIO CONSTITUENCIES

FOREWORD

THE ROYAL COMMISSION on Electoral Reform and Party Financing was established in November 1989. Our mandate was to inquire into and report on the appropriate principles and process that should govern the election of members of the House of Commons and the financing of political parties and candidates' campaigns. To conduct such a comprehensive examination of Canada's electoral system, we held extensive public consultations and developed a research program designed to ensure that our recommendations would be guided by an independent foundation of empirical inquiry and analysis.

The Commission's in-depth review of the electoral system was the first of its kind in Canada's history of electoral democracy. It was dictated largely by the major constitutional, social and technological changes of the past several decades, which have transformed Canadian society, and their concomitant influence on Canadians' expectations of the political process itself. In particular, the adoption in 1982 of the *Canadian Charter of Rights and Freedoms* has heightened Canadians' awareness of their democratic and political rights and of the way they are served by the electoral system.

The importance of electoral reform cannot be overemphasized. As the Commission's work proceeded, Canadians became increasingly preoccupied with constitutional issues that have the potential to change the nature of Confederation. No matter what their beliefs or political allegiances in this continuing debate, Canadians agree that constitutional change must be achieved in the context of fair and democratic processes. We cannot complacently assume that our current electoral process will always meet this standard or that it leaves no room for improvement. Parliament and the national government must be seen as legitimate; electoral reform can both enhance the stature of national political institutions and reinforce their ability to define the future of our country in ways that command Canadians' respect and confidence and promote the national interest.

In carrying out our mandate, we remained mindful of the importance of protecting our democratic heritage, while at the same time balancing it against the emerging values that are injecting a new dynamic into the electoral system. If our system is to reflect the realities of Canadian political life, then reform requires more than mere tinkering with electoral laws and practices.

Our broad mandate challenged us to explore a full range of options. We commissioned more than 100 research studies, to be published in a 23-volume collection. In the belief that our electoral laws must measure up to the very best contemporary practice, we examined election-related laws and processes in all of our provinces and territories and studied comparable legislation and processes in established democracies around the world. This unprecedented array of empirical study and expert opinion made a vital contribution to our deliberations. We made every effort to ensure that the research was both intellectually rigorous and of practical value. All studies were subjected to peer review, and many of the authors discussed their preliminary findings with members of the political and academic communities at national symposiums on major aspects of the electoral system.

The Commission placed the research program under the able and inspired direction of Dr. Peter Aucoin, Professor of Political Science and Public Administration at Dalhousie University. We are confident that the efforts of Dr. Aucoin, together with those of the research coordinators and scholars whose work appears in this and other volumes, will continue to be of value to historians, political scientists, parliamentarians and policy makers, as well as to thoughtful Canadians and the international community.

Along with the other Commissioners, I extend my sincere gratitude to the entire Commission staff for their dedication and commitment. I also wish to thank the many people who participated in our symposiums for their valuable contributions, as well as the members of the research and practitioners' advisory groups whose counsel significantly aided our undertaking.

Pierre Lortie
Chairman

INTRODUCTION

THE ROYAL COMMISSION'S research program constituted a comprehensive and detailed examination of the Canadian electoral process. The scope of the research, undertaken to assist Commissioners in their deliberations, was dictated by the broad mandate given to the Commission.

The objective of the research program was to provide Commissioners with a full account of the factors that have shaped our electoral democracy. This dictated, first and foremost, a focus on federal electoral law, but our inquiries also extended to the Canadian constitution, including the institutions of parliamentary government, the practices of political parties, the mass media and nonpartisan political organizations, as well as the decision-making role of the courts with respect to the constitutional rights of citizens. Throughout, our research sought to introduce a historical perspective in order to place the contemporary experience within the Canadian political tradition.

We recognized that neither our consideration of the factors shaping Canadian electoral democracy nor our assessment of reform proposals would be as complete as necessary if we failed to examine the experiences of Canadian provinces and territories and of other democracies. Our research program thus emphasized comparative dimensions in relation to the major subjects of inquiry.

Our research program involved, in addition to the work of the Commission's research coordinators, analysts and support staff, over 200 specialists from 28 universities in Canada, from the private sector and, in a number of cases, from abroad. Specialists in political science constituted the majority of our researchers, but specialists in law, economics, management, computer sciences, ethics, sociology and communications, among other disciplines, were also involved.

In addition to the preparation of research studies for the Commission, our research program included a series of research seminars, symposiums and workshops. These meetings brought together the Commissioners, researchers, representatives from the political parties, media personnel and others with practical experience in political parties, electoral politics and public affairs. These meetings provided not only a forum for discussion of the various subjects of the Commission's mandate, but also an opportunity for our research to be assessed by those with an intimate knowledge of the world of political practice.

These public reviews of our research were complemented by internal and external assessments of each research report by persons qualified in the area; such assessments were completed prior to our decision to publish any study in the series of research volumes.

The Research Branch of the Commission was divided into several areas, with the individual research projects in each area assigned to the research coordinators as follows:

F. Leslie Seidle	Political Party and Election Finance
Herman Bakvis	Political Parties
Kathy Megyery	Women, Ethno-cultural Groups and Youth
David Small	Redistribution; Electoral Boundaries; Voter Registration
Janet Hiebert	Party Ethics
Michael Cassidy	Democratic Rights; Election Administration
Robert A. Milen	Aboriginal Electoral Participation and Representation
Frederick J. Fletcher	Mass Media and Broadcasting in Elections
David Mac Donald (Assistant Research Coordinator)	Direct Democracy

These coordinators identified appropriate specialists to undertake research, managed the projects and prepared them for publication. They also organized the seminars, symposiums and workshops in their research areas and were responsible for preparing presentations and briefings to help the Commission in its deliberations and decision making. Finally, they participated in drafting the Final Report of the Commission.

On behalf of the Commission, I welcome the opportunity to thank the following for their generous assistance in producing these research studies – a project that required the talents of many individuals.

In performing their duties, the research coordinators made a notable contribution to the work of the Commission. Despite the pressures of tight deadlines, they worked with unfailing good humour and the utmost congeniality. I thank all of them for their consistent support and cooperation.

In particular, I wish to express my gratitude to Leslie Seidle, senior research coordinator, who supervised our research analysts and support staff in Ottawa. His diligence, commitment and professionalism not only set high standards, but also proved contagious. I am grateful to Kathy Megyery, who performed a similar function in Montreal with equal aplomb and skill. Her enthusiasm and dedication inspired us all.

On behalf of the research coordinators and myself, I wish to thank our research analysts: Daniel Arsenault, Eric Bertram, Cécile Boucher, Peter Constantinou, Yves Denoncourt, David Docherty, Luc Dumont, Jane Dunlop, Scott Evans, Véronique Garneau, Keith Heintzman, Paul Holmes, Hugh Mellon, Cheryl D. Mitchell, Donald Padget, Alain Pelletier, Dominique Tremblay and Lisa Young. The Research Branch was strengthened by their ability to carry out research in a wide variety of areas, their intellectual curiosity and their team spirit.

The work of the research coordinators and analysts was greatly facilitated by the professional skills and invaluable cooperation of Research Branch staff members: Paulette LeBlanc, who, as administrative assistant, managed the flow of research projects; Hélène Leroux, secretary to the research coordinators, who produced briefing material for the Commissioners and who, with Lori Nazar, assumed responsibility for monitoring the progress of research projects in the latter stages of our work; Kathleen McBride and her assistant Natalie Brose, who created and maintained the database of briefs and hearings transcripts; and Richard Herold and his assistant Susan Dancause, who were responsible for our research library. Jacinthe Séguin and Cathy Tucker also deserve thanks – in addition to their duties as receptionists, they assisted in a variety of ways to help us meet deadlines.

We were extremely fortunate to obtain the research services of first-class specialists from the academic and private sectors. Their contributions are found in this and the other 22 published research volumes. We thank them for the quality of their work and for their willingness to contribute and to meet our tight deadlines.

Our research program also benefited from the counsel of Jean-Marc Hamel, Special Adviser to the Chairman of the Commission and former

Chief Electoral Officer of Canada, whose knowledge and experience proved invaluable.

In addition, numerous specialists assessed our research studies. Their assessments not only improved the quality of our published studies, but also provided us with much-needed advice on many issues. In particular, we wish to single out professors Donald Blake, Janine Brodie, Alan Cairns, Kenneth Carty, John Courtney, Peter Desbarats, Jane Jenson, Richard Johnston, Vincent Lemieux, Terry Morley and Joseph Wearing, as well as Ms. Beth Symes.

Producing such a large number of studies in less than a year requires a mastery of the skills and logistics of publishing. We were fortunate to be able to count on the Commission's Director of Communications, Richard Rochefort, and Assistant Director, Hélène Papineau. They were ably supported by the Communications staff: Patricia Burden, Louise Dagenais, Caroline Field, Claudine Labelle, France Langlois, Lorraine Maheux, Ruth McVeigh, Chantal Morissette, Sylvie Patry, Jacques Poitras and Claudette Rouleau-O'Toole.

To bring the project to fruition, the Commission also called on specialized contractors. We are deeply grateful for the services of Ann McCoomb (references and fact checking); Marthe Lemery, Pierre Chagnon and the staff of Communications Com'ça (French quality control); Norman Bloom, Pamela Riseborough and associates of B&B Editorial Consulting (English adaptation and quality control); and Mado Reid (French production). Al Albania and his staff at Acart Graphics designed the studies and produced some 2 400 tables and figures.

The Commission's research reports constitute Canada's largest publishing project of 1991. Successful completion of the project required close cooperation between the public and private sectors. In the public sector, we especially acknowledge the excellent service of the Privy Council unit of the Translation Bureau, Department of the Secretary of State of Canada, under the direction of Michel Parent, and our contacts Ruth Steele and Terry Denovan of the Canada Communication Group, Department of Supply and Services.

The Commission's co-publisher for the research studies was Dundurn Press of Toronto, whose exceptional service is gratefully acknowledged. Wilson & Lafleur of Montreal, working with the Centre de Documentation Juridique du Québec, did equally admirable work in preparing the French version of the studies.

Teams of editors, copy editors and proofreaders worked diligently under stringent deadlines with the Commission and the publishers to prepare some 20 000 pages of manuscript for design, typesetting and printing. The work of these individuals, whose names are listed elsewhere in this volume, was greatly appreciated.

Our acknowledgements extend to the contributions of the Commission's Executive Director, Guy Goulard, and the administration and executive support teams: Maurice Lacasse, Denis Lafrance and Steve Tremblay (finance); Thérèse Lacasse and Mary Guy-Shea (personnel); Cécile Desforges (assistant to the Executive Director); Marie Dionne (administration); Anna Bevilacqua (records); and support staff members Michelle Bélanger, Roch Langlois, Michel Lauzon, Jean Mathieu, David McKay and Pierrette McMurtie, as well as Denise Miquelon and Christiane Séguin of the Montreal office.

A special debt of gratitude is owed to Marlène Girard, assistant to the Chairman. Her ability to supervise the logistics of the Commission's work amid the tight schedules of the Chairman and Commissioners contributed greatly to the completion of our task.

I also wish to express my deep gratitude to my own secretary, Liette Simard. Her superb administrative skills and great patience brought much-appreciated order to my penchant for the chaotic workstyle of academe. She also assumed responsibility for the administrative coordination of revisions to the final drafts of volumes 1 and 2 of the Commission's Final Report. I owe much to her efforts and assistance.

Finally, on behalf of the research coordinators and myself, I wish to thank the Chairman, Pierre Lortie, the members of the Commission, Pierre Fortier, Robert Gabor, William Knight and Lucie Pépin, and former members Elwood Cowley and Senator Donald Oliver. We are honoured to have worked with such an eminent and thoughtful group of Canadians, and we have benefited immensely from their knowledge and experience. In particular, we wish to acknowledge the creativity, intellectual rigour and energy our Chairman brought to our task. His unparalleled capacity to challenge, to bring out the best in us, was indeed inspiring.

Peter Aucoin
Director of Research

PREFACE

IN MODERN DEMOCRACIES, election campaigns are contested, to a large extent, in the mass media. From the days of the openly partisan press to the contemporary multi-media environment, political leaders have relied on mass media to mobilize electoral support. While the right to vote freely and the credibility of the ballot process are central to democracy, the conduct of campaigns and the flow of information to voters are also important. If campaigns are perceived to be conducted unfairly, the entire electoral process may become suspect. Concern for the legitimacy of the system is one of the primary reasons that most democracies have enacted regulations dealing with aspects of electoral communication. These regulations cover a wide range of media activities, including campaign advertising, election broadcasting and even some aspects of news and public affairs.

The Commission's research program on mass media and elections examined the major developments in electoral communication in Canada and other democratic countries in recent decades, in the context of electoral reform. The research studies were designed to cast light on major aspects of election media, whether amenable to regulation or not. Effective regulation requires an understanding of the entire system of campaign communication.

The results of the research program provided background for the Commission's report. Whatever their substantive focus, the studies examined issues such as fairness in electoral competition and public confidence in the electoral process, issues that are central to electoral reform. Some studies examined central elements in the campaign communication system, while others assessed its effectiveness in meeting the information needs of voters and the communication needs of parties. Several projects considered alternative forms of communication that might contribute to improved information for voters. The studies examined campaign media in the larger sense, including partisan advertising, free broadcast time, candidate communication strategies, new communication technologies and news and public affairs coverage, among other topics.

Research dealing directly with mass media and elections is reported in volumes 18 through 22. Volume 16, on opinion polling, and Volume 17, on the attitudes of Canadians toward the electoral system, were also part of the research program but include material on other subjects as well. Taken together, the seven volumes provide a comprehensive overview of the issues of campaign communication.

Volume 20 presents case studies of campaign communication in 10 ridings across Canada. Its purpose is to examine the information available to voters regarding local campaigns. Accordingly, the authors examined media use by local candidates, with emphasis on the availability of information to voters and the communication strategies of candidates, in order to improve the information flow. The studies were inspired, in part, by concerns about public perceptions regarding the relationship between citizens and representative institutions in Canada. Overall, the case studies found active local campaigns but only a limited effort to identify relevant local issues or to make clear to voters the local implications of national issues. The authors found that local candidates and local media often lacked the resources to articulate the local implications of national issues or to stimulate debate at the community level.

Under the direction of David V.J. Bell, who coordinated the project, five research teams each studied two ridings, one rural and one urban. The research consisted of interviews with local party and media personnel as well as some content analysis of local news media. The authors were asked to respond to a series of questions concerning the local information environment during the 1988 federal election. They developed a central core of common issues but approached the task of answering the questions posed to them from a variety of perspectives. The case studies contain rich detail and provide valuable insight into the nature of campaign communication at the local level. They address the Commission's concern with strengthening citizen participation and confidence in the integrity of the electoral process. Very little research has been done on campaign communication at the local level and, though limited by a relatively small sample of constituencies, this volume helps to fill a gap in what is known about Canadian election campaigns.

Because the studies were conducted in late 1990 and early 1991, the research teams had to reconstruct the local campaigns of 1988 after the fact. As a result, materials were not always available and memories were sometimes hazy. Nevertheless, by diligent research and careful cross-checking of sources, they have provided a reliable picture of local campaigns and recorded the observations of activists whose memories span several elections.

In order to assist the reader, an introductory study sets out the general framework for the research, identifies the central questions, and introduces the major issues. A concluding study summarizes the major findings, discusses areas of agreement and disagreement among the contributors, and places the issues in the larger context of electoral reform and the democratic process.

The studies reported here will be of interest not only to scholars and students examining the mass media and/or election campaigns, but also to party strategists and others concerned about campaigning at the local level. In particular, the thousands of citizens who make the system work by standing for office or helping to organize local campaigns will find something of interest in the case studies. More generally, the studies may stimulate useful discussion on how to deal with the widespread feeling that individual citizens are disconnected from the representative system. These discussions have implications beyond election campaigns but the issues raised in this volume in the narrower context of elections may stimulate consideration of the broader issues.

The Commission's research program on mass media and elections drew on the expertise of a wide range of communication scholars and political scientists in addition to those whose work is published in these volumes. Their assistance is greatly appreciated. Among those who participated as peer reviewers and advisers, several deserve special recognition: Peter Desbarats, Dean of the School of Journalism, University of Western Ontario; David Taras, University of Calgary; Holli Semetko, University of Michigan; and Marc Raboy, Laval University. The research program also benefited from the advice of individuals from the parties and the media: John Coleman, President, Canadian Advertising Foundation; Terry Hargreaves, Elly Alboim and Colin MacLeod of the CBC; Geoffrey Stevens, political columnist; Lynn McDonald, sociologist and former MP; and others who prefer to remain anonymous. On behalf of the authors and the Commission, I must also acknowledge our debt to the practitioners from the media and the parties, who attended our seminars or agreed to be interviewed and provided much valuable assistance and advice.

The administration of the research program depended heavily on the work of Cheryl Mitchell, who served as my assistant from the inception of the program, and our research assistants at York University: Catherine Bolan, Claudia Forgas, Marni Goldman, Todd Harris, Sharon Johnston and Sheila Riordon. We were also assisted most ably by the Commission staff. Peter Constantinou and Véronique Garneau had particular responsibilities for research in this area. The staff of the Department of Political Science, the Faculty of Arts, Calumet College, and the Faculty of Environmental Studies at York University were very accommodating.

The authors themselves deserve special acknowledgement for their willingness to try to meet tight deadlines, complicated by their normal academic responsibilities, and in particular to respond with cheerfulness and despatch to our requests for revisions. The conscientious peer reviewers were of major assistance to the authors and ourselves in preparing these studies for publication.

The unfailing good humour and encouragement of Peter Aucoin, the director of research, made an important contribution to the work. It was a privilege to work with the Commissioners, whose willingness to bring their experience to bear on the most esoteric of formulations was an inspiration. Pierre Lortie's overall direction and, in particular, his suggestions for research and incisive comments on various drafts made a vital contribution, which is reflected in these research volumes as well as in the Final Report of the Royal Commission. Working with the other research coordinators was a genuine pleasure. Richard Rochefort and his staff were crucial in bringing these studies to publication.

On a personal note, I wish to thank my wife and frequent collaborator, Martha Fletcher, for encouraging me to undertake this task, which I have found very rewarding, and for her direct advice on many aspects of the work, as well as for bearing more than her share of the burden of domestic management. My son, Frederick, reminded me that work, however important, must be balanced with other aspects of life but also that the future of the democratic process is worth working for.

Cheryl Mitchell brought dedication and skill to the work and must have an ample share of the credit for whatever contribution the research program has made. For errors in design and execution, however, I remain responsible.

With respect to Volume 20, I wish to acknowledge the assistance of Catherine Bolan, who participated in much of the editing, Kenneth Carty of the University of British Columbia, who provided both advice and data, and the many local party activists and media personnel who responded generously to requests for information. As always, it was a pleasure to work with David Bell.

Fred Fletcher
Research Coordinator

My personal thanks go first to Fred Fletcher, for inviting me to become involved in this project; to the members of the research team, each of whom made contributions to the entire project that went beyond the fine work they did on their own case studies; and to Catherine Bolan, who helped to coordinate the project as well as co-authoring the Ontario study with me.

David Bell
Project Coordinator

REACHING THE VOTER

1

ELECTORAL COMMUNICATION AT THE CONSTITUENCY LEVEL
A Framework for Analysis

David V.J. Bell
Frederick J. Fletcher

JOURNALISTS AND ACADEMICS alike often talk about federal elections in national terms and increasingly depict elections as "horse-races" between the party leaders. This image of elections has some validity, but it is partial and limited. Canada's single-member constituency, simple-plurality electoral system guarantees that the outcome of national elections depends on the individual electoral outcomes in each constituency. Yet there is a remarkable dearth of electoral case studies of individual constituencies. The unit of analysis for most electoral research is the country as a whole or large units such as provinces, on the one hand, or individual voters' preferences, on the other. Although this literature acknowledges the importance of learning more about the impact of constituency-level factors (i.e., candidates, local issues, constituency campaign strategies and local media coverage), few systematic studies have been done to explore these factors.[1] This lacuna is particularly regrettable for several reasons. First, as indicated, decisions made by individual voters at the constituency level, as aggregated through outcomes in each riding, determine overall national results. Second, individual MPs appear to be gaining a more important political role as a result of recent parliamentary reforms, yet little is known about how they are chosen (as candidates) or how political discourse in their individual riding affects their electoral results. Reforms intended to make the electoral system as a whole more democratic must take into consideration constituency-level factors.

There have been several studies in recent years that demonstrate a decline in public support for representative institutions and a widespread feeling that the link between representatives and citizens is ineffective. Indeed, public ratings of politicians and political parties after the 1988 election "were lower across the board than at any time since such surveys began" (Pammett 1990, 273). Price and Mancuso (1991, 198–99) note that there are in fact institutionalized links between members of Parliament and their constituents, but that tension between public expectations and parliamentary practice has been growing. Recent surveys indicate that a majority of Canadians believe that MPs should cast their votes in the House of Commons on the basis of constituency interests. This, however, contradicts the requirement of parliamentary government that MPs vote along party lines most of the time, a practice which now has little public support (ibid., 201).

The fact that a recent study in the United States (Kettering Foundation 1991, 5) revealed a widespread belief that the link between individuals and public officials has been severed indicates that the issue goes beyond representation. Party discipline is not a factor in the United States. The study found that many citizens felt disconnected from public debate because they perceived public discourse to be dominated by politicians, experts, organized interests and the media. A major flaw in the public debate, as the American respondents saw it, was that public issues were selected, framed and debated in terms that had no clear relevance to the communities in which they lived. They made it clear to the researchers that they felt issues should be localized to reflect their own concerns and to allow them to participate meaningfully in public debate. Such feelings appear to be common in Canada also. Election campaigns that distance voters from the central issues by failing to present them in local terms may be part of the problem.

Canadians are expressing concern over the increasing alienation and cynicism in our political and electoral process. The Royal Commission on Electoral Reform and Party Financing was established to examine the conduct of federal elections in Canada and to make recommendations that might lead to improvements in the electoral process. The goal of the Commission, described by its chair as "ambitious," is "to develop a blueprint for an electoral law that will effectively meet the needs of Canadians well into the next century, reinforce their confidence in our democratic process and their members of Parliament and reflect our values and democratic institutions" (Lortie 1990, 2).

The case studies presented in this volume focus on campaign communication but also deal with issues of candidate financing and selection. Spending limits, financial resources and services available to incumbents all influence campaign communication.

An overriding concern in these studies involved whether and how issues in the 1988 federal election were made salient to local voters. Local issues can be defined in various ways. In a narrow sense, local issues are unique to the constituency or community. More broadly defined, local issues capture the local implications of larger issues, such as the applicability of national tax reform to circumstances in the immediate community. Our researchers were asked to study the extent to which local issues – in both their narrowest and broadest definitions – were a factor in campaign communication at the local level, how they were expressed to voters through the media and how they were presented in relation to the major national issues of the 1988 federal election campaign.

In order to contextualize this question, Anthony Sayers (see following study) developed the framework of "issue space" to help us to understand the way in which the media and parties shape the local information environment facing voters. Issue space involves two aspects: quantitative – the number of issues politicized, i.e., that become a factor in the campaign – and qualitative – what issues are politicized. The size and content of local issue space are determined by a variety of factors. The most important of these are (1) the relationships within the political parties among local, provincial and national campaign organizations; (2) the balance of local, provincial and national concerns in the media that serve a particular constituency; and (3) the degree of distinctive community identification within the riding. Constituencies that encompass communities with a sense of local identity are likely to have more local issue space, but it will also vary according to the type of riding and the competitive situation among the parties.

THE LITERATURE ON CONSTITUENCY-LEVEL CAMPAIGNING

Notwithstanding the relative paucity of constituency-level studies, there are some fairly reliable research findings concerning the apparent impact of individual candidates on voters' preferences. Robert Cunningham (1971, 288) found that 26 percent of voters in the various Hamilton ridings he surveyed stated that the "local candidate" would be the "most important factor in determining" how they would vote in the upcoming election. More recent studies confirm this finding. Survey data from the 1988 election study indicate that 27 percent of those interviewed stated that "local candidates" were "the most important factor in voting" in that election. (This number was just over half of those citing "the party as a whole" [53 percent] but larger than those citing "party leaders" [20 percent].) Of this group, 57 percent stated that the candidate's position on "issues" was the most salient consideration, whereas 43 percent were influenced by the candidate's "personal qualities" (Pammett 1990, 271–72). Whether or not these responses reflect accurately the relative importance of local candidates in the vote decision, they do indicate that many voters believe the local candidate should be important.[2]

Furthermore, the literature contains numerous generalizations about the nature of campaign politics at the constituency level. Of central importance is the interplay between local factors (candidate's personal appeal, local issues, strength of individual riding campaign organization, use of local media for campaigning purposes, constituency demographics and previous voting practices, etc.) and national or regional factors such as appeal of party leaders, national issues and party platforms, national-level political advertising, media coverage and so on.

In a survey of the relevant literature, Fletcher (1987) identified the following generalizations:

- Journalistic practices and electoral regulations give an important electoral advantage to incumbents (353).
- Local campaign strategies (canvassing, literature "drops," telephone calls, etc.) make a difference that varies from riding to riding, but the magnitude of this difference and its variation across ridings is unknown (355).
- National parties increasingly target campaign activities to competitive constituencies; i.e., those that they think they must struggle to hold or win (357).
- Televised debates between candidates – particularly over local cable stations – have become increasingly common at the constituency level (358).
- Local candidates get little attention in the major media (360).

These generalizations tend to rest on impressions rather than solid evidence. Furthermore, little is known about "precise measures of media use" or specific "types and conditions" of influence (Fletcher 1987, 364), including "the content of political appeals" (368). Little or no research has been done to determine whether generalizations applied to the national level – e.g., "that leaders choose issues that can be explained simply on television," (367) – also apply to constituency-level campaigns. What is more important, it remains to be determined whether the national media so dominate local media that the link between voters and local candidates/issues is being seriously eroded. This volume explores these issues through qualitative case studies of campaign communication in 1988 in 10 constituencies.

CHOOSING THE SAMPLE

Each constituency, to paraphrase T.S. Eliot, is "unique and similar to others." Canadian constituencies vary according to size, competitiveness, demographic composition, region, urbanization and so on. (Data on these variables may be found in Eagles 1990.) In sampling constituencies for the purpose of this project, difficult compromises had to be made because time constraints precluded a larger sample. In the end, we decided to stratify our project by region, undertaking two case studies each in the Atlantic, Quebec, Ontario, the Prairies and BC. One of the constituencies chosen in each region was predominantly urban or suburban, the other predominantly rural. We examined ridings in which the campaign was taken seriously, i.e., the winning candidate had to contend with credible opponents who together had achieved at least 50 percent of the vote in at least three of the previous five elections. The 10 ridings are, of course, not representative, but they are sufficiently diverse to provide a reasonable basis for identifying problems in campaign communication and areas for possible reform.

On the basis of these criteria, the following constituencies were selected for analysis:

- British Columbia: Vancouver Centre and Kootenay West–Revelstoke
- Alberta: Calgary West and Macleod
- Ontario: Perth–Wellington–Waterloo and Markham
- Quebec: Frontenac and Outremont
- Nova Scotia: Annapolis Valley–Hants and Halifax.

ISSUES STUDIED

Each case study was designed to include all or most of the following:

- A brief profile of the central characteristics of the riding, including demographics, previous local issues and available media. (Here we were able to draw upon material contained in Professor Munroe Eagles' forthcoming Almanac, which provides a profile of each federal riding as well as other data available on federal electoral districts from Statistics Canada.)
- An analysis of campaign strategies used by each candidate in 1988 (based on interviews with candidates and/or campaign managers), especially with respect to focus on local vs. national or regional issues and use of the local media.
- An analysis of local media coverage of the 1988 federal election by the press and television, especially cable community channels

(based on interviews with key individuals in each outlet and some content analysis).

- An examination of the perceived importance of the local campaign in the eyes of campaign organizers.

OBJECTIVES OF THIS PROJECT

The term "media" comes from the Latin word for middle. Its application to communication, which is relatively recent, captures the notion that the means of communication, particularly mass communication, stand between individuals and some external reality. In modern politics, the media serve as the crucial link between parties and candidates on the one hand and individual voters on the other. Candidates do attempt to make personal contact with voters in a variety of ways, including "mainstreeting," going to work sites or shopping malls, or canvassing door to door. But only a tiny proportion of voters will have personal contact with the candidates or even get a chance to observe first-hand the candidates making a speech or engaging in a political debate. By far the majority of voters' information about candidates and their platforms is mediated through television, radio or print (including printed brochures, election signs, direct mail and so on).

For the purposes of this project, the local media environment consists of television, radio and newspapers. We did not systematically study the campaign literature circulated in most ridings by most candidates nor the use of direct mail or telephone banks; however, we did inquire about the use of these candidate-initiated forms of campaign communication in the constituencies studied. Our objective was to examine media use by candidates and news coverage at the local level so that we could determine the availability to voters of information regarding candidates, platforms and issues. We asked the researchers to consider the amount and type of information available and how the information flow might be improved.

In addition to candidate communication strategies, the authors were asked to examine the coverage practices of both broadcast and print media. The primary objective of the media analysis was to assess the balance in the media serving each constituency among local, provincial/regional and national concerns. This assessment involved an examination of the use of national news-service material relative to locally generated reports and, more importantly, the extent to which the campaign was framed as a "horse-race" among national leaders rather than a contest among local candidates. In this context, the media attention given to local candidates was analysed.

To help to gain an understanding of local campaign communication in general, the authors were asked to deal with a series of questions:

- Was the contest in the constituency presented as merely a surrogate for the national race?
- Did local candidates present themselves primarily as the local surrogate for the leader or as candidates in their own right?
- To what extent were the local campaigns dependent upon the national or provincial party organizations for campaign themes and materials? How much campaign literature was generated locally?
- To what extent did the local campaigns develop an agenda of issues different in content or emphasis from the national campaigns of their parties? What was the mix between local and national issues?
- What were the strategies of the local campaigns for reaching voters? How did they use the local media?
- How successful were the local campaigns in attracting media attention?
- How did the local media approach campaign coverage?

THE REGULATORY FRAMEWORK

During election campaigns, the broadcast media operate under a comprehensive set of guidelines issued under the authority of the *Broadcasting Act* and the *Canada Elections Act* by the Canadian Radio-television and Telecommunications Commission (CRTC). The guidelines were revised after public hearings in 1987 and are intended "to ensure that the public is informed of the issues involved so that it has sufficient knowledge to make an informed choice from among various candidates and parties" (CRTC 1987). The CRTC stipulates that broadcasters "shall allocate time for the broadcasting of programs, advertisements or announcements of a partisan political character on an equitable basis to all accredited political parties and rival candidates" (CRTC 1988). Partisan broadcasts are limited to a four-week period that ends one day before voting day.

The *Canada Elections Act* requires all broadcasters to make paid time available to registered political parties and, in addition, requires network operators to provide free time to the parties. Broadcasters are permitted, but not required, to make paid and free time available to candidates. If they choose to do so, they must make the time available to all candidates and allocate it on an equitable basis. At the national level, time is allocated among the parties on the basis of the number of seats in the House of Commons at dissolution and the percentage of the popular vote and the number of candidates nominated in the previous election. At the local level, many broadcasters and community cable channels chose to interpret "equitable" as "equal" in 1988 (Desbarats 1991).

The CRTC is required to issue guidelines to broadcasters as soon as an election is called. In releasing the guidelines for the 1988 federal election, the chair of the CRTC at the time, André Bureau, stated that "the purpose of these requirements is to ensure the public's right to be informed of the issues involved so that it has sufficient knowledge to make an informed choice from among the various parties and candidates ... The broadcaster's obligation as a trustee of the public airwaves is seldom greater than it is in respect to this exercise of the most fundamental democratic freedom" (CRTC 1988). The guidelines reminded broadcasters of their obligation to provide equitable treatment to all candidates and parties over the whole range of election broadcasting issues.

The four-week advertising period and the spending limits in Canada, along with provisions for some reimbursement of campaign expenses for candidates who receive at least 15 percent of the popular vote, ensure that the money-driven system in the United States cannot emerge here. In the U.S., effective candidacy for any major office is virtually impossible for anyone unable to raise hundreds of thousands of dollars to purchase television advertising. However, it has been suggested that the Canadian rules restrict the capacity of candidates, especially challengers to incumbents, to get their message out to voters.

The issue of equitable treatment was dealt with in some detail in the 1987 CRTC document (CRTC 1987). The main points can be summarized as follows:

- The requirement for equitable treatment applies to, and must be achieved within, each category of programming (paid time, free time, news, public affairs).
- Debates should include "all rival parties or candidates," even if this "requires that more than one program be broadcast."
- "Late entrants" to a campaign are entitled to "equitable coverage from the time they enter the campaign." They need not be compensated "for time previously afforded other candidates."
- On-air personalities who become candidates should be relieved of their on-air duties during the campaign.
- Decisions on which constituencies to cover are left to individual stations based on their service areas and practical considerations. Stations that re-broadcast much of their programming are expected nevertheless to endeavour to provide for the needs of the constituencies they serve.

This last requirement is complicated by the lack of fit between the broadcast reach of some media outlets and constituency boundaries. For example, some cable stations cover more than one constituency, while other constituencies are served by more than one cable outlet. Several of the following case studies discuss the implications of this problem.

It should be noted that these provisions are guidelines, not regulations. The extent to which they are enforceable is in doubt, though failure to make a reasonable attempt to fulfil them could affect licence renewal. In any case, the CRTC has traditionally been reluctant to intervene in the journalistic functions of the broadcast media. However, it does field complaints, almost all of which involve questions of equitable treatment of candidates, and attempts with general success to mediate between broadcasters and candidates during campaigns. The guidelines provide an overall set of norms and expectations for the broadcast media during campaigns.

THE "DEMOCRATIC CULTURE" OF ELECTIONS

Fair elections, openly contested by candidates who broadly represent their (local) community, are the touchstone of western democracy. Each society that claims to be democratic attempts to regulate the conduct of elections to ensure that these principles are realized. But no amount of regulation, no set of statutes and laws, could effectively guarantee that the electoral system operates fairly and equitably. Nor would extensive regulation be consistent with other principles, such as free speech, deemed equally crucial to the maintenance of democracy.

Political scientists have long recognized that democratic structures must be nurtured and reinforced by a supportive culture of democratic beliefs and values. One classic study argues that a successful democracy requires "a pattern of political attitudes and an underlying set of social attitudes that is supportive of a stable democratic process" (Almond and Verba 1963, vii). Democracy is a matter of "attitude and feeling" and not just structure and process. The more thoroughly members of a society understand and support democratic norms and values, the more democratic practices will flourish. This is especially true of the politically active segment of society.

In this volume, we are concerned about the extent to which political activists and journalists communicate these norms to electors, and about the information that voters need in order to make informed decisions.

The case studies in this volume provide diverse perspectives on a common set of themes and questions. We discuss the common findings and key areas of difference among the case studies in a concluding chapter, which also returns to the central questions posed above.

Leonard Preyra examines the conduct, style and content of electoral communication at the constituency level as it was shaped by three
sets of relationships: the intraparty integration of national and local
campaigns, the core–periphery news-gathering affiliations of the national
and local media, and the riding-specific factors of the campaign. This
"vertical integration" of the political and media organizations was
found to have substantial influence on the means, style and content of
electoral communications in the Nova Scotia ridings of Halifax and
Annapolis Valley–Hants. In spite of the uniqueness of the 1988 election campaign, with the predominance of the free trade issue, Preyra
argues that vertical integration will continue to promote the dominance
of national concerns in federal campaigns.

Luc Bernier's contribution examines the dynamics of media and
electoral politics in the Quebec ridings of Outremont and Frontenac.
His study traces the relationship between the local, provincial and
national levels of the political organizations, with reference to the impact
of the various sectors on the local campaign. He also explores the importance of a solid organizational base to the local campaign, especially
in terms of resources, motivation and tradition. Other topics in Bernier's
study include: the effect on the local campaign of a shortage of volunteer workers; election expenses, in particular, the "grey" areas that may
impede an overall fairness in the system; the role of incumbency, especially in Frontenac, where debate about the campaign of Marcel Masse
in 1988 was not whether the candidate would win, but by how much;
and the position of alternative parties in a local media environment
preoccupied with the established parties.

The study of two Ontario ridings by David Bell and Catherine
Bolan examines how local candidates attempt to reach their constituents
through the local media and, conversely, the practices of the local media
in covering the campaign. Their qualitative reading of newspaper articles, and personal interviews with key media and political figures, bring
forth some interesting observations on the similarities and differences
in the information environment in these ridings during the election
campaign. In addition, they explore the roles of new technologies and
campaign workers in the local political organizations, as well as the
impact of the increased importance of "minor" party and independent
candidates.

The study by Andrew Beh and Roger Gibbins on the 1988 election
campaign in the Alberta ridings of Macleod and Calgary West begins
with the question, "Do local candidates and constituency campaigns
count in federal election campaigns?" These constituencies were particularly suitable for their study, as both featured highly competitive

campaigns in 1988, an unusual feature in their history. The authors also explore the presence of Reform Party candidates, who played a significant role in these ridings. Finding a predominance of national themes and issues in media coverage, the authors, like Preyra, believe that local concerns are unlikely to be significant in future campaigns and that the free trade issue in 1988 exaggerated that tendency only slightly.

Anthony Sayers develops his concepts of issue space and local issue space in relation to the campaigns in the British Columbia constituencies of Vancouver Centre and Kootenay West–Revelstoke. He argues that issue definition and the importance ascribed to the various issues are likely to vary across the hierarchy of parties and the media, from local to national, horizontally across different constituencies and chronologically, as the campaign progresses and strategies are reshaped accordingly. Sayers conducted in-depth interviews with local candidates, activists, organizers, communications officers and key media figures. His study maps out succinctly the complex dynamics in campaigning as they vary from constituency to constituency. As a result, he argues that the impact of changes in the electoral process will vary among constituencies.

The concluding chapter summarizes the major findings and conclusions, explores the common themes and contradictions, attempts to identify problem areas and indicates possible areas for reform.

NOTES

1. Cf. Fletcher (1987, 346–47): "Election research in Canada has effectively isolated a number of important factors in the vote decision and has linked them with varying degrees of success to the campaigns of the national parties. However it has not yet examined in any depth the information environment within which voters make their choices. Regional and local factors have yet to be explored." Cf. also Eagles (1990, 289).

2. Notwithstanding these findings, one of the national party strategists interviewed in conjunction with the present project seriously questioned their validity. Although he acknowledged that "incumbency" is probably "worth 10–14 percent" in terms of votes, he viewed local factors per se as nearly irrelevant. Several others expressed similar views but placed the figure for candidate impact even lower, at 5–7 percent. This view has some support in the literature. See Cunningham (1971), Irvine (1982) and Ferejohn and Gaines (1991). The complexity of the vote decision and the weaknesses of the available data make the question a difficult one to resolve.

REFERENCES

Almond, Gabriel, and Sidney Verba. 1963. *The Civic Culture: Political Attitudes and Democracy in Five Nations.* Princeton: Princeton University Press.

Canadian Radio-television and Telecommunications Commission (CRTC). 1987. "Election Campaign Broadcasting." Public Notice CRTC 1987-209. Ottawa: CRTC.

———. 1988. "A Policy with Respect to Election Campaign Broadcasting." Public Notice CRTC 1988-142. Ottawa: CRTC.

Cunningham, Robert. 1971. "The Impact of the Local Candidate in Canadian Federal Elections." *Canadian Journal of Political Science* 4:287–90.

Desbarats, Peter. 1991. "Cable Television and Federal Election Campaigns in Canada." In *Election Broadcasting in Canada,* ed. Frederick J. Fletcher. Vol. 21 of the research studies of the Royal Commission on Electoral Reform and Party Financing. Ottawa and Toronto: RCERPF/Dundurn.

Eagles, Munroe D. 1990. "Political Ecology: Local Effects on the Political Behaviour of Canadians." In *Canadian Politics: An Introduction to the Discipline,* ed. Alain G. Gagnon and James Bickerton. Peterborough: Broadview Press.

Ferejohn, John, and Brian Gaines. 1991. "The Personal Vote in Canada." In *Representation, Integration and Political Parties in Canada,* ed. Herman Bakvis. Vol. 14 of the research studies of the Royal Commission on Electoral Reform and Party Financing. Ottawa and Toronto: RCERPF/Dundurn.

Fletcher, Frederick J. 1987. "Mass Media and Parliamentary Elections in Canada." *Legislative Studies Quarterly* 12:341–72.

Irvine, William P. 1982. "Does the Candidate Make a Difference? The Macro-Politics and the Micro-Politics of Getting Elected." *Canadian Journal of Political Science* 15:755–82.

Kettering Foundation. 1991. *Citizens and Politics: A View from Main Street America.* Study prepared by the Harwood Group. Dayton, Washington, New York: Kettering Foundation.

Lortie, Pierre. 1990. Opening Remarks by the Chairman at the First Public Hearing of the Royal Commission on Electoral Reform and Party Financing. Ottawa, 12 March.

Pammett, Jon H. 1990. "Elections." In *Canadian Politics in the 1990s,* ed. Michael S. Whittington and Glen Williams. Scarborough: Nelson Canada.

Price, Richard G., and Maureen Mancuso. 1991. "Ties That Bind: Parliamentary Members and Their Constituencies." In *Introductory Readings in Canadian Government and Politics,* ed. Robert M. Krause and R.H. Wagenberg. Toronto: Copp Clark Pitman.

2

LOCAL ISSUE SPACE
IN NATIONAL ELECTIONS
Kootenay West–Revelstoke
and Vancouver Centre

Anthony M. Sayers

I T IS ACCEPTED wisdom that deft handling of the media is an important part of a successful election campaign. Similarly, it is thought that the rise of national media and nationally orchestrated elections has reduced the role of local campaigns, candidates and issues in national elections. As a result of the lack of information about constituency level politics in Canada, these observations do not reflect the experiences of local campaign organizers.

This study aims to map some of the terrain of national elections at the local level, exploring the relationship between local, regional and national issues and campaign strategies, and the relationship between local campaigns and the media. Central to this analysis is the concept of issue space. This concept posits a notional space which represents the local information environment in which voters make their voting decisions. As such, it is the place where the various objectives and resources of candidates, parties and the media interact and compete to define the issues on which elections are decided at the constituency level. Given that the resources and objectives of each of these actors are likely to vary from constituency to constituency, we can expect the nature of issue space to vary between constituencies.

An issue space has both quantitative (number of issues) and qualitative (which issues are politicized) dimensions. In the following study we are interested in discovering what determines both the size and content of a local issue space. The interpenetration of local, provincial and national politics, political campaigns and media organizations creates

competition to define the content of local issue space, resulting in competition between local, regional and national issues for inclusion in this
space. As well, we can expect participants in the electoral process to
offer competing definitions of the election issues. One example of this
is the distinction between how the national wing of a political party
understands a "national" issue (in terms of both its definition and
importance to their campaign) and how its local branch defines such
an issue in light of local circumstances. Issue definition and the importance ascribed to the various issues are likely to vary vertically within
media and the parties – that is, across the hierarchy of parties and the
media from local to national, horizontally across different constituencies, and chronologically as the campaign progresses and strategies are
altered to address election contingencies.

To ascertain the various perspectives each of these groups of actors
brought to local election campaigns in 1988, a standardized personal
interview was conducted with various members of the print and electronic media, local candidates, party activists, party organizers and
party communications officers in the two constituencies studied. These
interviews attempted to assess the objectives, strategies and resources
associated with running and reporting a constituency contest, as well
as to look at the relations among different levels of the media and different levels of political parties.

The study is broken into four sections: first, a brief description of
the two British Columbia constituencies chosen for the study and the
rationale for these choices; second, an analysis of the role played by the
media in local campaigning, its relationship to the local campaigns,
and how these factors help define the content and size of local issue
space; third, an assessment of the interaction of local, regional and
national factors at the constituency level during national elections,
including the impact of these factors on the development of local issue
space; and finally, some concluding remarks and recommendations.

THE CONSTITUENCIES

The two constituencies chosen for the British Columbia section of
the study are Vancouver Centre (VC) and Kootenay West–Revelstoke
(KW-R). Vancouver Centre has a history of high-profile campaigns, where
candidates speak with some authority on party policy. The media took
advantage of this in 1988, and the parties provided many opportunities for the media to have access to candidates and leaders via this constituency. The Vancouver Centre campaign was given extensive coverage
by the local, provincial and national media, because Centre (as the riding is usually called) anchors one end of the continuum that connects

constituencies that have more than adequate access to media with those that have limited access to media. It can thus act as a reference point in assessing the different levels of media exposure experienced by various campaigns. KW-R represents the archetypal rural constituency in which the candidates are well-known locals. New Democrat and Progressive Conservative candidates had each represented the riding previously, the latter being the incumbent. While not of the same order of that found in Vancouver, KW-R has local media organizations that target local audiences and are capable of covering the local campaign.

Kootenay West–Revelstoke

This constituency is populated by home-owning families with relatively lower education levels but similar income levels to those found in Vancouver Centre. It is a large sprawling riding running north–south along the mountains, though the province's major highways run east–west. The riding has a number of towns (Revelstoke in the north, Nelson, Trail, Rossland and Castlegar in the south) whose economic interests include the large Cominco smelter in Trail, mining, forestry and tourism. Despite some boundary changes, transposing the 1984 results onto 1988 boundaries produces very similar vote shares and identical candidate rankings.

This constituency has proven to be very competitive. The straight NDP versus PC battle in this constituency is typical of the province. Two men have fought four successive elections, and the seat has swung back and forth so the MP faces a well-known, previous incumbent. This competition has been between the PC's Bob Brisco and the NDP's Lyle Kristiansen. Brisco won the seat in 1974, held it in 1979, lost to Kristiansen in 1980, recaptured it in the sweep of 1984, but then lost once again to Kristiansen in 1988. All these elections have been competitive. As seasoned campaigners, these candidates have intimate knowledge of local communication channels and well-developed organizations and strategies. They were joined in 1988 by Liberal candidate Garry Jenkins and Green Party candidate Michael Brown.

Vancouver Centre

The Vancouver Centre constituency, in the heart of Vancouver, contains a high proportion of rental accommodation which houses a relatively mobile, mostly single, well-educated and, by and large, middle class electorate. The constituency boundaries have remained fairly consistent over the last five elections, all of which have been highly competitive. The Liberals won the riding in 1974 and 1979, the Tories have been successful since then, and the NDP has had a strong showing as they control much of the area provincially. In both 1984 and 1988 the NDP ran second, and in 1988 the seat was won by under 300 votes. Encompassing the downtown core, this constituency has long been associated with the interests of the business community as well the ethnically and socially heterogeneous communities within its boundaries.

This constituency is of some special interest given the high profile of the local campaign in 1988. The retiring member, Pat Carney, had been a minister in the 1984–88 government and a central figure in negotiating the Free Trade Agreement, the main issue of the campaign. The three principal candidates were all high-profile figures: Kim Campbell, an ex-provincial politician who had sought the Social Credit leadership (and premiership) was widely touted as a rising star in the Conservative firmament (she subsequently was appointed Minister of Justice); Johanna den Hertog, federal president of the NDP; and Tex Enemark, one-time assistant to local MP Ron Basford, who was justice minister in the Trudeau government.

The following section considers the role of the media in shaping issue space at the constituency level. The media is the public arena for the competing definitions of election issues offered by local and nonlocal campaigns as well as those of the media itself. The number and size of media outlets that cover a particular campaign helps determine the size of issue space available to a campaign, and the priorities of the media help determine the content of that space.

CAMPAIGNS AND THE MEDIA

While campaigners from all sides in both constituencies were generally happy with the media coverage their campaigns received, the relationship between the campaigns and the media, and the way in which the campaigns were reported, differed considerably in the two constituencies studied. Elections are only part of the news that the media is expected to cover. The allocation of resources by the media reflects both their assessment of the value of a story and the broader resource constraints they face.

A priori, the factors that are critical to the role the media plays and the relationship between the media and the campaigns can be grouped in three ways: first, the characteristics of the constituency such as its electoral history, its profile in previous elections, and the demography and economic characteristics of the constituency; second, campaign-related factors such as the competence of campaign organizations and candidates, the profile of the current contest, and relations between the local party and non-local elements of the party; and, third, features of the local media such as its quality, the form and size of media that covers the contest, the priorities of that media, and the size and nature of its audience.

Kootenay West–Revelstoke

The type and number of media available in a constituency shapes a campaign's media strategy. Although it lacks a television station, Kootenay West–Revelstoke has a number of newspapers and radio stations as well as two cable television systems. Kootenay Broadcasting System (KBS) runs radio stations covering the southern half of the constituency, its broadcast area being nearly contiguous with the boundaries of the constituency. There are two smaller radio stations elsewhere in the constituency. With seven reporters including a news director, KBS is the largest news service in the constituency. It runs three AM and one FM station under its parent company, Four Seasons Radio, with wire services provided by the Satellite News Network which has its headquarters in Toronto. Local news is fed back to this service.

There are about 10 weekly or daily papers in the constituency. The main local papers are the *Trail Times*, the *Nelson News* and the *Castlegar News*. The first two are dailies and the last a biweekly. The dailies have circulations of about 6 000, while the *Castlegar News* has a circulation of about 5 000. At the time of the election, the *Trail Times* and the *Nelson News* were owned by the Stirling News Service of Vancouver, and the *Castlegar News* was an independent. All relied on the Canadian Press wire service which has its head office in Toronto. Shaw Cable is the local, independent cable network in the southern part of the constituency encompassing Trail, Castlegar and Nelson.

KBS was the only news organization to claim solid coverage of local election issues and to provide a breakdown of the events its reporters had attended. Reporters attended six candidates debates, which appears to have been greater than that of any other media organization. Hourly news bulletins often included election-related stories, both local and non-local. Editorial staff considered this to be unusually good coverage for rural radio and to be a reflection of the organization's news-oriented format. KBS sees itself as the main local news outlet. Such a conclusion is difficult to assess, but local campaigners were not convinced that there was a local leader among the media.

The local newspapers have newsrooms that range in size from one to four reporters. About one-half of any edition of each of these papers was given over to election coverage. A reporter at the *Trail Times* estimated that about 25 percent of reporters' time was spent on the election, including time spent editing press releases and "stripping" wire reports. No special arrangements were made to cover the election by any of the media, although KBS had much more flexibility in this matter given its larger news staff. Despite common ownership, the *Trail Times* and *Nelson News* did not coordinate their election coverage. Given the limitations on size and resources at the newspapers and radio, the use of syndicated materials was very common and usually accounted for anywhere between 50 and 75 percent of their election coverage. Only *Nelson News* reporters estimated local content to be slightly greater than syndicated material.

Strategies for covering the campaign typically consisted of an interview with each of the candidates and a column outlining their campaigns at the beginning of the campaign. During the campaign, attending two or three town hall meetings and eliciting candidate responses to such things as policy announcements made up the bulk of the reporting. Special events, such as the prime minister's tour of Cominco, were strong drawing-cards for the media, as were speaking engagements that promised to be lively, such as candidates' addresses to the union local. Campaign press releases often served to initiate stories, with the reporters sometimes following up the release by contacting the candidates. Some of the print media also covered cable and radio debates and put questions to the candidates.

Town hall and all-candidate meetings were well covered by the media early in the campaign, but once the candidates' basic message had been discerned, coverage declined. There were two cable debates during the campaign, one in Nelson, and one in Castlegar at the studios of Shaw Cable, which were arranged by the local Chamber of Commerce in each town. There were also two all-candidate meetings on local radio. Uncertainties about the size of audiences watching or listening make it difficult to assess the value of these events. Local debates were thought to have little impact on the election, whereas national debates were seen as having boosted the Liberals' chances, partly as a result of the local media consequently taking Liberal candidate Jenkins more seriously. Attendance by the party faithful at local debates was seen as a measure of the vitality of a campaign and thus may have influenced the reporters' assessment of whether a candidate was a serious contender for the seat.

Local reporters noted that anything that had the potential to generate a story was important, but it needed to be easily accessible given the limited resources of the local media. In general, particularly in the printed press, local copy or wire stories with local impact came first. Given this, news unrelated to the election often pre-empted election news and made front page. Stories about candidates ranked low as a result of a focus on issues, although, because they were rare, attacks upon other candidates were seen as providing good copy. Regional and national issues as well as stories concerning national leaders were all seen as important. However, the greater the local relevance of a non-local story, the better its chances of being run.

Further, reporters noted that while the local angle to a story is critical, the increasing interdependence of different levels of politics means that non-local politics can have implications for the local scene, and the two are difficult to distinguish. For example, management and unions at the Cominco smelter in Trail were publicly opposed on the free trade issue, and this gave local relevance to all stories concerning free trade. Moreover, although the media preferred to cover local election stories or tack local angles onto wire stories, the lack of resources often prohibited this.

Reporters were critical of their own reporting efforts and cited the lack of resources as a critical variable in limiting their capacity to cover the election, but they noted also that there were limits to the newsworthiness of the local electoral contest. The media considered its coverage, though insufficient, to have been both balanced and as good as could be hoped for given the circumstances.

The constraints faced by local media, particularly newspapers, are substantial. The local newspapers have news staffs that range in size from one to four reporters. Historically low staffing levels, chronic underfunding and competition from outside the area and from new forms of media have helped undercut the position of the papers in the local communities. The problem is exacerbated at some papers because of the use of junior reporters as well as high rates of staff turnover. The combination of poor resources and turnover in staff reduces the research and investigative capacities of the papers.

Relations between campaigns and the media also revolved around special events and town hall meetings. The provincial and national offices of the parties coached local strategists in how to create and market these events. Special events included press conferences, meetings with visiting party luminaries, speaking engagements and functions, as well as tours of various local businesses and the like. Only the NDP made the leader's visit into a local media event, using it to focus attention on free trade and union–NDP solidarity.

The size and character of a rural constituency presents party workers with a range of difficulties in their attempts to engage the media. Events had to be staged in a number of towns. The interests of these towns were not identical, so campaigning needed to be continually modified. Notably, Brisco's campaign strategy of attempting to convince each community that he had provided direct and substantial economic benefits to that community as a result of his efforts within his party and the Parliament required his campaign to address each community individually. With about 10 different newspapers, some daily, some weekly, all with different deadlines, and some with unusual printing technologies, coordinating the media campaign was difficult.

There was no polling independently funded and organized by any local campaign or media organization. The radio media made more use of polling results received from wire services than did the newspapers. The latter disliked the regional or national focus of polls. The local NDP had access to the extensive British Columbia section of national polls conducted by that party. Part of the sense of ineffectualness that was often expressed by local campaigners and the media appears to have resulted from the "big city" nature of polling. By emphasizing national and provincial politics and media, polling made the local campaign and politics appear electorally irrelevant.

Third-party advertising was not seen as an important factor in the campaign. The national "for" and "against" free trade advertising was seen as a little strident and out of place in a rural constituency where there is a neighbourly quality to campaigning. Other than complaints about the depth of local reporting, those interviewed were happy with the media coverage their candidate received.

Campaigners' assessment of the relative value of the various forms of media coverage depended on whether they were considering advertising or news coverage. Regarding news coverage, they often asserted that non-local news on television had reinforced the dominance of free trade and the national nature of the election. As the local media did not comment extensively on national debates, it was analysis by television and newspapers from outside the constituency that shaped the media view of the debates. Positive interpretations of Turner's performance were thought to have moved some anti–free trade support from the NDP to the Liberals. Regarding advertising, campaigners were very uncertain of the value of advertising in local media as, in their opinion, local media had limited credibility with voters. While newspaper advertising was less expensive than radio advertising, the decline in the status of local daily newspapers has encouraged campaigners to look to other media to put their message across. While radio offered an alternative to newspapers, most campaigners were reluctant to rely on it because they doubted its audience reach. Signs on the side of major highways were seen as particularly useful by a number of campaigners, while pamphlets were not highly regarded.

Campaign advertising is a good source of income for the local media and is placed by both local and non-local party organizations.

The national parties used radio as their major input into the local campaign, covering national election issues with "tag-ons" that mentioned the local candidate.

In addition to the amounts spent by the national parties, the local parties' spending on radio advertising accounted for 25 percent of the Tory advertising budget and 26 percent and 42 percent, respectively, in the case of the NDP and Liberal campaigns. This reflects the possibility of targeting certain high-listening times, such as the drive to and from work, the limited choices facing campaigners in terms of media, and the fact that the local radio audience area matches the boundaries of the constituency quite closely. The Tories' attempts to alter the content of the local issue space can be seen in the fact that their total advertising expenditure represented 43 percent of their total expenses, the largest of any of the campaigns. The NDP spent 36 percent of its total expenses on advertising, and the Liberals 35 percent. (See Appendix, table 2.A1.)

The main complaint from campaign managers was that, while getting the media to cover events was sometimes difficult, having them print press releases was not. Given the absence of full-time local reporters, the local campaigns supplied most of the basic information for media stories in the form of press releases. Local media were variously seen as lacking sufficient interest, too understaffed, or too inexperienced to cover an election adequately. The inability of local media to critique the local or national campaigns was seen as undercutting their standing with the voters and hence their value as a tool for influencing voters. Furthermore, because media outlets are by and large tied to a particular town, coverage of the campaign seemed variously episodic, disjointed, or repetitive as the campaigns moved around the constituency. This lack of versatility highlighted the inadequacies of the local media in the eyes of campaigners.

Although campaign strategists saw the local media as having only limited impact on voters, the lack of alternatives and congruence between the target audiences for radio and newspapers and the constituency boundaries facilitated the use of these media by local campaigns, particularly for radio. Conversely, this gave the media reason to cover the election for its audiences and was thus vital to ensuring adequate media coverage of the campaign. There was usually one campaign person working full time on media relations, writing and sending daily faxes to the media apprising them of the movements of the candidate and the issues he would be addressing that day, or phoning reporters to solicit their attendance at campaign events. Press releases often took their cue from issue sheets originating in head office that related to policy statements by leaders. Local workers added a "spin" linking the "fact sheets" to the local candidates' agenda and then released them to the local media.

Campaigners in the Kootenays expressed ambivalence about the impact of rural media on local campaigning. While necessary for candidates who wanted to be taken seriously, neither news coverage nor advertising were held to have much impact on voters' decisions. The lack of resources and the reactive nature of the media coverage of this race resulted in a different balance between various means by which campaigns communicated with the public. The importance of personal contact and debates was heightened. As well, it is possible to see how lack of media resources affects the issue space. Not only is it likely to be reduced in size, but forcing issues into (and out of) that space may be quite difficult, as the Tories discovered in their attempts to displace free trade.

Vancouver Centre

The range of media outlets that covered the Vancouver Centre (VC) contest was extensive. The following is a limited selection of those which covered the election in some detail: the local community newspapers, the *WestEnder* and the *Courier*; the main Vancouver television stations including the CBC, Radio Canada, BCTV and CKVU; several radio stations including both French and English CBC as well as CKNW; and the daily Vancouver newspapers, the *Vancouver Sun* and the *Province*. All of these have extensive affiliation arrangements for both receiving news from and distributing news to other parts of Canada, and, except for CKVU, all have local relays in other parts of British Columbia. The local Rogers cable station hosted an all-candidate debate. Vancouver Centre also attracted attention from the *Globe and Mail*, the *Toronto Star*, national editions of several news programs, and Dutch, West German, British and American television.

Major newspaper and television organizations approached the reporting of the campaign aware of the potential for manipulation of news by the media relations efforts of the campaigns. In contrast to Kootenay media, urban media had the resources to scrutinize campaign press releases before deciding whether they warranted a story. This scrutiny consisted of researchers and reporters following up the issues raised in the release, often with people other than the candidates. As in the Kootenays, the impact of free trade on industry and business was the focus of most reporting. Town hall debates were covered, but once the basic approach of each candidate became clear, it was thought too costly to cover them all, so coverage became more selective as the campaign progressed. Only a few notable clips from debates received air time, and at least as many dealt with audience participation as with statements by the candidates. Both the NDP and PC candidates were interviewed regularly, and the visits of their respective leaders provided a focus for coverage of the constituency. Turner's visits, on the other hand, tended to be centred in his own riding, Quadra, and thus brought less coverage to Centre and Liberal candidate Enemark than in the case of the other two leaders.

In terms of the credibility campaigners thought coverage bestowed on campaigns, television ranked first, followed closely by daily newspapers, with a clear break to community newspapers and radio, which vied for third and fourth ranking.

The logistics of television reporting encourage a focus on constituencies that are readily accessible. Unlike newspaper or radio reporting, the amount of equipment and people needed, plus the production work required before airing a nightly news report, limits the range of television. As well, the local urban seats made for good television as they were tightly contested with capable candidates who could be easily reached to speak to a number of local and non-local issues. Further, the party leaders spent a good deal of their BC tours in Vancouver and Victoria, resulting in a number of local stories surrounding the tours. Examples of this included den Hertog walking the downtown business district with Broadbent, Campbell meeting with Mulroney, and Enemark hosting a hastily organized lunch for Turner after bad weather prevented the leader from making a scheduled stop in Prince George.

As with other major media outlets centred in Vancouver that service province-wide audiences, television focused on a number of races it thought were of particular interest. The CBC chose Vancouver Centre and Quadra, Prince George–Bulkley Valley, Mission–Coquitlam, Kootenay East, Kootenay West–Revelstoke, Esquimalt–Juan de Fuca and six Vancouver Island seats. Reasons given for the selection included the way a constituency highlighted aspects of free trade (Prince George), the personal relationship between the member and the prime minister (Mission–Coquitlam), and the closeness of the race. The resources devoted to election coverage by the CBC were substantial. The CBC had eight camera crews, 15 reporters and 10 to 15 editorial people in the newsroom in 1988. At any one time, three or four reporters, three editorial people and one researcher were working on the election. Researchers compiled profiles of all the constituencies in the province for reporters, and extra funds were made available for travel expenses and overtime needed to cover the election. There was a special election night budget for the special show reporting the results.

The major party leaders spent 80 percent of their time campaigning beyond the BC border; lack of resources required that the CBC use affiliates to cover that portion of the leader tours. The other 20 percent was made up of the periods when local reporters were covering the BC section of these tours. Relations with affiliates were computerized, and all stories were filed through a central clearing house in Toronto. National coverage was worked out weeks in advance and finalized one day before the day in question. This coordination was particularly important when a leader tour was in Vancouver, because local television was at these times responsible for the national reports of the tour.

With respect to television news, British Columbia and local news about the campaign usually pre-empted national stories. Major announcements by the leaders were the only regular exceptions to this. CBC news reports were often related to poll results, notably CBC/*Globe and Mail* polls. The rules governing how polls are reported on the CBC are quite strict and include assessment of the statistical validity of the polls. Editors estimated that the content of news coverage favoured BC over national news by about three to two. Vancouver Centre stood out in this coverage partly because of the quality of the media relations which the campaigns maintained. The Campbell campaign was seen as the most organized in terms of both personnel and finances, while the NDP campaign was noted for its diligence with respect to informing the media of issues and candidates' movements. The understaffed Liberal campaign, while it relied heavily on media coverage to remain competitive, was seen by reporters as organizationally inferior to the other campaigns.

The major dailies in Vancouver, the *Sun* and the *Province,* are both owned by Southam but they operate independent newsrooms and did not coordinate their election coverage. The former had a circulation of around 200 000 copies as an afternoon paper, while the latter, a morning paper, had a circulation at the time of about 185 000 copies. As with television, the newspapers selected some constituencies on which to concentrate, one of which was Vancouver Centre, but the *Sun* also did a profile of every BC constituency. The *Province* divided British Columbia into a number of regions and assigned a reporter to keep track of the election in each region, using its Victoria bureau to cover Vancouver Island. About 60 percent of total coverage dealt with BC stories, and, as with television, a good local or BC story was seen as better copy than an equally good national story. Both papers had access to the Southam news service and the Canadian Press wire service, with the *Sun* favouring Southam and the *Province* favouring Canadian Press. Relations between the wire services and the local papers were close, with daily exchanges of stories. In particular, high-profile constituencies like

Vancouver Centre, where there were many press conferences and where leaders made a point of stopping on their tours, were often in stories sent from Vancouver to the various wire services.

Each paper used three reporters and two editors working exclusively on the election. The *Sun* could call upon 10 or so other reporters to help cover the contest from a total reporting staff of between 30 and 40, while the *Province* had a newsroom of 21 reporters. Special space was set aside in the papers every day for election coverage as was money and office space. As well, special funds were made available to allow the papers to cover leader tours while the leaders were in BC. Town hall debates and the like were covered more assiduously early in the campaign, but coverage decreased as the campaign progressed and the issues and candidates' positions became known.

Polls were used regularly as front page copy because they were often striking and provided a natural opening for a general report on the election. Poll results were also used by parties in their press releases, sometimes as the basis for canvassing local issues. Press releases were reviewed for suitable content, but the usefulness of faxed press releases was questioned. Indicative of the remarkable difference in the level of coverage in Centre as opposed to KW-R, one *Sun* reporter estimated that the paper performed 60 personal interviews with Centre candidates and attended 30 press conferences and 10 other events, such as town hall debates.

As local campaigns cannot afford to advertise on major television stations or in large dailies, the only options are radio and community newspapers, of which community newspapers are the least expensive. As a result of this, community newspapers are important to the conduct of the campaign. The community papers' explicit aim is to report news not covered by the dailies. The *WestEnder* and the *Vancouver Courier,* which were both independent newspapers at the time, carried the bulk of the advertising for the Centre campaign. The weekly *WestEnder* at the time had a staff of three reporters and an editor, while the biweekly *Courier* at the time had a staff of three reporters and two editors. Despite the windfall of campaign advertising, the papers did not expend a great deal of effort in covering the election. One reporter (or the equivalent in terms of time) spent the majority of his or her time covering the campaign with occasional help from a freelance reporter. The depth of local coverage appears to be a function of an individual reporter's commitment to covering the campaign. Reporters found the period taxing as few if any extra resources were made available for coverage.

The fact that the papers' distribution area includes other constituencies besides Vancouver Centre, including Vancouver Quadra,

John Turner's seat, strained the available resources. Except for the fact that the *WestEnder* and its affiliate the *EastEnder* shared some stories, there was no use of syndicated material or wire services in the *WestEnder* or *Courier*, nor did the papers try to cover anything more than the local angle of the election. The *Courier* covered all the town hall meetings, while the *WestEnder* covered the three major meetings as well as the nomination meetings. Most weeks the papers ran two or three stories on the election including rewritten press releases or stories initiated by press releases. As with the Kootenay papers, these papers relied on campaigns to keep the papers informed of the candidates' movements and the main issues of the campaign and picked up very local human interest stories such as how free trade would affect a local business. Polls played a part in community paper coverage, but, in general, they were not appropriate for the local slant of the papers.

While the campaigns put substantial effort into media relations in Vancouver Centre, the media pursued the candidates at least as vigorously as the campaigns pursued the media. Reporters noted that the proximity of Centre to media headquarters, the profile of the candidates, the closeness of the race, and the historical importance of the constituency in BC ensured that Centre was attractive to the media. The resources available to newspapers, radio and television allowed them to take advantage of this. As one candidate put it, the most important thing for a candidate to do was "to always be available to the media." As candidates were seen to speak with some authority on a range of issues, the local campaign might be reported as either a local contest, a provincial contest, or as an important contest in national terms. Some of the candidates reported spending up to 15 percent of their time dealing with national media, indicative of the national role played by local candidates. All of these reports would have been broadcast in Vancouver Centre, compounding the media exposure of the local candidates. In general, campaign managers and reporters expressed satisfaction with the way the other had done their job.

The three major parties had the equivalent of a full-time worker issuing press releases. As well, teams of volunteers created newsworthy events with the assistance of professionals such as media liaison experts, advertising design professionals and media analysts. Some of the latter were academics, while others were from the private sector. Only the Liberal campaign lacked the personnel necessary to compete with the other campaigns in these areas, perhaps because of the low level of party membership and the loss of some workers to the Turner campaign. Attempts to make up for the lack of door-to-door campaigning may account for the relatively large advertising budget of the

Liberal campaign. Liberals openly admitted that their campaign was "smoke and mirrors," designed to make it look competitive and its candidate a credible alternative to Campbell and den Hertog. The parties in Centre easily out-spent their Kootenay cousins on advertising. This spending accounted for approximately 67, 53 and 35 percent of the Liberal, PC and NDP total expenses, respectively (see Appendix).

The parties used the leader tours to attract the media, and press conferences called by groups of candidates were often held in Centre. Parties staged a number of other events to attract media attention. The Liberal party nomination was a high-profile event, but attendance was much less than expected. The New Democrat nomination attracted some media attention with the party going through the motions of a candidate search, but interest was reduced due to the widespread perception that den Hertog would be selected. The Progressive Conservatives did not announce Campbell as their candidate until three weeks after the writ had been dropped, and the party was trailing the NDP by 15 to 20 percent in the constituency. The intrigue surrounding the private search for a candidate helped attract attention to the campaign.

Local and national debates played a role in shaping newspaper reporting. In particular, the debate at Christ Church Cathedral, where Kim Campbell strongly defended free trade, enhanced her reputation as a serious candidate well worth reporting. Local press reporters who watched the cable debate thought that it and other debates tended to highlight the fact that the local contest was really between the New Democrats and the Tories. This may have helped these two campaigns in their relations with the media. The *Sun* organized a panel of "ordinary" people to watch the national English debates and detailed their responses. The apparent success of Turner in the national debates hurt the Tories in BC, and Mulroney's poor national performance did further damage. The failure of Broadbent to make an impact on the campaign nationally, exemplified in the debates, scuttled that part of the New Democrats campaign premised on his popularity.

The impact of Turner's and Mulroney's national debate indicates that the local issue space can be a component of the national issue space. For the majority of Canadians, the Liberals were the main opposition to free trade, and this was reflected in the way the national campaign was reported and in how the national media reported the Centre contest. Reporters from outside looking at BC tended to focus more on the Liberals than some campaigners thought was warranted by the party's level of support in the province. This emphasis in reporting, encouraged as it was by Turner's debate performance, had direct consequences for the local issue space in that local voters were subjected to it as part of the national coverage of the election. Coverage of leader tours in BC by national reporters treated Turner as the leader of the anti–free trade forces, much to the consternation of NDP workers and to the delight of Tory workers, who were happy to see the anti–free trade vote split.

As in the Kootenays, media interpretations of Turner's performance were a mixed blessing for the local Liberal campaign. While the local Liberal campaign received added media attention as a result of the debate, and morale and worker numbers improved, it was also "forced" to confront the free trade issue, an issue which divided the local organization. Many workers and strategists believed that the somewhat negative interpretation of Mulroney's debate performance and the dismal outlook for the provincial Tories were offset in Centre by the strength and expertise of the combined Campbell and Carney organizations.

Local community newspapers were often seen as equally or more important to the campaign than other media when both advertising and news coverage were taken together. But except for some NDP campaigners, workers did not think highly of these papers; they were simply all the campaigns could afford. Television and daily newspaper coverage maintained their value to the campaign because of the perceived impact of the news coverage of Centre provided by the major media. Radio usually ranked last, reflecting perceptions that its news coverage had little impact on voters. Cable, magazines, ethnic and lifestyle newspapers were not seen as particularly important, although some were used to advertise candidates' interests in specific issues.

DISCUSSION

The differences in the way the campaigns and the media interacted in the two constituencies studied were startling. In the Kootenays, limited resources constrained the role of the media and hence the breadth of the relationship between the local media and campaigns. The lack of influential media resulted in a local issue space of limited size and content. The number of towns in the Kootenays and the technical and geographical difficulties facing campaigners complicated relations between the media and campaigns and candidates. The Vancouver case reveals an abundance of media and a complex relationship between the media and campaigns based on proximity and symbiosis. This closeness resulted in a larger and more diverse issue space.

The importance of the media is based on two premises: the amount and type of coverage given a campaign is a major determinant of whether a campaign is perceived by the public as competitive; and, media coverage provides the basis for the mass communication of campaign messages in the form of both advertising and, most importantly, various news reporting formats. The latter are most valued because, in providing objective coverage, as distinct from party-produced campaign literature, campaigners believe the media has a higher standing with the public and consequently a greater impact on public opinion. In short, the media, in particular, well-financed independent media, can generate credibility for a campaign and get the campaign message across to the public. But this objectivity brings its own price, for the media may offer competing definitions of campaign issues and less than flattering analysis of party platforms. By providing the arena for debate and competing definitions of the issues, the media is a critical variable in the mix of factors that determine both the size and content of the local issue space.

The local Kootenay media were caught in an awkward position. Unable to afford in-depth reporting of the campaign and to some degree uncertain as to their role with respect to the campaign, they were forced to rely on campaign press releases and wire service feeds to cover the campaign. This hand-feeding of information further reduced their credibility in the eyes of local voters and campaigners, forcing the latter to rely on other means of influencing the local issue space. The apparent inability of local media to combat the intrusion of non-local concerns into the local campaign threatens the link between local media and local campaigns and holds the promise of an even more poorly defended local issue space in the future. The use of wire services to fill space in the local Kootenay media injected the free trade concerns of non-local media and campaigns into the local constituency, further entrenching it as the dominant local issue. Not only did the local radio network have the largest newsroom and arguably the best coverage of the local election, but advertising by the local campaigns in the Kootenays was much greater than in Vancouver, where there was basically no locally financed radio advertising. (The national parties advertised on radio in both constituencies.) It appears that the lack of alternatives to radio and the congruence of broadcast area and constituency boundaries, combined with the news-oriented nature of the Kootenay Broadcasting System, made radio a more valuable resource in the Kootenays.

Rural constituencies are less likely to attract the same sort of attention as a high-profile constituency such as Centre. Given the relative lack of integration between local and non-local campaigns, there is less overt competition to define the contents of this space, and campaigns in the Kootenays were free to attempt to alter the content and size of the local issue space. Rural campaigns must, however, deal with the potential loss of control over issue space which results when local concerns such as free trade coincide with a main issue of the provincial and/or national campaigns.

The growing use of polls aided the intrusion of the non-local campaign into the local issue space. Given that these polls nearly always focused on non-local issues and aggregate responses for provinces, they accentuated feelings of ineffectiveness among local campaigners.

In the Kootenays, non-media methods of affecting the local issue were labour-intensive. As a result, a campaign requires many volunteers if it wishes to alter the size and content of the local issue space. The local Tory and Liberal campaigns were unable to find sufficient means with which to overcome the dominance of the free trade issue. The strength of the local party organization is critical in the struggle for control of the local issue space.

The content of the local issue space in Centre was influenced by the particular perspectives and strategic concerns of a range of actors, both within the media and political parties. National and provincial media organizations as well as national and provincial party strategists sometimes competed and at other times colluded with each other and local party strategists in their attempts to shape the local issue space. This was in addition to the competition between political parties for control of the local issue space. In attempting to influence the content of the local issue space, the NDP and Liberal campaigns faced the difficulty of sharing the same anti–free trade message, a situation that competing political parties are not well adapted to deal with. Local issue space is a single means to a variety of ends.

The major media outlets in Centre had substantial resources to devote to covering the election. Special budgets, staff, office space and guaranteed air time or newspaper space were all available. The major Vancouver media played an important role in reporting the election in British Columbia to the rest of the country. The proximity of the riding to the news organizations and its high-profile candidates, who could speak effectively for their parties, made Centre a natural barometer of the performance of the parties in the province. These conditions promoted media attention to the local contest and facilitated a close relationship between the media and the local organizations.

While the above analysis implies that local campaigns in Centre had abundant issue space to work with, local issues did not dominate the campaign as much as some would have liked. As regional and national issues address large segments of media target audiences, these issues were often chosen for broadcast from the range of matters raised at local press conferences. Thus, only some of the local issue space gen-

erated by the media was available to the local campaign for addressing local issues.

As well, other non-local levels of the parties used this space to
address their concerns, with the local candidates acting as both provincial and national spokespersons for their parties. This left candidates
having to balance the priorities of other campaigns against those of the
local campaign. While it is likely that sufficient room exists for candidates to address local issues, there is no guarantee that the way in which
they are addressed is optimal for the local campaign. In contrast to
KW-R, campaigns in Centre had adequate issue space and many different media outlets capable of affecting the content of this space, but
they had to compete with definitions of the content of that space offered
by the media and other party organizations.

All this results in a symbiotic relationship between parties and
the media. The lack of adequately financed media in the Kootenays
had direct consequences for the size and content of the issue space
that developed and the sorts of activities undertaken by campaigns
as they attempted to alter the content of the local issue space. On the
other hand, the coincidence of major media and urban centres creates both the expectation and the resources necessary for high-
profile campaigns. The volume and quality of media available in
Vancouver encouraged campaigns to use professionals to oversee
their media relations, whereas the Kootenay campaigns relied largely
on workers with no particular media-related skills. The parties want
coverage, and the media wants contests that are exciting, informative
and close at hand.

By and large, party strategists were aware of the type and level of
media coverage that a particular constituency would receive during
an election campaign. As such, strategists attempted to tailor their campaigns to maximize their exposure and ensure this exposure was positive. The strategies used to gain favourable media coverage and the
way in which campaigns try to influence the size and content of local
issue space are the subjects of the next section.

ISSUES AND STRATEGIES IN LOCAL CAMPAIGNS

In the competition between local, regional and national issues, there is
little doubt that national themes dominated the minds of those that
worked on the 1988 election. This domination in part reflects the salience
of the free trade issue, selected by the overwhelming majority of interviewees as the single most important issue of the campaign. As well,
national leaders and party platforms were generally seen as more important to the electoral outcome than were local or regional factors.

Nevertheless, the style of local campaigns differed widely, and measures of local and regional content, such as where campaign literature originates and the main themes of the literature, reveal a clear local emphasis in most campaigns. By these measures, both local issues and local candidates are at least as important as regional, national and leader-related issues in shaping local issue space. This section explores how local issue space develops as a result of the interaction of local and non-local factors.

Kootenay West–Revelstoke

The demographic characteristics of a constituency provide the raw materials for any campaign. In Kootenay West–Revelstoke, the importance of primary and secondary industry provided an immediate focus for the free trade debate. Unions and management at the Cominco smelter in Trail, the principal industry of the region, squared off publicly over the issue. Proximity to the U.S. border and the sensitivity of some people to the question of relations with the United States contributed to the salience of the free trade debate. The free trade issue was, in the words of one reporter, "localized." As such, it is misleading to see free trade as a purely national issue. The distinction between local, regional and national issues is one that requires careful consideration. The issues space in the local campaign appears to have been dominated by the free trade debate in part because it was directly relevant to both the local and non-local issue spaces.

The incumbent, Progressive Conservative Bob Brisco, did not base his campaign on free trade. PC strategists felt that the anti-Mulroney feeling in BC, the difficulties over patronage associated with the prime minister and the union strength in the constituency made the issue difficult for the local campaign. As a result of this, the campaign decided to focus on Brisco's record as federal member and a number of local issues in an attempt to build on his strong personal following. In this sense, the local candidate was very important to the local PC campaign.

As with all the campaigns studied in both Vancouver and the Kootenays, PC campaigners estimated that 75 to 80 percent of their literature was locally produced. This local production of literature permits a local thrust to campaigning, but the uncertainty about its value in attracting supporters is as universal as is its use. The main literature of the Tory campaign listed various projects that had been funded by the federal government since Brisco had become federal member in 1984, emphasizing the fact that Brisco was the first local member to sit on the government benches in 50 years. It also focused on issues unrelated to free trade, such as the upcoming renegotiation of the Columbia River Treaty. With an eye to the strong environmental element in the com-

munity, the campaign included a plan to conserve local native archae-
ological sites.

The *Candidates Returns* reveal the financial strength of the Tories.
As well as collecting the most money, the Brisco campaign spent the
most. Of all the candidates in both constituencies, the Liberal candidate in KW-R was the only candidate to post a deficit. New Democrat
candidate Lyle Kristiansen was well financed (see Appendix). The
Tory campaign, with offices in Trail, Castlegar and Nelson was staffed
by between 20 and 30 full-time volunteers, over 100 regular part-time
volunteers and several hundred casual workers. The only worker to
receive any financial consideration was the campaign manager, who
had some of his expenses covered. Although these numbers seem
impressive, the chair of the Strategy Committee noted a lack of supporters compared with 1984 and a reduced level of commitment to the
campaign. In particular, workers noted that the organization of Brisco's
campaign and the recruiting of workers was hampered by his late start
in September. The demands of his work in Ottawa plus the ongoing
effects of a recent heart attack appeared to have strained relations
between the local association and Brisco, thus weakening his campaign somewhat.

The visit of Brian Mulroney to the constituency during the campaign highlighted one of the tensions that can face a local campaign
unhappy with its leader's profile. Brisco was a big supporter of
Mulroney, and the visit with its attendant press gallery should have
added credibility to the local Tory campaign. Yet the unpopularity of
the prime minister left the campaign uncertain as to how to use the
visit to its advantage. Local Tories saw the visit as designed more for
a national audience than for a local one.

In fact, the national Tory campaign appears to have been quite separate from the local campaign. The KW-R Tory campaign manager noted
that the local campaign was so distant from the regional or national
campaigns that it was "like working in a vacuum."

Moreover, while the national campaign spent more on advertising
on local radio than did the local campaign, there was no local input into
this advertising at all other than a mention of the local candidate's
name. Local campaigners complained that they could not even get a
schedule of how much and when the national party would be advertising in the local constituency.

According to figures supplied by Kootenay Broadcasting System,
the local radio network, the national Progressive Conservative campaign spent $5 149 on radio advertising during November of 1988, com-
pared with $2 629 spent by the local campaign. The national New
Democrat campaign spent $1 872 as opposed to the local campaign's

expenditure of $2 549, while the figures for the Liberal party were $1 057 and $1 425, respectively. The relative strength of the Conservatives' national campaign is clear from these figures, but this strength was applied through channels other than the local campaign organization. The local issue space was subjected to a good deal of interference from the national campaigns of the major parties and, in particular, the Tories.

The intraparty separation of local and national campaigns was not wholly unwelcome by the local Tory campaign strategists. Not only did they consider the national campaign and leader to be of dubious value in the local context, their campaign was sufficiently well financed that they could pursue their own strategies and attempt to distance themselves from other levels of the party. This strategic distance was facilitated by the geographic remoteness of the constituency. According to the Tory candidate, ties to the provincial party were closer than those to the national campaign, marked by regular contact with and visits from provincial strategists. Despite the efforts of the local party, however, the dominance of the free trade issue was not successfully challenged by the Tory campaign. Campaigners found the local media uninterested in other issues. The type of media available meant that an advertising blitz on other issues had little effect, and the campaign's ability to swamp the constituency with campaigners, the only other means of impacting on the issue space, was limited.

As well as creating a lightning-rod for free trade, union–management disagreement hardened the partisan nature of the campaign. A central theme in the New Democratic campaign was that "this is union country." NDP candidate Lyle Kristiansen had been involved in a high-profile scheme at a local mill where unions had taken over management of the mill. Localization of the free trade issue suited the NDP. Not only was its candidate a union man, but unlike either the Tories or the Liberals, the New Democrats embraced a well-organized provincial campaign whose aim of installing the party as the anti–free trade party in BC was well-suited to the local campaign. In contrast to the local Tories' experience, the visit of Ed Broadbent was a highlight for the local NDP campaign. It was used to push their anti–free trade stance and to advertise the NDP–union solidarity. Relations with the national campaign were enhanced by the fact that the media liaison person for the local campaign was from Ed Broadbent's office. A local man, he had his airfares to and from Ottawa paid by the local NDP campaign.

The New Democrats also had several campaign offices and claimed a central staff of about 15 people and another 100 volunteers. Although not as well financed as the Tories, the NDP were successful in getting large numbers of supporters to public events. As well, judging from the complaints of Progressive Conservative workers, the NDP found enough casual workers to erect more campaign signs than did other campaigns. Strong union support in the form of both time and money helped the campaign considerably. The local campaign was more than happy to ride the "coat-tails" of the provincial and, to a lesser extent, national party campaigns and utilized the party's links with the union movement.

The Liberal campaign faced even more difficulties than the Tory campaign in terms of finding issues to run on. The fact that Turner was the only national leader not to visit the constituency may be indicative of how the national party viewed its support in the area. The polarization of BC politics, fuelled in this case by free trade, and the fact that Brisco and Kristiansen had both held the seat previously were substantial hurdles for the Liberal campaign. The Liberals were uncomfortable when forced to deal with the strongly partisan politics of free trade, particularly as their anti–free trade stance was problematic for the local candidate, who noted that "the Liberal Party has historically supported free trade." Moreover, campaign workers noted the lack of a strong provincial campaign precluded a coordinated approach to provincial issues. Although the KW-R campaign manager was sent from the Vancouver office of the party, there was, in the words of Jenkins, "little contact and little help from the party ... The local campaign was left to its own devices." Although this might have enabled the local Liberals to steer an independent course, their lack of resources prevented them from doing so.

Excluded from centre stage in the free trade debate and faced with a weak provincial party which had little faith that KW-R could be won, the local Liberal campaign was very much on its own. The campaign had a handful of full-time volunteer staff, including a young enthusiastic volunteer campaign manager and about forty part-time workers. The Liberal campaign was also clearly more limited in its ability to raise funds. Their advertising budget was less than one-third of that of their opponents. Although he was seen as effective by both the media and Jenkins, the fact that the campaign manager did not come from the constituency reveals the weakness of the local association. In fact, there was some uncertainty as to whether the local association had the necessary number of members to fulfil the minimum requirements set by the party for association status.

Even if local Liberals had been more disposed toward the free trade issue, this was an issue the local union–NDP coalition was better placed to tackle. Liberals felt that only local issues were available to their campaign in the competition for control of the local issue space. These issues included forestry, sustainable development and renegotiation of the

Columbia River Treaty. In the end, they made little impact on the local issue space. Their exclusion from the central debate within the local issue space highlighted the marginal nature of their campaign, a fact further illustrated by their inability to muster support at town hall debates. One exception to the overall weakness of their campaign was the Liberals' use of fax material. This technological innovation facilitated contact between campaigns and the media and reduced the need for volunteers. The use of faxes by Liberal campaigners in the Kootenays may well presage a "fax war" during future elections, particularly in campaigns where there is a lack of volunteers. It was thought that this electronic innovation helped the Liberals appear to be running a serious bid for the seat.

In Centre, the campaigns had better resources and were central to the parties' provincial and national strategies. There was also a great deal of media interest in the contest. This led to a very different sort of campaign which reveals the double-edged nature of high-profile campaigns.

Vancouver Centre
The Vancouver Centre contest attracted high-profile candidates and a great deal of media attention. Some saw it as a "bell-wether" constituency which acted as a symbol of the support for the parties as the campaign progressed. Others saw it as a "swing" constituency which might well fail to elect a Tory to replace retiring cabinet minister Pat Carney. Whichever view they favoured, the parties and the media agreed that strong candidates and strong campaigns were essential in Centre. For their part, the media expects the parties to run good candidates and finds it to be both a convenient and, as a result of the type of candidates that have often run in Centre, an exciting contest to cover.

This constituency has in the past provided both Liberal and Tory cabinet ministers and has a national media profile. For the Tories, VC was one of the few BC constituencies where they might expect to hold on against the unpopularity of the Mulroney government in BC. The NDP saw an opportunity to take advantage of the growing strength of the party in Vancouver and provide a standard bearer for future provincial and federal success. To the Liberals, success in this riding would indicate their continued relevance in the West, especially given its propinquity to John Turner's constituency of Quadra.

Because the constituency was conveniently close to the headquarters of the province-wide media and parties and the local candidates were eminently qualified to act as party spokespersons, many issues were dealt with in the local campaign. Unlike the Kootenays, where the free trade issue was driven by the congruence of local and non-local factors, the debate in Centre appears to have been driven much more by the parties' desires to publicize their policies on free trade rather than by any local concern with the issue. There were very few local issues that could be brought into sharp focus as strictly free trade issues. This is not to say that there was no local interest in the issue, but rather that this interest was of a general, perhaps even abstract, nature at times. The debate was couched in national terms and, in this way, was a surrogate for the national debate. With respect to this characterization of the debate, it should be noted that the weakness of the Liberal party and the strength of the NDP in British Columbia gave rise to local debates that were variants of the national debate.

The fact that the constituency encompasses the downtown core encouraged an emphasis on free trade. The Liberals and Progressive Conservatives considered the support of the business community essential for justifying their views on free trade. Even the NDP appears to have pursued a policy of nonconfrontation with respect to the local business community. Parties stressed the professionalism of their candidate and had national leaders do several downtown "walk-throughs" with the aim of implying business support of their policies. Given that these events were for local, provincial and national media consumption, they further blurred the distinction between the various levels of the campaign brought about by the free trade debate.

Both the party officials and the media agreed that, in a potentially volatile constituency, a good candidate could be crucial to success. Strong candidates are an attraction for the media, so they tend to get reported. Their personal qualities are a vital part of campaigning and reporting, particularly since a member from Vancouver Centre may well be in Cabinet if his or her party wins office. The fact that the constituency had previously elected high-profile candidates meant that candidates' ability to "sell" their view of free trade came to be seen as a de facto measure of the candidates' political abilities and perhaps their chances of gaining future advantages for the constituency. The Tories and the NDP played heavily on the theme of "who is likely to help whom most." The NDP aimed its appeal directly to the "average" person, emphasizing the qualities of den Hertog as a "young, bright, concerned woman," while the Tories emphasized the protection of the constituency's economic base and linked this with the business and governmental experience of Campbell. The Liberals also emphasized Enemark's experience and his ability to extract favours from Ottawa if elected.

The local campaign focused on a range of issues other than free trade, partly in response to the nature of the constituency. The amount of media coverage received by this campaign underpinned the development of a large and varied issue space. Candidates were quick to establish their bona fides toward a number of issues including multiculturalism, women's affairs and gay concerns. Not only did local candidates wish to canvass local issues, but the level of media and élite attention made it an ideal platform from which to address the provincial audience concerning a number of issues. The downtown location of the riding was important because issues relevant to other areas of the province, such as fishing, forestry and mining, could be addressed using company or association spokespersons from their respective Vancouver headquarters. This allowed both parties and the media to simplify some of the logistical demands of a province-wide campaign.

As well as attracting provincial coverage, the local contest was also well covered in the national press. The parties acted to take advantage of these circumstances. The NDP, in particular, used the constituency as a stage for large press conferences which dealt with a wide range of issues. One such conference brought all women candidates in BC together to address women's concerns. The environment, lesbian and gay concerns and abortion were also issues treated in this manner. Partly as a result of this, there were complaints from campaigners that the balance of issues and the way they were treated was not optimal for the local campaign, but rather, was a function of the demands of their party hierarchy and of media preferences.

Party activists in all three local organizations claimed to have tried to distance the local campaign from their respective national campaigns, although the New Democrat and Tory candidates did not concur in this with their campaign workers. Local NDP campaigners felt constrained on a number of fronts. While happy with the extra emphasis given free trade by the provincial campaign as compared with the national campaigns' focus on leadership, den Hertog's campaign manager felt that her provincial campaign role as a spokesperson against free trade and on a range of provincial issues limited her local campaign. Moreover, her position as federal president was seen by some local volunteers as tying her too closely to the national campaign and the party establishment which focused on Broadbent's leadership, a non-issue in the West. Centre lost a number of workers to surrounding campaigns such as Svend Robinson's, where the chance to deal directly and mainly with local issues was attractive to some workers. As a result, some NDP insiders claimed that the local campaign suffered from lower than expected worker turnout and consequently was slow to get in stride. Campaigners estimated that the NDP campaign had about 10–15 full-time workers and 300 or 400 part-time workers.

The Vancouver Tories felt the provincial campaign was inadequate, although it focused on the free trade issue, and claimed to have ignored the national campaign. The weakness of the regional campaign did not hurt the local campaign which had the resources to run a strong campaign on its own. In fact, maintaining a certain distance from the gloom of the provincial campaign was seen as a good thing. The combination of what remained of the Carney organization and Campbell's provincial organization created a formidable campaign machine. Campaigners estimated the central staff at about 50 people and further claimed that the campaign had access to several hundred other volunteers. Both Liberal and NDP campaigners commented on the high levels of financial and volunteer support the Tories were able to muster.

The support for the Tories and the New Democrats was in sharp contrast to the 50 or so workers the Liberals could muster. There appears to have been a substantial leakage to the Turner campaign in the neighbouring constituency of Quadra. In fact, a number of important campaign workers admitted that they worked for Enemark out of a sense of personal loyalty rather than a sense of party solidarity. Thus, despite appearances, Vancouver Centre was really a two-way race.

The Liberal campaign was very loosely tied to the national campaign and attached to an almost non-existent local association and regional campaign. As in Kootenay West–Revelstoke, opposing free trade did not sit well with local workers, and since it was perceived that Centre had always given the Liberals a chance if they ran a good candidate, the campaign focused on the qualities of Tex Enemark. The weakness of the local organization and of the local campaign were reflected in the final results. The Liberal campaign's inability to muster support at town hall debates badly hurt its image and ensured that such debates became NDP versus PC events.

Indicative of the strength of the local financial support for the parties, the Centre Tories collected about twice as much as the other two major parties. Despite outspending the NDP on advertising two to one and the Tories three to two, the Liberals were renowned, at least among the media, for having a much weaker campaign than the others (see Appendix). That is prima facie evidence that non-media campaign activities which require good numbers of volunteers are critical to the credibility of a campaign.

In Centre, additional media space gained by virtue of the profile of the contest was not directly converted into additional issue space for use by the local campaign because of the increased demands placed on this space by other campaigns. Further, the mix of issues that made up the space reflected in part the preferences of the other campaigns and the media as well as the local campaign. This helps to explain why activists could claim a lack of local focus to the campaign.

As with the Kootenays, there were also parallel national and local campaign advertising strategies. The local Liberal and Tory campaigns appear to have had little input or relationship to the national advertising strategies. This was also true for the NDP, but was offset somewhat by the strength of the provincial campaign and the close ties between local and provincial strategies.

Finally, it is worth commenting on the importance of candidates in national elections. In a province that swung heavily against the government, and in a constituency controlled at the provincial level by the New Democrats, the Tories managed to elect Kim Campbell in Vancouver Centre. Campaigners tended to put quite a premium on the role of the candidate's personal qualities in this result. Their comments suggest the need for a modest re-evaluation of the notion of candidate influence on election results. This reassessment would consider a number of factors that appear to be related to the type of candidate selected to run for a seat: the resources which parties expend on a particular campaign by all levels of the party; the level of professional help available to the campaign; the organizational capacity of the campaign; the role played by the candidate in organizing and attracting good organizers to the campaign; the desire of the media to report on the candidate; the willingness of the party to use the candidate as a spokesperson; and the level of name recognition and credibility associated with a candidate prior to the campaign. As well, the assessment of the importance of the candidate should consider the nexus between high-profile candidates and high-profile constituencies.

DISCUSSION

The localization of the free trade issue in Kootenay West–Revelstoke illustrates the influence of local demographic factors on the content of local issue space. It also demonstrates the importance of the resources available to local campaigns and the relationship between local and non-local elements of the parties' campaign organizations. The near total dominance of the local issue space by the free trade debate resulted from the coincidence of local economic factors and the emphasis placed on free trade by the non-local campaigns. As a result, the local campaign was susceptible to national and regional politicking and politicization of the same cleavages as in the national campaign, a situation capitalized upon by the well-organized national and provincial parties. The success of the free trade issue in gaining dominance of the local issue space helped the New Democrats to control that space. The centrality of the issue to the voters and the community meant that the combined resources of the Tory and Liberal campaigns were unable to break its dominance of the local issue space.

The reproduction of provincial and national political cleavages at the local level gave the local issue space a very "national" appearance. Local campaigns hoping to open up the issue space to other issues were confronted with some local campaign support for free trade and with the campaigns of their own parties at other levels which focused on free trade. While the Tory and Liberal local campaigns had enough independence from these other levels to mount alternate campaigns, neither of them had the necessary combination of resources to break the stranglehold of this one issue.

As the degree of intraparty integration in campaign strategies was limited, the congruence between the local, regional and national issue appears to have been largely coincidental rather than the result of the interdependence of local and non-local campaigns. Only the local NDP experienced any integration of local and non-local campaigns, partly as a result of the strength of the provincial NDP and the fact that the focus of the non-local campaign was appropriate to the local campaign. Even in this case, the efforts at integration were limited. The positive attitude of local New Democrat campaigners to Ed Broadbent's visit highlighted the local campaign's willingness to ride the "coat-tails" of both the regional and national campaigns.

The strength of the national Tory campaign enabled it to make some attempt to link all the local campaigns, but this appears to have taken place in mainly province-wide media. The local campaigns competed to shape the mix of issues. The relationship between the major media and the campaigns shaped the local issue space. The level of resources available to these urban media was much greater than that of the rural media, and the local campaigns were better financed and in most cases better staffed. In particular, the level of professional help in everything from bookkeeping to advertising was much greater for urban campaigns than it was for their rural counterparts. Despite the limited local focus to the free trade debate, the interests of the provincial and national parties and media pushed it to the top of the agenda. Nevertheless, its dominance was markedly less than it was in the Kootenays. Local issues that did make it onto the agenda were often those which could be used by the parties and the media to address both local and non-local audiences. Thus, the content of the local issue space was not chosen by the local campaigns alone, but reflected the strategic considerations of a number of actors.

The desire of the non-local campaigns to take advantage of the high-profile media coverage of the campaign resulted in a greater integration of local and non-local campaigns than was the case in the Kootenays. The importance of media exposure was not lost on local campaigns, and the use of this media coverage became a matter of negotiation between the various party levels. The provision of professional media relations volunteers indicates the premium placed on the media by the campaigns. As a result of this integration, local candidates were more closely associated with their party's platform. The integration of non-local campaigns into the local campaign added more issues to the local issue space as parties strove to get their message out using the local campaigns. In a strategic sense, this meant running on those issues deemed important in the context of the larger campaign and losing the ability to appear flexible when local conditions might warrant it. This was particularly true of the NDP campaign. The reduction in the local campaign's control of this large space because of the high profile of the local campaign and the media attention it garnered, was a striking feature of the VC campaign.

In the Kootenays, the strength of the provincial NDP campaign meant that the local New Democrat campaign was more heavily integrated than either of its major contenders. This integration limited the local NDP campaign's ability to respond to local issues. The Tories appeared to have responded better to local issues. The local Liberal campaign was nearly totally isolated. While not directly constrained by the demands of other levels of the party, it did have to deal with what it perceived to be the negative consequences of Turner's success in leading the national anti–free trade fight. The organizational weakness of the Liberals in BC (ironically one of the reasons for their freedom), reduced the local campaign's ability to collect and focus the necessary resources to affect the local issue space.

In passing, it should be noted that of all those associated with the campaigns, the candidate generally tended to be most aware of and favourably disposed toward the efforts made by other levels of the party to coordinate the local and non-local levels of the campaign. This was especially true for sitting members, and may indicate that candidates, perhaps by their close and extended contact with the party, tend to have a more national view of the election than do their workers.

CONCLUSION

This study has presented the concept of issue space as a means for understanding the way in which parties and the media shape the local information environment facing voters. There are two aspects to issue space. One is quantitative, that is, the number of issues that can be politicized at a local election. The other is qualitative, that is, what issues are politicized.

The size of the local issue space is determined by a number of factors: the number and type of media that cover the local contest; the profile of the local campaign and candidates; and the level of resources brought to bear by the parties in publicizing their campaigns.

The content of this issue space is a function of factors closely related to the above: the demography of a constituency; the degree of congruence in and integration of the priorities of the local, provincial and national campaigns and media; and the outcome of the competition between the various local campaigns for control of the issue space.

Events in Kootenay West–Revelstoke and Vancouver Centre suggest that the notion that there are clearly differentiated local, regional and national issues needs to be treated cautiously. Some local issues have national aspects, and some national issues have local aspects. The free trade issue was localized in the Kootenays, while in Centre, local issues melded with the provincial and national campaigns.

This study discovered two distinctive types of local issue space; one, in the Kootenays, which is best described as *parallel issue space,* and one, in Centre, which is best described as *component issue space.* The content of a parallel issue space is not dependent on any interaction between it and other non-local issue space. While it may resemble provincial or national issue space, this resemblance may result from either the local acceptance of non-local definitions of important issues or the failure of local campaigners to define alternative issues. A component issue space is one in which there is clear and intended interdependence between the local and non-local issue spaces. The content, size and means for controlling these two types of issue space are likely to be very different. Campaigns in constituencies with component issue spaces are connected to and play a part in non-local campaigns. Campaigns in constituencies with parallel issue spaces will be left much more to their own devices.

The abundance of media in Vancouver resulted in the local issue space having to respond to demands made on it by local, provincial and national media and political parties, thereby creating a local issue space that was both large and diverse in content. The demands made on the local issue space by this range of local and non-local actors creates competition for control of the local issue space and may reduce the control exercised by local campaigns over the content of that space. The interdependence of local and non-local factors meant that the issue space in Vancouver Centre became a component of the non-local issue space, and, as a result, the campaigns became components of the national campaign.

Kootenay West–Revelstoke experienced a relatively low-profile campaign in which local campaigns (except the NDP) tried to run on local issues other than free trade. Although local campaigns suffered less from competition for control of the local issue space, they were also confronted with far fewer media resources with which to influence the content of that space. On the whole, the relatively less important role played by the media in this constituency resulted in the campaigns favouring more traditional forms of communicating their message to the public. The local issue space was overwhelmed by the national campaign from a distance, partly because of the local salience of free trade. The separation of the local and non-local issue spaces meant that the issue space in Kootenay West–Revelstoke ran parallel to the non-local issue space, and as a result, the local campaigns were parallel but separate from the non-local campaigns.

Possible Reforms

In general, this study suggests that, at national elections, the choice of issues that are canvassed at the local level is at best only partially controlled by local campaign organizations. Moreover, as this study shows, the dynamics of campaigning are complicated and vary a great deal across constituencies. As a result, the impact of any changes to the laws governing campaigning will have different effects from constituency to constituency.

In addition, and given the number and complexity of elements operating in the electoral process, any change to the laws providing the context for local campaigning will produce effects which are unpredictable and may even have consequences which are at odds with the aims of enhancing local participation in campaigning.

Ballot Design
Removal of party names from ballots   While this may reduce the information available to voters at the point of voting, it will encourage campaigns to focus on candidates in their electioneering.

Media
More media access for local campaigns   It would strengthen local campaigns, if a proportion of the free and paid time that broadcasters are obliged to make available under current regulations were required to be set aside for local candidates. Time on radio and cable community

channels might be more useful. Mandatory local candidates debates might be worthy of consideration.

Requirement that all party advertising placed in local media be endorsed by the appropriate local campaign committee This would ensure that local parties could influence the thrust of campaigning in the local constituency by provincial and national campaigns. A reform such as this might more appropriately be a matter for the parties than for electoral regulation.

Requirement that local media state the statistical validity and local relevance of all polls published This would help voters decide what weight to give polls and should include the number of respondents that reside in the constituency(ies) within which the poll is published.

That the Canadian Radio-television and Telecommunications Commission increase its efforts to remind broadcasters of their obligation to provide local campaign coverage The CRTC guidelines require effective and equitable coverage and the Canadian Association of Broadcasters accepts this obligation. However, some broadcasters do not provide as much coverage as might be expected.

BIBLIOGRAPHY

Canada. Library of Parliament. Information and Reference Branch. 1982. *History of the Federal Electoral Ridings 1867–1980: Volume One.* Ottawa: Library of Parliament.

———. Statistics Canada. 1988. *Federal Electoral Districts – 1987 Representation Order Part 1: Profiles.* Ottawa: Minister of Supply and Services Canada.

Caplan, Gerald, Michael Kirby and Hugh Segal. 1989. *Election: The Issues, the Strategies, the Aftermath.* Scarborough: Prentice-Hall Canada.

Eagles, Munroe. 1991. Unpublished almanac of federal riding profiles.

Fraser, Graham. 1989. *Playing for Keeps: The Making of the Prime Minister.* Toronto: McClelland and Stewart.

Frizzell, Alan, Jon Pammett and Anthony Westell. 1989. *The Canadian General Election of 1988.* Ottawa: Carleton University Press.

APPENDIX

Table 2.A1
Campaign expenses and finances in Kootenay West–Revelstoke and Vancouver Centre
(dollars)

Expenses	Kootenay West–Revelstoke			Vancouver Centre		
	NDP	PC	Liberal	NDP	PC	Liberal
Radio	3 614	4 689	4 881	—	—	100
Television	—	—	—	—	—	—
Other media	10 453	13 718	6 698	17 553	24 602	32 438
Total media	14 067	18 407	11 579	17 553	24 602	32 538
Salaries	9 644	1 941	2 400	8 924	—	2 500
Office	10 975	17 997	9 608	16 249	13 259	12 344
Travel	1 858	2 127	2 686	—	—	—
Other	1 877	1 713	5 281	7 524	7 625	884
Total expenses *(1)*	38 421	42 185	31 554	50 250	45 486	48 266
Percentage of limit spent	80.9	88.8	66.4	97.6	88.3	93.7
Reimbursement	17 149	23 609	16 896	24 329	23 029	24 309
Contributions	42 998	61 232	—	66 615	116 488	54 053
Total Income *(2)*	60 147	84 841	16 896	90 944	139 517	78 362
Balance *(2 - 1)*	21 726	42 656	-14 658	40 694	94 031	30 096

Source: Canada, Elections Canada. "Candidates' Returns Respecting Election Expenses" (1988).

3

THE CAMPAIGN–MEDIA INTERFACE IN LOCAL CONSTITUENCIES
Two Alberta Case Studies from the 1988 Federal Election Campaign

Andrew Beh
Roger Gibbins

T HERE IS NO question that candidates and constituency campaigns play an important role in the democratic mythology that envelops election campaigns in Canada and other Western democracies. Voters identify the local candidates as an important part of their voting calculus, even when the candidates' stance on the issues, and often their names, are unknown. There is, in short, a normative reluctance to reduce election campaigns to struggles among national parties and leaders; we believe that the local candidates should count, at least to a degree, and that the choice among local candidates should be more than a proxy for our preference among national parties and leaders. For their part, local candidates have no choice but to believe that the constituency campaign counts, and may in fact be decisive. Only with such a belief firmly in place can candidates face the emotional turmoil, personal dislocation and financial risk of the campaign.

Although political mythologies are often well rooted in reality, the linkage is far from certain with respect to the actual role played by constituency campaigns. Election studies support the normative appeal of the mythology but, as discussed below, offer little empirical support. Thus, an important tension exists between the way we feel voters should behave – carefully weighing the strengths and weaknesses of the candidates running in their constituency – and the way it seems they do behave – using their vote to express a national preference with little regard for, interest in, or even knowledge of the local candidates. The present study addresses this tension by asking, once again: Do local candidates and constituency campaigns count in federal election campaigns? Do local candidates, and the local campaigns more broadly defined, have a significant impact on the constituency outcome of a national campaign? Or are the local candidates and the campaign organizations they have cobbled together overwhelmed by the national campaign, by the national parties, leaders, media and issues? Put more positively, what are the means by which local candidates and campaigns can find some leverage on the national campaign and thus become, to some degree, the masters of their own fate while riding the turbulent seas of a national campaign?

What sets this inquiry apart is not the questions asked, for such questions have been asked before. Rather, the difference stems from the way in which the questions are answered, from the research methodology employed. The primary concern lies with the relationship between local campaigns and the mass media, not with the perceptions of voters or candidates. In short, this study explores the extent to which the media provide local candidates and campaign organizations with some significant purchase on the national election campaign within which they are engulfed.

This exploration takes place within a political environment that is hostile to, and perhaps uniquely hostile to, the emergence of significant constituency-level effects. First, the research focuses on the 1988 general election, an election that served to some significant extent as a national referendum on the proposed Free Trade Agreement (FTA) with the United States. The dominance of the free trade issue in the 1988 campaign could only increase the likelihood that voters would use their ballots to register their support for or opposition to the FTA, and not to register preferences among local candidates. Second, the research examines two federal constituencies within Alberta, a province not known for closely fought constituency battles. (In the words of Allan Fotheringham, Alberta voters tend to stampede rather than choose.) Indeed, it had been in 1968, two decades previously, that an Alberta candidate other than a Progressive Conservative had last been elected in a general election. As a consequence, the political culture within the province had come to reflect the view that any Progressive Conservative candidate would be elected and, conversely, that even Mother Teresa would be defeated if she were to run under Liberal or

New Democratic colours. In short, the electoral environment was such that the impact from individual candidates or constituency campaigns would only be expected to shade the size of Conservative pluralities. Thus the 1988 FTA election in Alberta provides a very tough test for the emergence of constituency-level effects.

The study that follows builds upon the literature review of Fred Fletcher (1987, 346–47), which identified seven general characteristics of federal campaign politics at the constituency level:

- the national campaign and national issues dominate public consciousness;
- journalistic practices and electoral regulations give an important electoral advantage to incumbents;
- local campaign strategies (canvassing, literature "drops," telephone calls, etc.) make a difference that varies from riding to riding, but the magnitude of this difference and its variation across ridings are unknown;
- local candidates are wary of media coverage by journalists visiting the riding on behalf of major news organizations, preparing feature reports or riding profiles;
- national parties increasingly target campaign activities to "marginal ridings";
- televised debates between candidates – particularly over local cable stations – have become increasingly common at the constituency level; and
- local candidates get little attention in the major media.

The present analysis provides particular amplification for three of Fletcher's observations: first, that the national campaign and issues dominate public consciousness; second, that televised debates between candidates – particularly over local cable stations – have become increasingly common (or at least are considerably important) at the constituency level; and third, that local candidates get little attention in the major media. These three observations are explored within the context of three questions:

1. Is the constituency campaign merely a local surrogate for the national race?
2. What strategies do candidates employ for reaching constituents through the media?
3. How successful are they in attracting media attention?

The relationship between candidates and the media in the 1988 general election is examined in two Alberta ridings, Calgary West and Macleod. In keeping with parallel studies conducted in British Columbia and Ontario, these particular ridings were chosen for two reasons. First, they cover both urban and rural environments (Calgary West, the former and Macleod, the latter), and therefore capture quite distinct media environments; and second, both ridings featured competitive races in 1988, a rarity in a province known for lopsided electoral outcomes. In the 1988 campaign, the competitiveness came in large part from the emergence of the Reform Party of Canada. Although the Reform Party was only created in October 1987, and was not a major player in most Alberta ridings in 1988, it did play a significant role in Calgary West and Macleod, and has gone on to become a major player on the current political scene.

The methodology for this study covered three interrelated stages. The first was to interview media representatives who were making decisions during the campaign as to what would and would not be covered. For television stations, this meant interviewing news directors or producers; for newspapers, it meant interviewing editors-in-chief or managing editors. The second stage involved interviewing candidates, campaign managers and media relations agents. The third stage was both quantitative – measuring how much newspaper space was devoted to what sort of campaign coverage – and qualitative – analysing the content of the coverage. The third stage covered the *Calgary Herald*, and, to a lesser extent, the *Calgary Sun* and local newspapers in the Macleod riding. A limited examination of television coverage was also undertaken in this study.

CALGARY WEST

Calgary West Constituency Profile
Calgary West is one of six federal ridings in Calgary – the other five are Calgary Centre, Calgary North, Calgary Northeast, Calgary Southeast and Calgary Southwest. The riding contained 15 percent of the 657 118 people who lived in Calgary at the time of the 1988 election (see table 3.1).[1]

At the time of the 1988 election, over 14 percent of Calgary West residents had at least one university degree, and only 5.1 percent had less than a grade nine education (the provincial average is 8.2 percent). Calgary West was exclusively urban and largely middle class: the mean and median family incomes were $40 053 and $33 435 respectively. Both the University of Calgary and Mount Royal College are located in

Table 3.1
Demographic details of Calgary West

Total population	98 661
Area (km^2)	1 249
Population density (population/km^2)	79

Calgary West. At the time of the election, unemployment in the Calgary West riding was 9.6 percent, 0.1 percent below the provincial average. It should also be noted that the six Calgary ridings were and are reasonably homogeneous with respect to their socio-demographic composition; Calgary West did not stand apart from the other five in any particularly salient or significant way.

The Progressive Conservative candidate and incumbent MP in Calgary West was Jim Hawkes, who was first elected in 1979. Hawkes had served in a variety of posts from parliamentary secretary to the deputy prime minister to vice-chair of the Parliamentary Task Force on Employment Opportunities in the 1980s. The 1988 election had added interest since Hawkes's closest competition came from his former (1985–86) legislative assistant, Steven Harper, who had also worked on Hawkes's 1984 election team. Harper subsequently became the chief policy officer for the Reform Party of Canada, and the party's 1988 candidate in Calgary West. John Philips represented the Liberals, Richard Vanderberg the NDP, Brent Morin the Confederation of Regions, and David Faren the Libertarian party. Both Hawkes and Harper, and their parties, supported the Free Trade Agreement (FTA), while Philips and Vanderberg opposed it.

The entry of Harper and the Reform Party explains Hawkes's 15.6 percent drop in support from 1984. Nevertheless, Hawkes still received 58.5 percent of the 1988 vote while his nearest competitor, Harper, received only 16.6 percent. Liberal and NDP support was 12.6 percent and 11.6 percent respectively, neither of which was significantly different from the 1984 results. The 1988 turnout rate was 78.8 percent of registered voters (see table 3.2).

The data on campaign financing show that the Conservatives garnered $43 298 in donations – only $1 550 less than all the other parties combined (see table 3.3). They were also more liberal with their spending; Hawkes's PC campaign spent $29 745, considerably more than any other party. Here it should be noted that neither the Liberals nor the NDP had any reasonable expectations for success in Calgary West, that

Table 3.2
Voting results in Calgary West, 1984 and 1988

	Percentage of popular vote		
	1988	1984	Change, 1984–88
Conservative	58.5	74.1	−15.6
Liberal	12.6	11.4	+1.2
NDP	11.6	11.3	+0.3
RPC	16.6	—	+16.6
Other*	0.7	3.2	−2.5

*This includes Confederation of Regions party and the Libertarian party.

the riding was not targeted by their national campaign organizations, and that as a consequence campaign expenditures were modest. Only the Reform Party had any grounds for optimism, although even it was caught in the dilemma of supporting the FTA in a campaign where the federal Conservatives had an armlock on the pro-FTA vote.

Calgary West Media Environment

The two major newspapers serving Calgary West, the *Calgary Herald* and the *Calgary Sun*, both cover the entire city and surrounding metropolitan area. Calgary West does not have differentiated or segmented media outlets, a fact that has some considerable bearing on media coverage of the constituency campaign. As a consequence, for example, a story on the Calgary West campaign would be of no direct

Table 3.3
Campaign financing in Calgary West, 1988

	No. of donations	Total $ value	% of limit spent
Conservative	297	43 298	68.7
RPC	143	25 344	46.8
Liberal	46	12 800	18.8
NDP	3	6 654	12.3
Libertarian	1	50	0.0
COR	0	0	0.0

interest or relevance to almost 90 percent of the *Calgary Herald*'s readership, whereas a story on the national campaign would be of potential interest to all readers. Such calculations also come into play with respect to the three major Calgary-based television stations[2] which cover the riding: CBC; Channels 2 and 7 (independent); and CFCN, a CTV affiliate. Channel 10 – occupied by two small independent broadcasting stations tied to Calgary North Cable TV/FM in the northern half of Calgary, and Rogers Cable TV in the southern half of the city – also broadcasts programming relevant to this study.

Both papers serving Calgary West are affiliated with sister papers across Canada through newspaper chains centred in Toronto. The *Herald* is part of the Southam chain, and the *Sun* part of the *Sun/Star* chain. Both papers rely heavily on story contributions from their sister papers, and it is of little surprise, therefore, that much of the 1988 election coverage pertained to campaigns in those cities in which sister papers existed. Thus, by reading either the *Sun* or the *Herald*, Calgarians could have learned a considerable amount about local campaigns in Metropolitan Toronto.

At the present time, the *Herald* distributes approximately 140 000 newspapers per day in Calgary and roughly 8 800 throughout the Macleod riding. The *Sun* distributes approximately 100 000 newspapers per day in Calgary and roughly 3 100 in Macleod. Representatives of the two newspapers maintain that the current circulation figures are reasonably close to circulation figures during the 1988 election campaign.

The *Sun* directed 10 to 15 reporters, on at least a part-time basis, to cover the 1988 campaign in Calgary and its immediately surrounding areas. The *Herald*, with its larger circulation, devoted 15 to 20 reporters to covering the campaign in the greater Calgary area during the seven-week period. In addition, the *Herald* had a High River (a town in the Macleod riding) bureau with one chief correspondent.

An assessment of the media environment should also note the broader political context within which media outlets function. At the time of the 1988 campaign, the Progressive Conservatives had dominated federal politics in the province since 1972, and provincial politics since 1971. This monochromatic partisan landscape appears to have had two offsetting effects. In the first place, the major media outlets have developed a comfortable and perhaps even cozy relationship with the incumbent provincial and federal Tory governments. At the same time, however, the very lack of an effective opposition partisan voice in the province has led the media to pick up the opposition banner from time to time, to fill the oppositional void created by enfeebled opposition parties. Thus, media outlets tend to be relatively supportive in their editorial policies, and relatively critical in their news coverage.

Analysis of Calgary West Newspaper Coverage

Introduction   The examination of newspaper coverage of the 1988 campaign involved both quantitative analysis – measuring how much space was devoted to what sort of coverage – and qualitative analysis – reading the content of the coverage – of the morning edition of the *Calgary Herald,* and a qualitative analysis of the morning edition of the *Calgary Sun.* Given that initial inspection revealed little difference in the coverage pattern of the two papers, the labour-intensive quantitative analysis was restricted to the *Calgary Herald.* The purpose was to determine not only how much and what kind of coverage was given to the 1988 election, but also *why* that coverage occurred. Indirectly, this meant determining how successful local campaign organizations were in attracting media coverage.

A number of analytical distinctions were made in the quantitative analysis, the first of which was the distinction between news articles with a national emphasis and articles with a local emphasis on one or more of the Calgary or Calgary-metropolitan ridings, including Macleod. The former articles discussed issues with respect to national party leaders, national parties, or both; the latter dealt with issues with respect to the local campaigns and candidates.

Because the 1988 federal election was essentially a one-issue campaign, almost the entire discourse of the election concerned the advantages and disadvantages of the proposed Free Trade Agreement (FTA). It was, therefore, not an environment that encouraged a nuanced discussion of local issues or candidates. Articles focusing on local candidates were almost entirely cast in terms of the national FTA debate, while only a very small number of articles addressed the purely local impact of free trade. Hence, the distinction between local and national stories rests essentially on whether the article discussed national issues in terms of the national impact of those issues, the national leaders or national parties, or in terms of local impact or local candidates. Those articles about the local campaign that did not have to do with the national FTA debate were usually of two sorts: humorous anecdotes – reports of personality clashes between candidates, yelling matches at forums – or announcements of forums, meet-the-candidate opportunities and rallies. There were no salient campaign issues that were purely local in character. The vast majority of local articles, when discussing issues rather than the campaign race, consisted of local candidates discussing national issues, and doing so with respect to the national impact of those issues.

The second distinction was between those articles initiated by the local campaign organizations, and those initiated by the newspaper. While it was difficult to be certain of this distinction in every case, articles that had been initiated by a campaign organization were usually stated as such. For example, coverage of a press conference is usually a clear instance because the reporter would often report that he or she was attending a press conference. Rallies, demonstrations and "media events" are also relatively clear examples. An article containing comments from several Liberal candidates regarding free trade, however, is not so clear unless the article had stated that the reporter was covering a press conference or perhaps a high school forum at which Liberal candidates were in attendance.

It is clear from interviews with both media representatives and campaign organizers that communication flowed freely and in volume from campaign organizations to the newspapers. Campaign organizers attempted to achieve media coverage by constantly communicating with the newspapers' election reporters: press releases and phone calls telling of scheduled events constituted the bulk of this communication. (The Macleod campaign organizers, however, claimed that they made only a modest effort attempting to attract the two Calgary newspapers.) To this limited extent, the campaign organizations "initiated" a good deal of the campaign coverage. However, in a more substantive sense, what counts is how the newspapers decided to handle this flow of relatively routine campaign information. What events did they decide to cover, which speeches were reported, and which were not? It is in this sense that newspaper initiation is discussed. Nonetheless, the distinction is not sharp, and thus the numerical findings should be seen as suggestive only.

The third distinction required an effort to segment articles dealing with the substance of the proposed FTA. In order to qualify for this distinction, an article must not have involved a discussion of what politicians on the campaign trail thought of the Agreement. Rather, the focus would have been on the projected impact of the Agreement, on editorial reaction, or on analyses from individuals outside the partisan arena.

There was no differentiation in measurements among pictures, text and font type or size. This study is concerned only with how much space was devoted to differing aspects of the election. It should also be noted that letters to the editor and political cartoons have been considered as articles, and have been categorized in the same manner as other articles. This strategy was adopted because letters to the editor and political cartoons are a significant component of election coverage, and because differentiating between font sizes and types – not to mention compression and tracking ratios – cannot be achieved with precision.

Analysis   Table 3.4 illustrates how much coverage, in terms of area, was given to the election by the *Herald* between 2 October – the day the election was called – and 22 November 1988 – the day after the campaign had ended. (Appendix A provides information on the distribution of articles within the *Herald*.) Table 3.4 distinguishes among three types of articles:

- National articles: coverage of issues from the vantage point of either national leaders or local campaigns outside metropolitan Calgary, or both;
- Calgary articles: coverage of local candidates or campaigns in any of the six Calgary ridings initiated either by the campaign organizations or by the newspapers; and
- FTA articles: coverage of the Free Trade Agreement itself.

In the *Herald*, over six times as much space was devoted to national issues, leaders and campaigns, and to contests outside Calgary, as to all other campaign coverage. Although coverage of the Calgary campaigns outnumbered FTA articles by a ratio of just over two to one, the point to stress is that local campaigns in their entirety accounted for only 13 percent of the *Herald*'s 1988 election coverage.

Table 3.5 provides a snapshot of the *Herald* on 19 October, one day of the campaign. The main stories of the day included a stand-off between Premier Don Getty and the Lubicon Lake Indian Band, a major

Table 3.4
Area and percentage of campaign coverage, *Calgary Herald*, 2 October to 22 November 1988

	Area devoted (cm²)	% of total election coverage	% of total newspaper space
National	151 378	81	2.46
Calgary	24 808	13	0.40
FTA	11 357	6	0.18
Total	187 543	100	3.04

Table 3.5
Area and percentage of coverage, *Calgary Herald*, 19 October 1988

	Area devoted (cm^2)	% of total newspaper space
National election	4 491.5	4.066
Calgary election	277.6	0.003
FTA	114.8	0.001
General news*	37 350.5	33.814
Food section*	12 995.2	11.765
Entertainment*	14 619.6	13.235
Classified*	17 868.4	16.176
Sports*	9 746.4	8.824
Business*	12 995.2	11.765
Total	110 459.2	99.649

*The corresponding numbers include advertisements.

forest fire in Yellowstone National Park, and a retrospective look at the 19 October 1987 stock market crash. Election stories included a preview of the upcoming leadership debate, a description of Maureen McTeer's election campaign in Carleton–Gloucester, and coverage of party leaders' comments on the free trade issue. The principal local story brought together a number of critical comments on MP Alex Kindy's re-election campaign in Calgary Northeast.

Table 3.6 encompasses those articles dealing with Calgary-area campaigns, and distinguishes between those initiated by campaign

Table 3.6
Area and percentage of coverage initiated by the *Herald* and by campaign organizations, *Calgary Herald*, 2 October to 22 November 1988

	Area devoted (cm^2)	% of total coverage
Calgary Herald initiated	21 052	85
Calgary campaign initiated	3 756	15
Total	24 808	100

organizations and those initiated by the *Herald*. The table thus includes but is not restricted to coverage of the Calgary West campaign.

Table 3.6 shows that the *Herald* was almost seven times as likely to initiate election coverage as it was to react to promptings for attention from campaign organizations. This suggests in turn that, for candidates running in Calgary, garnering newspaper attention was a difficult task indeed. Of the total 1988 campaign coverage, only 2 percent was initiated by all of the Calgary-area campaign organizations combined. This represents a very small drop in a rather large bucket.

It was difficult to determine a simple pattern of articles that the newspapers decided to print from the qualitative analysis of both the *Herald* and the *Sun*. Usually, newspaper-initiated articles regarding the Calgary campaigns were not about all-candidate forums or press conferences, but instead covered mishaps, personality clashes or generally sensational events. Unlike the *Herald*, the *Sun* had no special section of the newspaper devoted exclusively to election coverage. Indeed, the *Sun*'s coverage constituted a relatively smaller proportion of the entire newspaper.

The *Sun*'s coverage also stressed personalities and conflicts somewhat more than the *Herald*. Typical events were PC candidate Harvie Andre running door-to-door in his sneakers, or swastikas painted on campaign signs in northeast Calgary. The only other sorts of articles were simply announcements of formal events staged by campaign organizations or by special-interest organizations. Generally, the Calgary newspapers concentrated on "personalities" and conflicts rather than on the policies and platforms that were expressed at staged events such as press conferences.

Stories initiated by the campaign organizations were more likely to involve policies and platforms, although even here the final press stories often focused on personalities and conflicts. In one *Herald* story about an all-candidates forum, for example, the focus of the story was on how PC candidate Bobbie Sparrow was attacked for her stand on free trade by the constituents attending the forum.

Some of the party representatives interviewed actually decided to forego totally attempts to garner attention from the *Herald* or *Sun*. Media representatives, for their part, claimed that the lack of purely local emphasis was a result of the lack of freshness and excitement in local constituency politics. Media representatives criticized local campaigns for rehashing the same information at each press conference and public forum. Not one media representative thought that his or her coverage was too heavily slanted toward national parties, leaders and issues. Therefore, they saw no reason for local campaigns to change media strategies to garner more attention because more media attention would not have been forthcoming. Media representatives felt that coverage was balanced between local and national, whereas local campaign representatives interviewed expressed frustration with the *Herald*'s and *Sun*'s indifference to local campaigns.

Tables 3.7 and 3.8 sharpen the analysis somewhat by examining the *Herald*'s specific coverage of the Calgary West and Macleod campaigns. In both cases, newspaper-initiated stories take on even greater weight.

These two tables show that the amount of campaign-organization-initiated coverage is greatly outweighed by the amount initiated by the *Herald*. The ratios are 49 to 1 in the case of Calgary West and almost 12 to 1 in the case of the Macleod riding. The relative success of the Macleod campaign organizations in attracting the *Herald*'s attention might be an artifact or consequence of geography; the Macleod riding stretches a great distance from Calgary, thus making it difficult for the *Herald* to initiate stories about the Macleod campaign. However, the *Herald* also has a dedicated bureau in High River, enabling and encouraging more detailed attention to be given to the riding; the establishment of a bureau means some corresponding commitment to print

Table 3.7
Area and percentage of Calgary West campaign coverage initiated by the *Herald* and campaign organizations, *Calgary Herald*, 2 October to 22 November 1988

	Area devoted (cm^2)	% of coverage
Calgary Herald initiated	2 721	98
Campaign initiated	43	2
Total	2 764	100

Table 3.8
Area and percentage of Macleod campaign coverage initiated by the *Herald* and campaign organizations, *Calgary Herald*, 2 October to 22 November 1988

	Area devoted (cm^2)	% of coverage
Calgary Herald initiated	1 785	92
Campaign initiated	158	8
Total	1 943	100

what the bureau provides. It should also be noted that, for both the *Herald* and the *Sun,* most of the coverage initiated by the Macleod campaign organizations had to do with announcements of forums, meet-the-candidate opportunities and so on. Similar announcements about Calgary West occurred far less often in both papers.

Conclusion   This brief analysis unequivocally supports two of Fletcher's observations: that the national campaign and national issues dominate public consciousness; and that local candidates get little attention in the newspaper media. From these general observations, three more specific conclusions can be drawn.

1. The race in the constituency is merely a local surrogate for the national race. All media representatives in Calgary and members of varied Calgary West campaign organizations who were interviewed claimed that local candidates did not play a significant role in the media coverage. Even apart from FTA coverage, little was written about the candidates themselves. The candidates were vessels for the national debate, and not objects of interest in and of themselves. Three of the four Calgary West candidates and three of the four Macleod candidates made almost no attempt to attract the *Herald* or *Sun* because such effort was seen as better placed elsewhere.

2. The primary and usually sole media strategy of all campaign organizations was to inform reporters about scheduled, formal events. Campaign organizations appeared to lack the creativity and/or skill necessary to sustain a more proactive, high-impact media campaign. It was also made clear by all involved that serious and substantial coverage of the local campaigns by the Calgary newspapers likely could not have been increased. It is not surprising, as a consequence, that the newspapers themselves initiated the great bulk of the campaign coverage.

3. The strategy adopted by the campaign organizations was not very successful. Despite the fact that most campaign organizations interviewed for this study said that media representatives were well informed as to scheduled campaign events, little coverage of these events materialized. Simply put, campaign events involved endless repeating of the same information and were therefore of little interest to the media.

The quantitative analysis of the *Herald*'s coverage, and the more qualitative analysis of both the *Herald* and *Sun,* show that local candidates were lost in the jungle of stories pertaining to the FTA, and to the national campaigns, leaders, parties and issues. This conclusion highlights the difficulties encountered by local candidates trying to increase their public profiles and to spread their political messages through the print media. The 1988 election campaign at the constituency level was clearly the national campaign writ small. "Local" coverage meant, in almost every case, coverage of national issues using the words and actions of local candidates. The extent to which this is a result of the peculiarities of the 1988 campaign, the ways in which the print media cover elections, the Alberta political environment, and/or the systemic impact of national election campaigns that are increasingly presidential in style is difficult to determine.

Calgary West Television Coverage
Calgary West is served by four Calgary-based television stations:

- Cable 10 TV/FM;
- CBC;
- Channels 2 and 7 (based in Calgary and affiliated with the Lethbridge 2 and 7 stations that provided the parent station in Calgary with occasional information about southern Alberta ridings including Macleod); and
- CFCN (an affiliate of CTV).

In order to cover the election:

- CBC drew upon eight reporters (two of whom devoted full-time attention to the election);
- CFCN had a staff of 10 reporters in Calgary and six in Lethbridge, none of whom were charged with covering the election on a full-time basis;
- Channels 2 and 7 had approximately 10 reporters in Calgary and four in Lethbridge, none of whom were responsible exclusively for covering the federal election; and
- Rogers Cable TV and Cable 10 TV/FM devoted one interviewer each to cover the election.

Voters in Calgary West, and the rest of Calgary, were treated to a variety of election coverage. All television media representatives interviewed stressed the importance of keeping the coverage fresh. According to one news producer, this meant actually avoiding staged press conferences and "media events" because platforms and policy stands were merely repeated from one rehearsed venue to another. CBC and CFCN representatives stressed a need to keep the stories new and interesting, and expressed the obvious limitation of television in conveying in an exciting fashion staged campaign events. This means, of course, that "institutional" stories such as coverage of news conferences and the like were not avidly pursued. As a result, there was a clear discontinuity between the media strategy of campaign organizations – publicizing forums and speeches – and the appetites of the media. The CBC held a political forum comprising a handful of representatives of the public in Calgary, and featured several small discussions during the evening news program with representatives of the three major parties. The Reform Party was not included.

Of considerable interest to this project is the role played by community television stations. People in northern Calgary receive Cable 10 TV/FM, and in the south, Rogers Cable TV, stations that are owned and operated as totally separate companies. Both stations split the ridings in the city and provided political forums for all candidates in all ridings. Cable 10 TV/FM held the televised forum for Calgary West, one that was taken seriously by candidates despite the community television venue. (Calgary West PC candidate Jim Hawkes pulled himself out of bed despite a serious illness to attend the forum.) In total, the two community stations held eight political forums, six for Calgary ridings, one for Cochrane and one for Airdrie.

Channel 10 potentially reaches some 138 000 southern viewers and 130 000 in the North. The northern half of Channel 10 reaches residents in the outlying towns of Cochrane and Airdrie, but Rogers Cable TV is limited to the southern half of the city only. Thus in total, both community cable stations potentially reach over one-quarter of a million viewers, almost all of whom live within Calgary city limits. It is unlikely, however, that this potential was reached by the Calgary West forum. Certainly the events of the forum did not ripple through other media outlets.

Cable television representatives estimated viewership of these forums to be "substantial," but precise figures are not available. Nonetheless, while the cable audience may not have been large, all campaign organizations took the forums seriously; they were viewed similarly to town hall forums with larger audiences, and the open debate style was seen by the campaign organizers as an effective means of presenting their ideas and candidates.

MACLEOD

Macleod Constituency Profile

The Macleod riding was created as a new constituency for the 1984 federal election, replacing the former ridings of Bow River (64.8 percent of the population in the new Macleod riding) and Lethbridge–Foothills (35.2 percent of the population). Although a Macleod riding had existed prior to the 1980 redistribution, the boundaries of the old and new ridings were not identical. The new Macleod constituency covers 27 130 square kilometres in Southern Alberta, ranging from the south-east Alberta community of Crowsnest Pass and the British Columbia–Alberta border, east to the boundary with the Lethbridge–Foothills riding, and north to the Bow River (see table 3.9).

There are only five small urban centres in the constituency with populations greater than 2 000: Crowsnest Pass (constituted by the formerly separate municipalities of Bellevue, Coleman and Blairmore), Claresholm, Fort Macleod, High River and Okotoks. Notable ethnographic features of the Macleod constituency include:

- a large number of people with a British ethnic origin (30.8 percent), along with a considerable number of German descent (7.9 percent);
- 4.8 percent of the riding is made up of Aboriginal people, over twice the provincial average of 2.2 percent; and
- the constituency has the smallest proportion of people in Alberta claiming French as the language used at home (0.12 percent).

Macleod has an essentially agriculture-based economy; almost one-fifth of the workforce is employed in agriculture (19.9 percent), with the service sector employing 10.4 percent. Much of the service sector activity is targeted at the agricultural sector. Mining, which takes place almost exclusively in the Crowsnest Pass area, accounts for 6.9 percent of the labour force and most of the riding's industrial activity. Unemployment

Table 3.9
Demographic details of Macleod

Total population	65 664
Area (km^2)	27 130
Population density (population/km^2)	2.4

Table 3.10
Voting results in Macleod, 1984 and 1988

	Percentage of popular vote		
	1988	1984	Change, 1984–88
Conservative	50.5	74.6	-24.1
RPC	31.2	—	+31.2
Liberal	9.4	6.6	+2.8
NDP	8.6	10.7	-2.1
Commonwealth	0.3	8.0	-7.7

Table 3.11
Campaign financing in Macleod, 1988

	No. of donations	Total $ value	% of limit spent
Conservative	186	42 845	82.4
RPC	325	53 443	82.7
Liberal	58	13 275	36.0
NDP	2	11 909	8.2
Commonwealth	0	0	0.0

in Macleod was 8.0 percent at the time of the 1988 election, 1.7 percent below the provincial average.

From the late 1970s through to 1984, the Bow River riding, spanning much of the new Macleod constituency, was represented by PC Gordon Taylor. When Taylor retired, Ken Hughes became the PC candidate for Macleod. Hughes's background included posts as special assistant to then External Affairs Minister Joe Clark, and executive assistant to the president of Bow Valley Industries. Like Calgary West, Macleod was considered to be a Conservative stronghold. Nonetheless, Ken Copithorne, a local rancher with deep roots in the community, ran a spirited campaign as the Reform Party candidate. The Liberals were represented by Ernie Patterson, the NDP by Gary Taje, and Tex Hover represented the Commonwealth of Canada. Free trade dominated the campaign, as it did in Calgary West. PC and Reform Party candidates supported the proposed FTA, while the Liberal and NDP candidates opposed it. Hover, the Commonwealth of Canada candidate, was not sure where he or his party stood on the issue.

The Macleod riding had almost three times as many rural polls as urban polls. In the 1988 election, 76.5 percent of the registered voters went to the polls and gave the PC candidate, Ken Hughes, a 19.3 percent margin of victory over Ken Copithorne (see table 3.10).

The strength of the Reform Party vote is reflected in the pattern of campaign contributions. As table 3.11 shows, the Reform Party organization in Macleod garnered over $10 000 more in contributions than did the Conservatives, and over two times that collected by the Liberals and NDP combined.

Macleod Media Environment

There are 10 weekly newspapers in the Macleod constituency, with mean and median circulations of 3 999 and 3 305 respectively. The circulation per newspaper ranges from 1 780 in Fort Macleod to 10 475 for the Okotoks *Eagle View Post*. The number of people living in the towns in which the newspapers are produced varies markedly, from 7 000 in the new municipality of Crowsnest Pass to 1 564 in Nanton. The mean in-town population for the 10 towns is 4 479; the trading area populations range from 26 000 for the Okotoks *Eagle View Post* to 4 500 for the Nanton *News*. The size of the trading area is perhaps the most significant factor when considering the relative importance of any given newspaper (see table 3.12).

Table 3.12
Macleod newspaper circulation and populations

Newspaper	Circulation	Population in town	Population in trading area*
Blairmore Pass *Herald*	2 750	7 000	16 000
Claresholm *Local Press*	2 169	3 500	10 000
Crowsnest Pass *Promoter*	3 472	7 000	8 000
Fort Macleod *Gazette*	1 780	3 180	7 500
High River *Times*	3 375	5 100	15 000
Nanton *News*	1 348	1 564	4 500
Okotoks *Eagle View Post*	10 475	5 676	26 000
Okotoks *Western Wheel*	8 512	5 676	15 000
Pincher Creek *Echo*	2 799	4 000	10 500
Vulcan *Advocate*	3 305	1 600	8 000
Total	39 985	44 296	120 500

*Trading area refers to the actual total population reached by the newspaper.

There are also three Alberta-based television stations: CBC, Channels 2 and 7 (either the affiliate based in Lethbridge or the one in Calgary) and CFCN (either the affiliate based in Lethbridge or the one in Calgary).

Analysis of Macleod Newspaper Coverage

The analysis involved both a quantitative and a qualitative analysis of the 10 papers. Like the analysis of the *Herald* and *Sun*, the central purpose was to determine the extent to which local campaigns received coverage in the print media. Once again, a distinction was made between campaign- and newspaper-initiated coverage, and between national articles and those dealing with the Macleod campaign. (No attempt was made to measure the very small amount of space devoted to non-partisan discussion of the proposed Free Trade Agreement.) As was the case in the Calgary papers, articles focusing on local candidates were cast almost entirely in terms of national issues, and particularly in terms of the national debate over free trade. Virtually no articles addressed purely local subjects.

All 10 newspapers are weeklies, and thus the campaign coverage period for each paper varies according to the day of the week on which it is printed. This analysis began with the first issue after the election announcement on 2 October, and ended with the first issue giving the election results after 21 November.

Table 3.13
Absolute and relative campaign coverage, Macleod riding newspapers, 2 October to 30 November 1988

Newspaper	National coverage (cm^2)	Local coverage (cm^2)
Blairmore Pass *Herald*	2 700	1 583
Claresholm *Local Press*	843	4 827
Crowsnest Pass *Promoter*	787	6 790
Fort Macleod *Gazette*	590	1 636
High River *Times*	2 620	10 930
Nanton *News*	2 031	2 251
Okotoks *Eagle View Post*	1 309	1 482
Okotoks *Western Wheel*	2 449	4 152
Pincher Creek *Echo*	3 807	5 651
Vulcan *Advocate*	543	2 605
Total	17 679	41 907

Table 3.14
**Ratio of national to local campaign coverage, Macleod
riding newspapers, 2 October to 30 November 1988**

Newspaper	Ratio
Blairmore Pass *Herald*	1.7:1.0
Claresholm *Local Press*	1:5.7
Crowsnest Pass *Promoter*	1:8.6
Fort Macleod *Gazette*	1:2.8
High River *Times*	1:4.2
Nanton *News*	1:1.1
Okotoks *Eagle View Post*	1:1.1
Okotoks *Western Wheel*	1:1.7
Pincher Creek Echo	1:1.5
Vulcan *Advocate*	1:4.8

Tables 3.13 and 3.14 show the relative coverage of the national and local campaigns. The contrast with Calgary West is dramatic, as the Macleod newspapers concentrated much more heavily on the local candidates and campaigns. However, it should be stressed again that the local articles tended to cast the Macleod campaign in the context of the national campaign, and of the free trade debate. Local coverage did not mean that local issues existed, much less prevailed, or that differences among the candidates were explored at any length.

Overall, the local candidates and campaigns received more than twice the space devoted to the national, non-Macleod campaign. As table 3.14 shows, the ratio of local to national coverage was greater than four to one in some of the smaller papers. Admittedly, this finding is not by itself all that startling. Local weekly papers do not have the resources to provide independent coverage of the national campaign, and any interesting wire service stories are likely to be picked up by the *Herald* or *Sun*. Thus, weeklies in Macleod do what only weeklies in Macleod are able to do and are interested in doing: they cover the Macleod campaign.

At the same time, it must be stressed that the great bulk of election coverage to reach Macleod voters came through the *Calgary Herald,* the *Calgary Sun* or Calgary-based television stations. Therefore, the Macleod coverage in the weeklies provided, at best, a very modest counterweight to the national coverage emanating from the Calgary-based media.

While Macleod voters may have had more access to constituency news than did voters in Calgary West, the national campaign still dominated total newspaper coverage in both constituencies.

Most print media coverage in Macleod was initiated by the campaign organizations. Interviews took place in conjunction with "main-streeting" visits to the local community; candidates would take a break from handshaking to drop into the local newspaper office. Local newspapers were routinely alerted to forums and staged events, although it is unlikely that the weekly editors needed to hear from campaign organizations to know what events were taking place in their towns. It is worth noting that almost all local stories revolved around staged, "institutional" events, something that was not typical of the Calgary coverage. The following article nicely illustrates why newspapers in the Macleod riding tended to provide "institutional" coverage:

> A reader has phoned in to complain at the high degree of coverage the Echo has given the Reform Party.
>
> She raised a valid point. Most voters rely on the media for information about the respective parties and their five candidates in Macleod.
>
> If it's details rather than superficialities that they look for then the local weekly is the best means to discover such facts. If that information is not there, then how can people vote on a factual basis?
>
> It's true the Reformers have received a lot of coverage in this paper. This should not necessarily be seen as an endorsement, but they have shown a strong aptitude to getting themselves into the news ...
>
> One has to define just what is "news." Public meetings are news; Reformer Ken Copithorne held a well-attended public meeting in town a fortnight ago. This was written up as a news story.
>
> The other four parties have not (yet) held any public meetings. Presumably this is due to strategic or other reasons. Pounding pavements, hammering on doors and kissing babies is another way to win votes, but it's hardly dramatic or headline-grabbing.
>
> Neither has Pincher Creek enjoyed (or suffered) visits from Broadbent, Mulroney or Turner, so the Echo can print no banner headlines from party top brass promising more government spending for less taxation, etc., etc.
>
> The Echo takes political reporting quite seriously. It has interviewed the five candidates, and their answers to direct questions are being published in the next two issues. All are treated fairly.
>
> Reporters went over to Claresholm last Thursday where all five candidates faced the audience in a forum. This is news, and all faced

the same questions under equal conditions ...

All the Echo can do is report what people say and do. Whether voters are convinced or repelled with what is written is another matter. After that it's up to you as citizens to cast your vote according to reason or prejudice. (Breeze 1988, A5)

Unlike most other newspapers in the riding, the *Pincher Creek Echo* did initiate its own interviews. These interviews, however, were subsumed in the greater mass of campaign-initiated stories. According to all interviewed, the reason for this imbalance is simply a matter of resources – with an average of only two reporters on staff, there was little if any time available for newspaper-initiated coverage, much less investigative reporting. Covering an all-candidate forum in town was clearly the easiest and most effective means by which to cover the constituency campaign. Several editors also claimed that this sort of "institutional" coverage was not only necessary, but was also the sort of coverage that was desirable. The *Pincher Creek Echo* article quoted above certainly captures this sentiment.

Although all campaign and print media representatives in the Macleod constituency attested to the central importance of the local candidates, the "local" coverage nevertheless had very much a "national" flavour. In this respect, and notwithstanding the fact that Macleod weeklies gave relatively greater play to the local campaign, the election coverage by Macleod newspapers was in some important ways similar to that of the Calgary newspapers. In both cases, the national campaign dominated; the race in the constituency was a local surrogate for the national race. Although Macleod media representatives argued that local candidates were important, and although the local candidates figured largely in local articles, the emphasis was essentially national. While the Macleod coverage contained relatively more "local" coverage, this meant in reality increased coverage of the national campaign, leaders and/or issues as viewed through the prism of the constituency campaign.

In summary, local candidates played a relatively prominent role in the Macleod newspaper coverage of the 1988 election. However, this conclusion does not mean that local issues were also prominent. In fact, even more clearly than in Calgary, campaign coverage at the local level was the national campaign writ small. "Local" coverage in reality meant, in almost every case, coverage of national issues using the words and actions of local candidates.

Macleod Television Coverage

As noted above, the Macleod riding is served by three Alberta-based television stations. A limited number of Macleod residents would receive both Lethbridge and Calgary affiliates of CFCN and Channels 2 and 7. Most residents receive:

- CBC (based in Calgary);
- Channels 2 and 7 (either the affiliate based in Calgary or in Lethbridge); and
- CFCN (either the affiliate based in Calgary or in Lethbridge).

In order to cover the election:

- CBC was able to draw upon eight reporters, two of whom devoted full-time attention to the election;
- CFCN had a staff of 10 reporters in Calgary and six in Lethbridge, none of whom had to cover the election on a full-time basis; and
- Channels 2 and 7 had approximately 10 reporters in Calgary and four in Lethbridge, none of whom had just the federal election to cover.

The 1988 CBC coverage is important to note, for the Calgary-based station was taken off the air in late November 1990. In the next election, CBC coverage of the Macleod riding will originate from Edmonton, and will have to compete for air time with all ridings in Alberta. As a consequence, Macleod voters and, indeed, voters across the southern half of the province who watch CBC television news will see very little and quite likely no coverage of their own constituency campaigns. The election will therefore be stripped of any local character, giving even greater play to the national campaign. It is difficult to argue that Macleod voters will be well served as a consequence.

During the 1988 campaign, residents in Macleod north of, and including, High River and Okotoks, received Channels 2 and 7 and CFCN broadcasts originating from Calgary. Those south of High River and Okotoks received the Lethbridge affiliates. Programming was almost entirely the same for both the affiliates and parent stations, with one relevant exception: news programming. Reporters based in Lethbridge were able to concentrate on local coverage without being overwhelmed by the Calgary campaigns. This is the only significant difference between the election coverage received by voters living in Macleod and those living in Calgary constituencies. CBC broadcasting originated in Calgary, and emphasized coverage of Calgary campaigns.

Macleod residents were able to view the same CBC election forums as were seen by Calgary voters.

Unlike Calgarians, Macleod voters did not have access to community cable television. This fact, combined with the fact that television signals received by Macleod voters are broadcast from outside the constituency, leads to the conclusion that television played a relatively small role in informing Macleod residents about their local campaign, a conclusion supported by interviews with campaign organizers and media representatives in Macleod. To some degree, radio coverage filled the electronic void, but for campaign organizers radio placed a distant second to the importance of newspaper coverage.

CONCLUSIONS

For most voters, media coverage provides a critically important window on national election campaigns. Apart from infrequent and brief direct contact with the campaign – a candidate ringing the doorbell, campaign literature left in the mailbox or on the lawn – voters see the campaign through the media. Thus, an analysis of the media coverage of election campaigns can provide useful insight into how the campaign is seen by voters. More indirectly, it also provides a tentative indication of the extent to which local candidates and campaign organizations are able to leave a significant mark on national election campaigns. We can ask, then, does the local campaign matter? Does it stand out against the broader canvas of the national campaign?

In this study, conditions were not propitious for the emergence of significant constituency-level effects, first because the debate on the proposed Free Trade Agreement dominated the election, and second because Alberta has not been noted for closely fought constituency battles in which individual candidates could turn the tide through their own effort, attributes and skill. It should not come as a surprise, therefore, that national leaders, parties and issues dominated the 1988 media coverage in Calgary West and Macleod. While the local candidates and campaigns did not vanish without a trace, they were clearly overwhelmed and all but submerged by the national campaign. Not only did coverage of the national campaign dominate, albeit to a lesser extent in the Macleod weeklies, but local coverage tended to be cast in terms of the national campaign. Instead of local issues, there were local perspectives on national issues. The constituency campaigns in Calgary West and Macleod essentially were little more than the national campaign writ small. Although such perspectives may have nuanced the national debate, the nuances seem to have had a limited impact on electoral behaviour.

There is, however, an important if somewhat hypothetical question that remains. Might we expect more pronounced constituency-level effects in an election that was not dominated by a single issue, and that was fought in a more competitive electoral environment than the one found in Alberta in 1988? Probably not. The patterns of media coverage outlined in this study are probably not tied to the idiosyncratic features of the 1988 campaign in Alberta. In short, national coverage will most likely prevail under different conditions. Legislative changes are not foreseen that would dramatically enhance the attention paid by the media to the local campaign, or that would increase the leverage that local campaign organizations and candidates might have on media coverage and the election outcome. If such changes can be envisioned by others, it would still be necessary to ask if constituency-level effects should be increased. Here it is suggested that the appropriate normative answer is no, that the reality observed in Calgary West and Macleod is not at odds with the role that national elections should play in Canadian political life.

NOTES

1. City of Calgary Census (April 1988).

2. Without cable, Calgary viewers receive CBXFT (French CBC). With full cable service, viewers receive 19 Canadian-based channels and 10 American-based channels.

REFERENCES

Breeze, Philip. 1988. "Covering the Election." *Pincher Creek Echo*, 8 November, A5.

Fletcher, Frederick J. 1987. "Mass Media and Parliamentary Elections in Canada." *Legislative Studies Quarterly* 12 (August): 341–72.

APPENDIX

Table 3.A1
**Number and location of articles concerning the federal election, *Calgary Herald*,
2 October to 22 November 1988**

A (840)		B (463)		C (553)		D (743)		F (436)	
No. of articles	Page no.	No. of articles	Page no.	No. of articles	Page no.	No. of articles	Page no.	No. of articles	Page no.
71	1	10	1	31	1	3	1	2	1
64	2	3	2	29	2	1	2	1	3
17	3	2	3	15	3	1	3	1	4
87	4	10	4	10	4	1	4	1	7
41	5	7	5	8	5	7	5		
49	6	28	6	1	6	5	6		
5	7	2	7	17	7	2	7		
35	8	10	8	1	12	1	8		
10	9	1	9			1	9		
7	10					2	10		
10	11					5	11		
11	12					4	12		
1	13								
31	14								
21	15								
5	17								
42	18								
10	19								
7	21								
12	22								
7	23								
	E	(492)							
	G	(156)							
	H	(110)							
	Total	3 793							

Note: Figures in parentheses are total number of pages in that section during that period.

Sections E (492), G (156) and H (110) are not included as there were no articles concerning the federal election on those pages.

4

THE MASS MEDIA AND FEDERAL ELECTION CAMPAIGNING AT THE LOCAL LEVEL
A Case Study of Two Ontario Constituencies

David V.J. Bell
Catherine M. Bolan

IN 1980, PIERRE ELLIOTT TRUDEAU defeated Prime Minister Joe Clark in an election no one expected would occur so soon after Clark's surprising defeat of Trudeau the previous spring. Ed Broadbent ran third. In 1984, Prime Minister John Turner lost to Brian Mulroney thus concluding the second shortest term as prime minister in the history of the country. Ed Broadbent again ran third. Then in 1988, despite a surprisingly strong performance in the English-language nationally televised leadership debates, John Turner again suffered a crushing defeat at the hands of Mulroney, who thereby secured the first back-to-back majority governments in 40 years. Once again Broadbent placed third.

The foregoing brief history of federal electoral results in the 1980s seems quite straightforward. There is nothing unusual about treating electoral results, the outcome of hard-fought struggles carried on in nearly 300 ridings from coast to coast, as personal contests between party leaders. Sports commentators often do something similar – describing the outcome of the bruising struggle on the football field or the ice as a victory of one coach over another, even though the coaches never come onto the playing surface during the entire game. To the millions of fans who have been watching the players on television, the personalization of team victories as triumphs for the coach seems a bit peculiar (not to mention how it strikes the players themselves). But the personalization of electoral victories as achievements of the leader is accepted almost without question. Chances are, the political spectators have seen much more of the leaders on television than they have observed the local "players" running for office in their own constituency. Indeed nearly two-thirds of Canadian anglophones and 70 percent of Canadian francophones watched at least one of the two televised leadership debates in the 1988 election (Clarke et al. 1991, 102). It is unlikely that nearly that many Canadians saw their local candidates in person or on television at any time during the 1988 campaign. Paradoxically, however, 27 percent of 1988 voters surveyed reported the "most important factor" in their vote decision was the local candidate. This number exceeded those citing the party leader as most important factor[1] (see figure 4.1).

Figure 4.1
Most important factor in vote decision: 1974–88

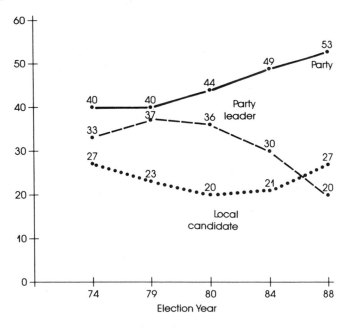

Source: Clarke et al. (1991, 115).

This study of the 1988 local campaign in two Ontario ridings, one predominantly urban, the other predominantly rural, has a special emphasis on the role of the mass media. The main objective of the study was to find out the extent to which the constituency campaign is merely a surrogate or miniature replica of the national race. How local candidates attempt to reach their constituents through the media was also examined and, conversely, what strategies the media employ in their attempt to "cover" the campaign. Through pursuing these questions and analysing actual media coverage of the campaign, we discovered how successful local candidates were in attracting media attention. Finally, we explored some questions related to campaign financing and opinion polls.

In order to investigate these issues, we relied primarily on interviews of campaign activists (candidates and campaign managers) and key media figures (newspaper editors and television news directors) in each riding.[2]

THE CONSTITUENCIES

The two ridings chosen for this study – Markham and Perth–Wellington–Waterloo – display demographic and political characteristics that make them particularly interesting and appropriate for this project. Both were affected by the 1987 electoral boundaries redistribution.

Markham

Markham, located on the northeast boundary of Metropolitan Toronto, was created largely out of what had been the York North riding. The western section of the old riding was lopped off and replaced by the addition in the north of the town of Whitchurch-Stouffville, previously belonging to York Peel.[3] Even after redistribution Markham had a population of over 130 000, making it the third largest constituency in the country. It was also one of the most affluent with an average family income of $59 095 (fifth in Canada). Markham had the third highest proportion of residents in managerial/administrative positions (20.3%), while boasting the country's lowest unemployment rate in 1988 (3.8%) and second highest proportion of home-owners (over two-thirds of all households). Its fast growth in population (second highest in Canada between 1981 and 1986) was matched by high growth in jobs: more workers travelled into the riding every day than left to work elsewhere. The Markham labour force was employed in manufacturing (18%), retail trade (13%), business service (9%), wholesale trade (8%) and the hospitality industry (7%).

Before redistribution and during the late 1960s and 1970s, the riding had been won by Liberal cabinet minister Barney Danson.[4] In 1979, the

Tories took it under John Gamble, who held on to win re-election despite the Liberal national victory in 1980.

In 1984, dissatisfaction with John Gamble on the part of many Tories, coupled with an equally strong dislike within the Liberal party of their own candidate, opened the way for a successful candidacy as an Independent by long-time municipal politician Tony Roman. With support from disaffected Liberals and Conservatives, Roman was the only Independent to win a seat in the House in 40 years. His incumbency was short-lived, however. In 1988 he declined to seek re-election federally, choosing to return to the municipal fold. Meanwhile, Bill Attewell, who had won the Don Valley East seat for the Conservatives in 1984, saw his riding boundaries drastically altered by the 1987 redistribution and looked to Markham for a new base. Because the riding was technically "new," John Gamble was forced to do battle for control of the new constituency executive. But Gamble's right-wing views, given national prominence in the course of his spectacularly unsuccessful bid for the national leadership in 1983, had alienated a number of key Conservative party members in the area. At a meeting held in February 1988, Peter Atkins (son of Norman Atkins, a prominent Tory éminence grise) engineered a successful take-over of the key executive positions of the new riding association, occasioning Gamble's decision to withdraw from the party to run as an Independent. This paved the way for Attewell's successful bid for the nomination.

The contest for the Liberal nomination in 1988 was also quite colourful. Jag Bhaduria, a Hindu who had immigrated to Canada in 1968 and worked for the Liberal party under Trudeau, won a bitter contest after signing up over 2 000 new members, many of them of South Asian background who had moved into a new subdivision in the riding (Millikin Mills) since the 1984 election. Bhaduria spent a considerable sum of his own money to win the nomination, but was then abandoned by the local executive (who all resigned) and given little assistance from the party after taking on as (paid) campaign manager a former Chrétien supporter, Diarmuid O'Dea.

The NDP nomination went to Susan Krone in an uneventful ceremony (understandably so in a riding where the NDP had never previously managed even to recover its deposit).

The final candidate in 1988 was Libertarian Ian Hutchison who allowed his name to stand yet took almost no active part in the campaign.

Perth–Wellington–Waterloo
The 1984 riding of Perth, whose boundaries coincided with those of Perth County, was enlarged by nearly 40 percent through the addition of

portions of adjacent Waterloo and Wellington–Grey–Dufferin–Simcoe constituencies. Located between Kitchener and London, the riding is in the heartland of old Ontario in an area often called Ontario's "Bible Belt" (McNaught and Roe 1988). A mixture of rural and urban residents (nearly two-thirds of polls are rural), the riding's largest urban centre is Stratford, a small city of 27 000. Some of its rural residents observe traditional Mennonite customs. Despite its lower average family income ($36 863), it is relatively prosperous for a rural/urban constituency. (It does, however, have more than twice as many low-income families as Markham: 9.6 percent as compared to 4.4 percent.) Perth–Wellington–Waterloo has nearly eight times the area of Markham (3 313 km^2 compared to 424 km^2) but less than three-quarters of its population (92 026 compared to 129 732). Famous for the Stratford festival, this riding contains a number of light manufacturing plants that employ nearly a quarter of all workers in the area. Sixteen percent are employed in agriculture and related industries, 11 percent in retail trade, 7 percent in the hospitality industry and 6 percent in construction.

With fewer than 10 percent of the population comprising immigrants, mass mobilization around the politics of ethnicity was non-existent. In its place, however, was an equally significant issue – abortion. The nomination of Liberal Mike Stinson was conducted in convention-like style with a throng of several thousand at the Stratford Coliseum. Stinson's declared pro-life position attracted hundreds of supporters and probably guaranteed him the nomination. His subsequent efforts, however, to play down this issue and emphasize other planks in his platform, may ultimately have cost him the election. More than 2 000 votes went to Christian Heritage party candidate Stan Puklicz whose strong pro-life stand eclipsed Stinson's support for the pro-life position. The Tory incumbent, Harry Brightwell, was stunned to see his enormous victory of 1984 shrink to a plurality of less than 1 000 votes over his second place opponent, Stinson. In third place was NDP Linda Ham, whose relatively strong showing (19 percent of the popular vote) foreshadowed the NDP victory in the provincial election two years later. Finishing in fifth place was Libertarian Joe Yundt who had also run in 1984. (Data on voting and campaign financing in the two ridings are presented in tables 4.3, 4.4, 4.6, and 4.7.)

MEDIA PROFILE

Markham

From a media viewpoint, Markham stands in the shadow of Metropolitan Toronto, which features at least four major television stations (CBC, CTV, Global and City), three large daily newspapers (the *Globe and Mail*, the *Toronto Star* and the *Toronto Sun*),[5] and numerous radio stations. Nevertheless, Markham has a local cable station (Classicomm) and a number of local newspapers, several of which have been in existence since the 19th century. Because there are 33 ridings in the viewing or circulation area of the greater Toronto–based media outlets, individual suburban ridings such as Markham receive little attention from these larger Toronto media. (We found only one story in the *Globe and Mail* on Markham; one in the *Toronto Star*, actually part of a profile of all 33 Metro-area ridings; and five in the weekly insert to the *Toronto Star* called "Neighbours North," two of which appeared on 11 October, one on 15 October, and two in the aftermath of the election on 27 November.) Consequently, residents must rely on the local media to provide coverage of the campaign in their own constituencies.

Classicomm, the local cable TV station, covered each nomination meeting, gave some news coverage to the candidates and invited each one to the studio for a "profile" interview lasting about 20 minutes. The station also hosted an all-candidate debate rebroadcast several times throughout the campaign. There are no reliable data on how many Markham voters watched the debates but informal indications are that a large number did. Eighty-nine percent of Markham residents subscribe to Classicomm, this number comprising 95 percent of the station's 90 000 subscribers. The remaining 5 percent of their subscribers live in the (new) riding of York North. Classicomm's station (Channel 10) is seen by an average of 60 000 viewers each week. (The close "fit" between Classicomm's coverage area and the riding boundaries is atypical of most urban Ontario ridings.)

No single local newspaper covers the entire constituency, which comprises a number of fairly distinct communities, each served predominantly by its own local paper. Many homes in the southwest section of the riding receive the *Thornhill Liberal* published just north of Thornhill in the town of Richmond Hill. To the east and slightly north of Thornhill are the communities of Unionville and Markham, served by the *Markham Economist and Sun*. The *Liberal* and the *Economist* were established in the 19th century, but are now owned by Metroland Printing, Publishing and Distributing, a conglomerate controlled by the *Toronto Star*. Finally, Stouffville has its own newspaper, the *Stouffville Sun*, owned in 1988 by Uxbridge Printing but now part of the Laurentian chain.

None of these three papers is published daily, and each has a relatively small staff, as table 4.1 shows. (Their number and diversity is again atypical of most urban ridings.)

Table 4.1
Newspapers serving the Markham riding during the 1988 federal election

Name of paper	Where published	Ownership	Frequency	Circulation	Editorial
Thornhill Liberal	Richmond Hill*	Metroland	2 times a week (now 3 times)	28 500	1 editor 1 news editor 1 sports editor 4 reporters
Markham Economist and Sun	Markham	Metroland	3 times a week (now twice)	50 000	1 editor-in-chief 3 sub-editors 2 reporters
Stouffville Sun	Stouffville	Uxbridge Printing (now Laurentian)	once a week	(delivered free)	3 editorial

*Also covers York North riding as the Richmond Hill Liberal.

Perth–Wellington–Waterloo

Most of this constituency is served by Grand River Cable station located in the city of Kitchener and owned by Rogers Cable. Because the station's licensed territory includes Kitchener, Stratford, St. Marys and Brantford, it covers three federal constituencies as well as Perth–Wellington–Waterloo. Although nationally 85 percent of Canadians subscribe to cable, the figure is lower in ridings that have large rural areas making cable installation economically impractical. (The relevant figure for Perth–Wellington–Waterloo is 50 percent.) The situation is further complicated in this riding by the presence of Mennonites, the more traditional of whom do not have electricity on their farms. In view of these constraints, among the all-candidates debates in the riding, two were held on broadcast media: one on cable television, the other on the local Stratford radio station, CJCS. Both included a phone-in component so that viewers or listeners (screened to ensure a variety of issues raised) could pose questions directly to candidates. In addition, Grand River Cable provided each federal candidate with three minutes of air time to speak on topics of their choice. Their messages were recorded at the beginning of the campaign period and rebroadcast up to three times throughout.

The newspaper environment in Perth–Wellington–Waterloo is in many respects more complex than in Markham. Two local dailies have a significant number of readers in the area. The Stratford Beacon Herald has a circulation of 14 000: 8 000 within the city of Stratford and 6 000 outside. A recent survey determined that 80 percent of those who subscribe to the Beacon Herald read no other newspaper. Although virtually all of its readers live in the Perth–Wellington–Waterloo constituency, the *Beacon Herald* sees itself as a local newspaper with obligations to provide national and even international coverage. Indeed, the newspaper is one of the few remaining local "independents" still operating in Canada.

The *Kitchener-Waterloo Record* is a strong daily with an even larger operation than the *Beacon Herald*. The *Record* defines its area of coverage to include the bulk of central southwestern Ontario, spanning at least a dozen ridings. Precise circulation figures for Perth–Wellington–Waterloo were not available but the paper has a "strong readership" in the constituency and accordingly attempted to provide good coverage of the campaign. In addition to these two strong dailies, the riding has a number of smaller newspapers serving towns and communities. Most of these papers are published weekly and have circulation to only portions of the riding. Their nature, size and operation are summarized in table 4.2.

Table 4.2
Newspapers serving the Perth–Wellington–Waterloo riding during the 1988 federal election

Name of paper	Where published	Ownership	Frequency	Circulation	Editorial
Beacon Herald	Stratford	family	daily	14 100	1 managing editor 4 desk editors 5 city reporters 1 district reporter 2 photographers
Kitchener-Waterloo Record	Kitchener	Southam	daily	n.a.	21 writers
Listowel Banner	Listowel	Newfoundland Capital Corp. (NCC chain)	weekly	4 700	1 editor 2 reporters
Mitchell Advocate	Mitchell	Signal Star	weekly	2 500	1 editor 1 reporter
Milverton Sun	Milverton	NCC	weekly	n.a.	1 person
Journal Argus	St. Marys	family	weekly	4 500	1 editor 2 reporters 1 photographer
New Hamburg Independent	New Hamburg	Fairway Group (Southam)	weekly	3 900	1 editor 2 reporters

n.a. = not available.

THE CAMPAIGN AND THE VOTE: GENERAL COMMENTS

Overlap with Ontario Municipal Elections

In Ontario, the federal election date followed by exactly one week the date of provincewide municipal elections, held on 14 November.[6] The coincidence of the two campaigns had a profound impact on candidates, voters and the media. Voters were faced with a bewildering onslaught of campaign advertisement, epitomized in forests of road and lawn signs. Some federal candidates had to scramble to find workers, many of whom had long-standing commitments to work for municipal candidates. Some candidates themselves had considerable involvements in both elections. A candidate for council in King City (a small town northwest of Markham) was also the returning officer for York North, a riding in which there were many allegations of irregularities. But the most serious consequence of the overlap between the two campaigns affected the media, who found it virtually impossible to provide thorough coverage of both campaigns. In most instances, editors or news directors were forced to give one election priority over the other in terms of coverage.[7] In Markham, the municipal election was emphasized because there was a feeling of "who else will cover it." Several newspapers in Perth–Wellington–Waterloo had a different perspective, however. Given that they serve as the primary source of both national and local news, they felt a strong obligation to cover the federal election at the expense of the municipal one on the premise that "no one else would do it." This was exacerbated in Perth–Wellington–Waterloo by the large dimensions of the riding, making it difficult for the already overextended staff of the weeklies to cover many events. As a result, nearly all of the smaller newspapers tended to focus on aspects of the campaign which occurred in their immediate areas.

No one interviewed regarded positively the timing of the federal election. Many expressed the opinion that overlaps between municipal and federal (or provincial) elections should somehow be prohibited. One of the most outspoken criticisms appeared in an editorial in the *Thornhill Liberal* on 12 October (1988c), entitled "Don't Let Federal Vote Overshadow Ontario Vote":

> There's no perfect time to call a federal election, but it's a real shame that Mulroney and his boys had to pick a date in November so close to Ontario's municipal election.
>
> Unfortunately for you voters, the big media will focus its spotlight on the three federal leaders and the national campaign in general. The municipal election is likely to be an afterthought for the dailies and

television news stations, meaning you'll get a much less complete and thorough preparation on the issues and the people in the Nov. 14 municipal election.

That's unfortunate, because interest in local elections is poor at best. Traditionally only about 30 percent of eligible voters in Ontario bother to vote, yet the local mayors, councillors and school trustees are the politicians who affect voters' lives every day.

You can't call up Brian, John or Ed when the pothole in front of your house threatens to swallow your car. It won't do you much good to lobby Ottawa about crowded portables at your child's school, either.

These are the ordinary, but vital, issues behind the municipal election. Before Nov. 14, take a little time to get to know which council hopefuls are running in your ward and who wants to be your trustee. Just as important and fascinating, watch the jostling and listen to the promises made by the mayoralty candidates. There will be some close and interesting races for mayor in Richmond Hill, Vaughan and Markham.

These people will affect your lives as much, if not more, than any federal politician. If you don't get all the information about the municipal election you need from the big media, watch your weekly newspapers and come out to a few all-candidates meetings.

Give the November 14 election at least as much attention as the November 21 vote.

The decision to call a federal election for 21 November was obviously made in full awareness of the overlap. Whether the Conservatives hoped to obtain an advantage from what they must have known would be a period of information overload and therefore relative inattention from the media; or whether this date was chosen reluctantly, despite its inconvenience, because of larger factors, is impossible to determine. Even the Conservatives interviewed regretted the timing, and felt that they might have done better without having to compete with the municipal elections for media attention, resources and workers.

Single-Issue Election

The other central factor in the 1988 election was the overwhelming predominance of the free trade issue.[8] Few, if any, federal elections have been so dominated by a single issue. For example, of those Canadians surveyed in the 1988 Canadian National Election Study, 88 percent mentioned free trade as the "most important issue" in the election. This was nearly double the second highest clustering of opinion around a single issue, namely inflation, cost of living, wage and price controls mentioned by 46 percent of those surveyed in 1974. Third was oil prices, development, energy policy mentioned by 31 percent in 1980 (see Clarke et al. 1991, 70). But the 1988 election did not begin as a single-issue campaign,[9] and when it took that direction as a result of the national leaders debates it caught some party strategists and media people by surprise, including those at the national level.

Free trade was an issue with several dimensions. Some viewed it in straight economic terms and tried to evaluate it purely with regard to its economic consequences. But even this proved to be difficult and complex. Expert opinion was divided. Economic consequences were hard to anticipate. The range of possible effects covered a great spectrum of economic aspects, including employment, interest rates, the value of the Canadian dollar, consumer prices and future economic growth, among others. Much discussion focused on the possible effect of free trade on social programs and cultural industries. For others, free trade had symbolic importance – in terms of Canadian sovereignty and national identity – that went far beyond even the broadest economic considerations. Finally, as Johnston et al. (1989, 1) point out, "the electoral significance of the Free Trade Agreement was not just for the economy or the welfare state. The Agreement also got caught up in a debate over how much the government could be trusted, a debate which turned on retrospective considerations, many of which had nothing to do with economics." Given the enormous range of implications attributed to free trade, it is not surprising that it was a national issue with diverse local implications and manifestations. With its high numbers of professional and managerial residents, many Markham voters were solidly pro–free trade. Perth–Wellington–Waterloo was much more divided. Those in the arts community voiced concern about the Agreement's effect on cultural policies. Farmers worried about the implications for marketing boards.[10] Workers feared jobs would be lost with local industries relocating south of the border. But some voters anticipated free trade would increase economic opportunities by ensuring better access to the American market. Whatever the specific arguments, clearly free trade was both a national and local issue, depending on the perspective taken. This point should be kept in mind during our discussion and analysis of the local campaigns.

New Communication Technology and Liaison with Party Headquarters
Not surprisingly, aspects of the 1988 campaign were affected by the latest communication devices. In several instances fax machines or direct computer link-ups were used to facilitate communication with

national party headquarters. This permitted virtually instantaneous communication between the constituency office and national strategists.[11] At least, this was what was supposed to happen. But for various reasons, including technical difficulties getting the systems to work reliably, problems finding trained workers not intimidated by the technology, or lack of time to devote to these exercises, campaigners complained of communication difficulties between their office and the central party. Several also lamented the lack of advance training that left local campaign organizers on their own and sometimes in the dark as far as national initiatives were concerned. Many respondents contrasted the tight planning and preparation undertaken by national party organizers in 1984 with the rather haphazard arrangements in 1988. Whether 1988 was exceptional or not, almost all campaign managers expressed the view that they had considerable autonomy in planning and implementing campaign strategy. This extended to the preparation of campaign literature, although each party had available, at some cost to the local candidate, packages of campaign material. These could be personalized by the insertion of pictures of the local candidate with the leader, or some reference to local issues.

Although new communication devices were relatively minor factors in this election, one can expect in future, with the bugs worked out, they will play a major role. This role will be strongly "biased" (in Innisian terms) in favour of increased control of local campaigns by the central party office.

Good Help Is Hard to Find

Perhaps because of the overlap with municipal elections; perhaps because of modern lifestyles with more single-parent families or both spouses working outside the home, or because of a growing disenchantment with politicians, volunteer campaign workers were hard to find for several candidates interviewed. Consequently, few candidates, if any, were able to canvass their riding thoroughly, and therefore were severely limited in their ability to "pull the vote" on election day.

Paid versus voluntary work on election campaigns is a factor which can present problems for workers and for the campaign. One campaign manager had to take a leave of absence from his civil service job to accept his position with the campaign. In another instance, the role of media liaison was a part-time voluntary position. The individual who held this responsibility also had full-time paid employment. As a result, most contacts between press and the campaign were conducted through the campaign manager and the campaign room manager who were available on a more regular basis but were also committed to other duties.

The Fragmentation of the Electorate and the Proliferation of Parties

Profound disenchantment with "old line" parties is contributing to increased voter volatility, evidenced clearly in the 1990 Ontario election. Many of those who voted NDP in 1990 had probably never voted that way before and defected from one or both of the other major parties. Their support for the NDP is anything but permanent; they may shift once again in a new direction. This volatility has created exciting opportunities for what used to be called "fringe" parties, now more appropriately designated "alternative" parties. In the two ridings studied, only two alternative parties were active (Libertarian and Christian Heritage). Paradoxically, the effect of the alternative party candidates in the media was to direct coverage away from local issues, largely because of the topics of discussion favoured by these candidates. For example, in Perth–Wellington–Waterloo the Libertarian candidate raised issues of ideology (e.g., government intervention) at debates and in interviews. These discussions were not framed in local perceptions, as they were largely philosophical in nature. This had the effect of diffusing and de-centring debates from local issues. In the same riding, Christian Heritage party candidate Stan Puklicz actually argued against a local focus: "We have to shift our attitudes. We're voting for Canada as a whole, and people are conditioned to think of their individual riding. I'm saying that I'll do a lot for our individual riding but I want to do it on a national level, what is good for all of this country and shift out of the 'me' mentality. The MP that is elected goes to Ottawa to represent the whole country and discuss national issues" (Henrich 1988c).

In the next election in various regions across the country, we can expect serious electoral campaigning by the Reform Party, the Green Party, the Family Coalition, the Bloc québécois, the Confederation of Regions party, and possibly others as well. This will fundamentally challenge efforts to apply any sort of fairness doctrine to media coverage. Guidelines will need to be carefully thought through.

THE CAMPAIGN IN MARKHAM

One issue in the Markham campaign surfaced even before the writs were issued for the election. During his campaign for the Progressive Conservative candidacy, Bill Attewell had buttons printed saying "Bill Attewell, MP, Markham." His opponents accused him of trying to give the impression that he was the incumbent. This was reinforced when just prior to the election call he distributed his MP's newsletter (originally prepared for his Don Valley East constituents) to Markham constituents. He fended off the more serious criticism, the allegation that it was done at public expense, by claiming *he* had paid for the extra run of pamphlets and associated distribution costs. Since these were sent just prior to the election, the costs did not have to appear on his statement of election expenses.[12]

The campaign in Markham featured only a handful of all-candidates debates, most of which took place in retirement homes or high schools. The only debate readily accessible to the public was hastily organized by the NDP and held in Stouffville. One reason for the lack of open public forums can be traced indirectly to the municipal elections. The *Markham Economist and Sun* staff were "too busy" to organize the debate they usually sponsor in Markham.

At the first debate, at a senior citizens' home in Thornhill, candidates were heavily criticized for putting too much emphasis on free trade and not addressing issues considered by their audience to be more pressing. Each candidate, however, did have other issues to discuss. Attewell stressed his own experience and the good economic record of the Mulroney government (especially in job creation). Liberal candidate Jag Bhaduria talked about the need for improvements in law and order, and attacked the Conservatives over free trade and the deficit. Susan Krone, the NDP candidate, emphasized the relative credibility of the leaders, and expressed concern over daycare, housing for battered women and other women's issues. She also emphasized the negative effects for Markham and Canada of free trade. Independent John Gamble criticized the Meech Lake Accord and warned of an impending national sales tax. Ian Hutchison, of the Libertarian party, complained about the growth of government interference in individuals' lives across a range of areas.

Coverage of this initial debate differed in terms of the issues mentioned. Both the *Stouffville Sun* (Mason 1988) and the *Thornhill Liberal* (1988a) were anxious to find a "winner" and to evaluate the candidates' reception by voters.[13] "Bill Attewell appeared to be walking into enemy territory ... Residents ... directed most of their questions – and anger – at Mr. Attewell ... The other three candidates in the riding also took their share of shots at Mr. Attewell," wrote the *Sun*. The *Liberal* reported that "Conservative Bill Attewell was put on the hot seat." A commentary column in the same issue, entitled "Gamble Gets the Edge in Debate," reported that "the fiery lawyer and one-time Conservative scored only a few points with his policies, but when it came to speaking with emotion and passion, Mr. Gamble won hands-down." When the coverage did get down to the issues raised in the debate, the *Sun* wrote almost exclusively on free trade, while the *Liberal* stated pensions, tax reform, free trade and Meech Lake were prominent issues, although the latter two dominated the reporting. Discussion of the issues was reported in an exclusively national context, as was found to be the case with all coverage of the candidates debates.

The media played a major role in shaping the local political debate. With few public meetings to cover, some newspapers attempted to generate a comparative profile by asking candidates to state their position on a specific set of topics, including free trade, abortion, leadership and supermailboxes. Apart from these features, and a few about all-candidates meetings, there was relatively little reporting of the federal election and still less that was analytical or issue-oriented. In all, stories tended to be about what candidates were doing or saying. Reports of all-candidates meetings often focused on the sparks that flew at the meeting but had little to say about the substance of the issues discussed. The Toronto media had very little interest in the Markham race. The *Globe and Mail* ran one fairly extensive story in which it said the "spotlight was on John Gamble" (Webb-Proctor 1988).

Our analysis of local newspaper coverage of the election revealed that no editorial or guest editorial referred to local federal candidates by name. The few editorials that discussed the federal election largely bypassed the local campaign. In its one editorial on the election, the *Markham Economist and Sun* (1988) referred to national leaders, but not to the local campaign or candidates. Two of its guest editors discussed housing (Swarbrick 1988) and free trade (Davidson 1988) but neither discussed implications of these issues in local terms, nor did they refer to the local campaign or candidates. The *Stouffville Sun* ran an editorial on 2 November in which Jim Mason presented "some questions for your federal election candidates when they come calling in your neighbourhood over the next three weeks," which involved the Senate, supermailboxes in Stouffville, a federal airport in Pickering, and the financial implications of election promises. Again, while reference was made to local issues in the campaign, candidates were not mentioned by name. In the *Thornhill Liberal*, letters to the editor, editorials and columns centred largely on free trade and its implication in national terms. An editorial by David Teetzel (1988) was the most explicit about the relevance of local candidates in the federal campaign but again did not mention the individuals seeking election.

Arguably the most important reportage of the election was the televised debate by the local cable station, Classicomm. Here again media figures helped structure the issue questions posed to the candidates from a media panel, not from a studio audience or from viewers through a phone-in.

A leader's visit was always good for some press. However, Turner did not show up, and Broadbent made only a brief appearance early in the race. This made Mulroney's visit, although brief, a good media event for Bill Attewell. He got front-page headlines ("PM hosts free trade rally in Thornhill") and a picture of the two men at a Party event in the 22 October *Liberal*. However, the rally inspired a highly critical editorial column by David Teetzel, who complained that people who came out to see the prime minister "ended up being extras in a TV show," thus encountering "the truth about national campaigns in the TV age: the candidates aren't here for the people's benefit, the people come out for the candidate's benefit." Teetzel was

Table 4.3
Voting behaviour, Markham
(percentages)

	1988	1984	% change
Conservative	53.1	36.0	+17.1
Liberal	31.8	15.3	+16.5
NDP	9.0	9.0	+0.0
Other	6.1	39.8	- 33.7
Percentage margin of victory	21.3		
Total ballots 69 329			
Rejected ballots 263			
Percentage turnout	75.6		

Source: Eagles et al. (1991).
Note: Rural polls = 0; urban polls = 251.

Table 4.4
Campaign financing, Markham

	Number of donations	Total value ($)	Election expenses ($)	% of limit spent
Conservative	160	55 981	50 576	90.2
Liberal*	155	29 390	44 712	79.7
NDP	53	11 657	10 163	18.1
Independent	52	21 886	21 918	—
Libertarian	—	—	—	—

Source: Canada, Elections Canada (1988).

*The "Summary of Revenue" in the Candidate's Return Respecting Election Expenses breaks amounts into (1) contributions received ($29 390) and (2) operating loans ($19 029). While the *Report of the Chief Electoral Officers* (Canada, Elections Canada 1988) does not include this second figure, it could explain the higher amount of the candidates' election expenses compared to those received through contributions.

quick to acknowledge Mulroney was not the only leader to run a "stage managed" campaign. All leaders do, including Broadbent, who spoke in Aurora (north and west of Markham) at the outset of the campaign. Moreover, Teetzel laid some of the blame for these media practices on the media themselves. He concluded: "The upside of this is that we do have local candidates. When the cameras and lights are turned off, they're the ones who will knock on your door, explain the policies and treat you with the respect you deserve. It's time we took the emphasis off the figureheads running for prime minister and paid some attention to the people on the grass roots level" (Teetzel 1988).

The key to the outcome of the campaign, and Attewell's impressive victory (he won with the biggest plurality [14 000+] of any Ontario Conservative) probably had less to do with media coverage than with his superb organization[14] (built up effectively in his quest for the nomination) and his good relations with a number of key ethnic groups. For example, Attewell's role as chair of the all-party Parliamentary Group for Soviet Jewry enhanced his support from the 9 000 Jewish voters in Markham.

In an editorial on the federal election, the *Markham Economist and Sun* provided a fitting epigram for both the election and media coverage. Entitled "Free trade – Ready or Not," the editorial lamented that "A vote either way is based on scant information." Readers carefully following newspaper reports on the election would be poorly informed about the precise local effects of free trade. They would have been told many times, however, that it was either generally good or bad. Neither the candidates nor the media appear to have made serious attempts at public education in regard to an issue which in the end virtually everyone agreed was crucial and significant.[15]

THE CAMPAIGN IN PERTH–WELLINGTON–WATERLOO

The most striking contrast between the campaign in Markham and that in Perth–Wellington–Waterloo is the latter's vastly greater amount of local media attention and the much higher level of activity. Whereas the two largest local papers in Markham had a relatively small staff with time and attention split between two elections, the *Beacon Herald*, for example, was able to assign one reporter to each federal candidate for the duration of the campaign. And it published six days a week. With the *Kitchener-Waterloo Record* circulating in several ridings, "local" coverage was achieved by running feature stories on pertinent ridings. We found five articles specifically on Perth–Wellington–Waterloo, the focus of which were redistribution of electoral boundaries (two articles), free trade, agriculture and women's issues. The latter three issues were

discussed largely in a "national" context, with no specifics on their relationship to the riding. The *Record* is the only newspaper in the riding
receiving wire feeds from a parent, which is Southam. This added a
wider dimension to the election coverage with articles on general topics
such as campaign literature and leader image in television, among others.
This, however, had the effect of taking away from the regional focus.

In contrast to the handful of all-candidates meetings in Markham,
Perth–Wellington–Waterloo candidates met fifteen times, including in
two broadcast debates (one on radio, one on television). The hosts of
the meetings represented a broad range of interests in the riding, from
local business to women's groups. Furthermore, six high-profile
campaigners visited the riding – four for the Progressive Conservatives,
one each for the Liberals and the NDP. (See list of events in table 4.5.)

The most significant "local issue," though not viewed in partisan
terms, was the recent redistribution that increased the size of the riding
by nearly 40 percent. Many of the local élite viewed this as a break in
the natural integrity of the Perth County boundary, still maintained in
the provincial election. In the easternmost end of the riding, Wilmot
Township remains anchored to Waterloo through its municipal and
regional governments. This created confusion among voters who were

Table 4.5
Important dates for campaign activities in Perth–Wellington–Waterloo

Visits to riding	
Jake Epp, Health and Welfare Minister	27 October
Brian Mulroney, Prime Minister	9 November
Eugene Whelan, Former Minister of Agriculture	11 November
Allan Blakeney, Former Premier of Saskatchewan	18 November
Charlie Mayer, Minister for the Canadian Wheat Board	18 November
All-candidates meetings	
Elma Memorial Community Centre	24 October
Northwestern Secondary School	27 October
Perth Women Voters in Action	29 October
Rotary Club	3 November
Mitchell District High School	7 November
New Hamburg Arena	7 November
Perth Federation of Agriculture	8 November
Business and Professional Women's Club	9 November
Brunner Nursing Home	14 November
Waterloo-Oxford Secondary School	15 November
Central Secondary School	16 November
CJCS Radio Stratford	17 November
Rogers Cable TV Kitchener	17 November
Listowel District Secondary School	18 November

being canvassed by candidates all new to them.[16] Voters also felt that because Wilmot Township primarily reads the *Kitchener-Waterloo Record*, they did not receive comprehensive election coverage of their riding. Perth residents resented the addition of portions of Wellington and Waterloo, several expressing a mild resentment that a non-Perth resident (Mike Stinson) won the nomination.

The newspapers in this largely rural constituency claimed that they gave the federal election priority over the municipal election. This appears to be accurate, however one candidate complained the more experienced reporters had been assigned to the municipal election, and that press reports of the federal campaign were lower in quality due to the lack of experience and depth of the junior reporters. "When they don't understand an issue they can slaughter you." The weekly papers saw it as their responsibility to focus on the local campaign, leaving the national election to the dailies.

Fair treatment of the candidates by the press was an issue of much concern to the local media. "Fairness" tended to be defined in terms of space and attention. (One paper even counted column-inches.) The *Beacon Herald* and *New Hamburg Independent* ran a series of candidate profiles, obtained through sit-down and telephone interviews, all of them virtually equal in length. There was some resistance to this practice, however, one editor claiming that equal coverage was not a reflection of reality; it resulted in an imbalance because alternative candidates "got more coverage than they deserved." Others kept their coverage of the campaign to a bare minimum because of time and space constraints, and reported on "events" such as rallies, visits to the riding or the opening of campaign offices. They acknowledged that this practice favoured the "big three" parties and incumbency, but claimed that sit-down interviews with candidates and riding profiles were simply not possible. In cases where candidate profiles were run, it was usually a result of initiatives taken by the campaign organization to contact the media through press reports and bios.[17]

The press's definition of fair treatment was not shared by some of the candidates who were more concerned with the qualitative than the quantitative aspects of coverage. The issue in this case was media coverage of abortion, on which the candidates represented the complete spectrum of viewpoints. These perspectives did not correspond to any party line for most candidates, as reflected in the free vote on the issue held in Parliament before recessing for the election campaign. Liberal candidate Mike Stinson held a strong anti-abortion position. New Democrat Linda Ham believed that women should have choices and that those needing abortions should have access to that medical service.

Tory incumbent Harry Brightwell, a self-proclaimed "middle-of-the-road" person, supported a law which neither restricted abortions nor permitted total freedom for abortions. Stan Puklicz upheld his Christian Heritage party's belief in the family as the basic unit in society, calling abortion a moral issue for which "rights" did not exist. One candidate admitted that he suffered from the single-issue perception of his campaign. Another went so far as to contact one of the newspapers to protest his labelling as a one-issue candidate.

The large geographic area of the riding imposed tremendous constraints on the time and efforts of politicians and media personnel alike. Most candidates needed several campaign offices in various parts of the riding. One advantage here was that the opening of a campaign office was always good for coverage in the press. Harry Brightwell had a toll-free line installed in the town of Wellesley in the northeast end of the riding. Candidates faced the onerous task of crossing the riding to and from the many activities and all-candidates meetings scheduled throughout the campaign. In the most extreme example, the two live phone-in debates on radio and on television occurred on the same evening in two different cities 30 to 40 minutes travelling time apart. The Rogers Cable debate was the fifth time candidates had met in four days and the tenth in two weeks, with another scheduled the following morning in the north end of the riding. Furthermore, Perth–Wellington–Waterloo is a riding where personal contact with candidates is highly valued. There was a strong emphasis on canvassing and literature drops. One candidate noted that: "People get offended if you don't come to call." Linda Ham found the rural/urban split in such a large territory made it difficult for her campaign, especially since the NDP tended to have more support in urban Stratford.

It was widely held that apart from the riding boundary change, there were no "local" issues in Perth–Wellington–Waterloo, that is, issues unique to the constituency. This may be explained in part by the municipal campaign which encompassed community concerns of recycling, low-income housing, planned development, the environment, tourism and improvement of the downtown core. National issues dominated the federal campaign; local implications were rarely drawn out. For example, during a visit to the riding, Health Minister Jake Epp discussed the implications for Canada's health care system under free trade without addressing the imminent concerns of the riding. This pattern may have been exacerbated by the seemingly endless stream of visits to the riding by federal politicians who tended to discuss issues in national contexts. The overlap between municipal and federal campaigns may have reinforced the separation between local and national issues through media coverage. One issue of the *New Hamburg Independent* (Henrich 1988a, 1988b) featured front-page stories about the municipal and federal election campaigns, effectively delineating a clear separation between local and national issues.

The prominence of broadcast media in Perth–Wellington–Waterloo is another way in which this riding is distinguished from Markham and the media environment there. CJCS Radio, in Stratford, held the only radio debate in either constituency. Candidates were given two to three minutes for their opening and closing remarks. This was followed by a phone-in segment in which callers directed their questions to particular candidates, with the others having a chance to respond. The station was generally pleased with this formula and measured its success by the high levels of caller response. This all-candidates meeting was the only way the station could effectively cover the local election. Aside from this venue, its only reporting of the local campaign was achieved through sparse coverage of debates throughout the riding or through national advertising which might mention local candidates. Harry Brightwell spent nearly $5 000 on spot ads and on radio ads scripted in the campaign office and recorded by the candidate himself. These ads were run on CJCS in Stratford, on CKNX, an easy listening station in Wingham, and on a country and western station in Kitchener. The national party provided taped music used as background for these ads, which focused on various issues not receiving attention in the national campaign.

Rogers Cable also hosted an all-candidates meeting.[18] The 90-minute event consisted of an opening statement by each candidate (speaking order drawn by lot) with a one-minute rebuttal to the others' remarks. A host presented a series of issues which had been tracked during the campaign and through press reports. Each issue was presented with every candidate having the chance to respond. This was followed by an open-line segment to the general community. Callers were screened initially, then asked their questions live on the air; they could then remain on-air and respond to the candidate's answers. Attempts were made to broaden the debate by distributing calls on as many topics as possible. Although estimates on viewership are difficult to obtain, the station feels that its debate formula works, based on viewer response. (The station operates a phone-in service and encourages viewer response.)

The higher prominence of broadcast media was reiterated through press reports on the radio and TV debates. The *Beacon Herald* ran an extensive story on 18 November entitled "Federal candidates face new issues in TV, radio debates." With the late date of these events, on 17 November, it is unlikely any of the weekly papers would have covered them since their next issues were dominated by the election results.

Table 4.6
Voting behaviour, Perth–Wellington–Waterloo
(percentages)

	1988	1984	% change
Conservative	39.1	55.8	- 16.7
Liberal	37.0	28.5	+8.5
NDP	19.0	15.5	+3.5
Other	4.9	0.2	+4.7
Percentage margin of victory	2.1		
Total ballots	46 121		
Rejected ballots	149		
Percentage turnout	71.9		

Source: Eagles et al. (1991).

Note: Rural polls = 123; urban polls = 76.

Table 4.7
Campaign financing, Perth–Wellington–Waterloo

	Number of donations	Total ($)	Election expenses ($)	% of limit spent
Conservative	210	31 716	42 716	92.9
Liberal	218	39 949	40 066	87.2
NDP	126	21 398	31 312	68.1
Christian Heritage	143	15 025	14 900	32.6
Libertarian	9	1 000	—	—

Source: Canada, Elections Canada (1988).

PRINCIPAL FINDINGS

Local vs. National Issues

The local campaigns we examined were indeed miniature replicas of the national race in many important respects. The main focus was on free trade (particularly after the national leaders debates). Both Meech Lake and the impending national sales tax were largely ignored. Though discussion of other issues did take place, those issues were framed in "national" terms. Hence, even when the focus shifted away from free trade, the discourse of the local campaign echoed national themes and arguments. Many national issues had important local implications, and might have been researched and debated in terms of their local impact, yet neither candidates nor the media approached them in this fashion. (In this respect, they conform to Gilbert and Sullivan's satirical portrait of the MP who "always answered the Party's call, and never thought of thinking for myself at all.") Local candidates assume their task is to "speak the party line." They may write their own speeches, but as far as campaign themes and issues are concerned they seldom think their own thoughts. Local issues scarcely exist in their minds, and they are ascribed little significance. National issues are discussed in rhetoric borrowed from the national party "line."

Local factors (though not issues) did, however, play an important part in the contests for the candidacy. A significant recruitment of new Liberal party members occurred around the politics of ethnicity[19] in Markham and the politics of abortion in Perth–Wellington–Waterloo. The quest for the Conservative nomination in Markham also involved recruitment of new party members, this effort carrying over into the election campaign, providing a source of campaign workers.

Principal Factors in the Campaign

Our research process involved asking the political and media élite in both ridings to comment on several specific factors in the campaign. The objective was to examine their importance in forming the information environment in which voters made their choices. Certain factors mirrored the themes running throughout this research, such as the tension between local and national issues, and the role of leaders and parties, along with the media coverage of them, in shaping the campaign. Political respondents were asked about the importance of advertising, canvassing and all-candidates meetings, along with other media of communication like campaign literature, and new technologies such as direct mail. In all, the findings indicate there were both common and unique features in the information environment of voters in Markham and in Perth–Wellington–Waterloo in the 1988 campaigns.

When asked about the relevance of local issues, media and political élites held strikingly different views. Virtually all media respondents claimed local issues played a very significant, and in some cases, crucial role in their coverage of the campaign. Political respondents, however, placed a relatively low significance (and in certain cases none at all) on the importance of local issues in their campaign. Some interesting information can be gleaned from tables 4.8 and 4.9. This did not differ between constituencies, as one might expect, given the salience of free trade in Perth–Wellington–Waterloo; but it did reflect the commonly held view that there were no identifiable local issues unique

Table 4.8
Significant factors in the campaign (media)

Interviewee	Local issues	Candidates' strength	Attacking other candidates	Regional issues	National issues	National leaders	Party platform	Incumbency
Markham								
A	4	4	2	3	4	4	3	2
B	4	2	3	2	2	3	2	3
C	2	2	1	2	3	3	3	N/A
D	3–4	2–3	2–3	2	2	2	2–3	3
Perth								
A	1	2	1	1	4	4	4	4
B	4	4	1	4	4	4	2	1
C	4	2	3	2	3	2	3	3
D	4	1	1	2	4	4	4	3
E	2	3	1	1	3	3–4	3	3
F	3	2	2	2	4	4	4	2
G	3	2	1	1	2	2	3	4
H	3	1	2	1	2	2	4	2
I	4	1	2	3	3	2	2	2

Question: How significant were the following factors in your coverage of the campaign?
1. not significant at all; 2. somewhat significant; 3. very significant; 4. absolutely crucial.
N/A = not applicable.

to either riding. Candidates and campaign managers placed much more significance than did the media on national issues, which in many cases were viewed as absolutely crucial factors in the campaigns. Regional issues were also perceived as having a significant impact, although to a lesser degree in Markham. The same pattern held for regional issues among the media respondents.

One of the most marked differences between ridings involved the issue of incumbency. In Markham, it was claimed incumbency was a relatively insignificant issue in the campaign. In fact, two respondents stated the issue of incumbency was irrelevant because of boundary changes in the 1987 redistribution. In Perth–Wellington–Waterloo however, also a new riding, it was commonly held incumbency was a major, if not deciding, factor in Harry Brightwell's 961-vote (2.1 percent) margin. (Thus resurfaces the debate over the importance of the local candidate.) Candidates' strengths were perceived as less important among the media than among the political respondents in the two ridings, and the majority of respondents claimed that attacking other candidates held little, if any, significance in the campaign. On average, party platforms were perceived as playing a very significant role in the organization of campaigns and media coverage in both constituencies.

Table 4.9
Significant factors in the campaign (political)

Interviewee	Local issues	Candidates' strength	Attacking other candidates	Regional issues	National issues	National leaders	Party platform	Incumbency
Markham								
A	2	3	2	1	4	4	3	3
B	1	3	2	2	4	4	4	2
C	1	2	1	1	3	3	3	2
D	3	3	1	3	4	4	3	1
E	1	1	2	3	4	4++	2	N/A*
F	2	3	3	2	4	4	3	1
G	2	4	1	1	4	3	4	3
H	1	2	1	1	3	3	2	3
I	N/A	N/A	N/A	N/A	N/A	N/A	N/A	N/A
Perth								
A	3	3	1	4	3	3	2	4
B	2	4	3	2	4	4	4	3
C	2	2	1	1–2	3	3	3	3
D	1	4	3	3	3	1	3–4	2–3

Question: How significant were the following factors in your coverage of the campaign?
1. not significant at all; 2. somewhat significant; 3. very significant; 4. absolutely crucial.

N/A = not applicable.

*Not applicable owing to redistribution in 1987.

Candidates and campaign managers were asked about the importance of several campaign factors in shaping their strategies (see table 4.10). In Markham, there was a great disparity of opinion on the issue of canvassing. This contrasts with the commonly held view in Perth–Wellington–Waterloo that canvassing was of the utmost significance in the election outcome. This is perhaps not surprising in a largely rural area which, throughout our research, was repeatedly described by media and political sources as a "person" riding. (Note the pessimistic conclusions of Black 1984.) The canvassing aspect of the campaign process was in fact the most highly rated activity in the riding.

Opinion was also sought on a number of other campaign factors. In general, media coverage was perceived as a very important aspect, while direct mail was not a factor in most campaigns in these ridings.[20] Most respondents ranked literature drops from very important to absolutely crucial. For example, in Perth–Wellington–Waterloo, one organization placed crucial significance on campaign literature, scheduling two to three drops per household or business. Another organization downplayed this strategy, favouring instead face-to-face canvassing

Table 4.10
Campaign activity rankings

Interviewee	Advertising	News coverage	All-candidates meetings	Canvassing	Literature drops	Direct mail	Meet-the-candidates	Getting out the vote
Markham								
A	4	3	2	4	3	1	4	N/A
B	3	3	3	4	4	1	2	4
C	1	1	2	3	N/A	N/A	N/A	3
D	1	3	2	3	4	1	2	3
E	4	3	1	1	4	1	2	4
F	2	2	3	1	3	1	3	1
G	2	2	4+	4	4	1	4	1
H	4	3	4	4	4	3	4	4
Perth								
A	3	4	3	4	4	2	3	4
B	3+	3	1+	3+	3	3	2	2
C	3	2–3	2	4	1–2	N/A	3	2
D	N/A	N/A	N/A	N/A	N/A	N/A	N/A	N/A

Question: In terms of your campaigning, how would you rank the importance of the following activities?

1. not significant at all; 2. somewhat significant; 3. very significant; 4. absolutely crucial.

N/A = not applicable.

with voters through more contact canvassing. Opinion varied on the importance of all-candidates meetings. Surprisingly, there were no identifiable patterns of response according to riding, given the notably different roles these events played in the campaigns. There was a lesser range of opinion on meet-the-candidate gatherings, which were, on average, perceived as very important. Finally, while the issue of getting out the vote elicited a variety of responses, on average it was perceived as a very important factor in the campaign, with no significant disparities between ridings.

Some interesting observations emerged from political respondents on the importance of the various types of media targeted for the campaign (see table 4.11). In both ridings, it was felt local TV stations played a relatively unimportant role during the election period. This contrasts with the high level of importance attached to the role of local newspapers and other print media. This distinction confirms the point raised earlier of the primacy of newspapers in media strategies of local election campaigns over radio, cable TV, and commercial television.[21] Radio was an unimportant factor in the Markham campaigns, while it was regarded as an important element in the rural Perth–Wellington–Waterloo contest.

Table 4.11
Importance of various media in the campaign

Interviewee	Local TV stations	Local cable stations	Local newspapers	Other newspapers or magazines	Radio
Markham					
A	1	2	2.5	N/A	N/A
B	2	1	4	3	N/A
C	1	2	3	N/A	N/A
D	1	3	2	2	1
E	1	4	4	4	1
F	4	3–4	3	3	1
G	1	4	4	4	1
H	2	2	3	2	1
Perth					
A	1	3	4	4	2
B	3	2	3	N/A	3
C	2	2	2	3	2
D	1	2	4	N/A	2.5

Question: In designing the media side of your campaign, how much importance did you give the following?

1. not significant at all; 2. somewhat significant; 3. very significant; 4. absolutely crucial.

N/A = not applicable.

Local cable TV stations were important factors in media strategies in both ridings, more so than local commercial stations and slightly less so than the print media. This suggests that despite the difficulty in tracking viewer estimates for cable TV, this medium is valued as a campaign tool.

Media Coverage of the Local Campaign

Televised debates between local candidates are becoming the most important events in the local campaign. These debates also function as a "miniature replica" of their national counterpart. It is expected viewership of these debates will increase, and that a "phone-in" component will become more common. In urban areas, televised debates may soon eclipse other types of campaigning, including all-candidates meetings. (These appear to be in decline in Markham.) In rural ridings, radio debates will probably continue so long as cable is less widely subscribed to.

The quality of issue coverage is poor in both print and broadcast media. In large part this reflects the low level of analysis and debate offered by the candidates themselves. This in turn can be traced to an absence of research personnel and resources on the one hand, and a lack of appropriate expectations within the political culture on the other. These various factors reinforce each other in a vicious circle:

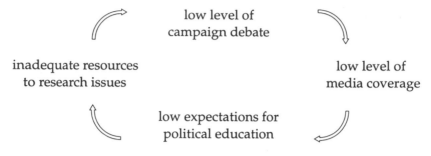

low level of
campaign debate

inadequate resources
to research issues

low level of
media coverage

low expectations for
political education

It may be possible to break out of this cycle by improving the resources for researching local implications of national politics and issues. One way to accomplish this would involve setting up a series of constituency internships for senior undergraduate students in political science and related disciplines to undertake research on constituencies. Research findings and analyses would be made available to local media, and to parties and candidates active in the riding.[22] These internships could be organized under the auspices of Elections Canada and supervised by university faculty.

In 1988, the local media in the urban setting saw their primary role as that of reporting on the municipal campaign. This left a relative gap in coverage of the federal election that no other media filled. We assume this problem stemmed from the overlap between the two campaigns. Coverage in the rural riding was much more extensive and thorough. Media leaders in both settings indicated a desire to provide fair coverage and might welcome a set of guidelines, similar to those used for broadcast media by the CRTC, to help cover the campaign in an appropriate fashion. They might also welcome a workshop or conference where these issues could be discussed. This is a service Elections Canada might also provide. In the end it may be more productive than requiring or subsidizing "free advertising space" in local newspapers.

Campaign Financing and Expenditures

The main interest of this study in campaign financing pertained to its impact on media strategies. The interviews conducted yielded a great variety of interesting comments. Opinion ranged across a wide spectrum. One candidate noted, "I ran a perfectly respectable campaign for about $8 000. There is no need whatsoever for such high spending limits." At the other extreme, several activists felt it impossible to run a "half decent" campaign for $50 000, the bulk of the money disappearing into unavoidable fixed costs for rent or campaign literature before the real campaign even begins. Effective TV advertising is particularly infeasible given current restrictions. One campaign manager recommended removing limits altogether, letting those who can raise more, spend more. An alternative to unlimited spending is more subsidized "free time" or "free space," or encouraging parties to devote more TV resources to local constituencies rather than emphasizing the national level exclusively. Finally, one candidate, who drew extensively on personal financial resources to pursue the nomination, complained current regulations may lead to the exclusion from candidacy of the less well off. "Anyone should be able to seek the nomination, not just individuals who can come up with their own money." He urged imposing limits on expenses for seeking the nomination in order to prevent a monopoly by the wealthy or by those who are effective fund-raisers. (Perhaps these guidelines could be modelled after current restrictions on candidates for party leadership.) Several respondents recommended possible tax deductions for individuals contributing to nomination campaigns. Others pointed out that if existing spending limits are maintained, large-scale paid TV advertising will continue to be infeasible for local candidates. Given that Canadians increasingly turn to television as their major source of information about politics, this may be problematic. To avoid giving undue advantage to wealthy parties or candidates, it may be preferable, instead of raising spending limits, to extend free time requirements to local cable stations. A few of those we interviewed discussed possible requirements for "free space" in local newspapers. (This suggestion was warmly endorsed by some but bitterly opposed by others. In general, people's responses reflected their basic ideological viewpoint on government action versus privatization.) Several candidates recommended that regulations concerning financing be simplified so that official agents and others involved in the campaign would find them more comprehensible. This goal might be achieved by more direct communication with the central party in order to educate individuals involved in the process.

Polls

The 1988 campaign was as much the "poll campaign" as it was the "free trade election." There were more than twice as many published polls in 1988 than in 1984, and they attracted a great deal of media attention. Fletcher (1990) found that reporting of polls figured prominently in approximately 30 percent of TV and newspaper campaign coverage. The depth and extent of our respondents' criticisms of polls were surprising. Most critics complained that polls generated a bandwagon effect. Few spoke of the obverse effect associated with "strategic voting" even though Johnston et al. (1989) present persuasive evidence that it was fairly extensive in the 1988 election. Most critics said they would prefer a ban on polls during election campaigns though none believed this was a feasible response to what was nevertheless regarded as a serious problem. As Marney Beck (1988) put it in a 2 November editorial in the *Thornhill Liberal*, "Do the polls influence people how to vote, or do they accurately reflect the whims of the voters' preferences? It's the 'chicken and egg' question and the whole thing makes the electorate look like a bunch of turkeys."

Though banning polls completely is out of the question, consideration should be given to generalizing the *Globe and Mail* policy of refusing to commission polls in the last 10 days of the campaign.[23]

CONCLUSION

Our study of two Ontario constituencies has uncovered both similarities and differences in the information environment of voters during the 1988 federal election campaign. Overall, there was a contrast in the amount of attention given the campaign by the media in Perth–Wellington–Waterloo and in Markham. This may be attributable to the different social and political demographies in rural and urban environments. In Perth–Wellington–Waterloo, perceived as a "person" riding, much more emphasis was placed on personal contact with the candidate both in terms of campaign strategies and in media coverage. While the two ridings underwent electoral boundary changes in 1987, the impact was felt more strongly in Perth–Wellington–Waterloo. In this riding, a candidate from the "new" section was perceived as an outsider in some circles. The differing media emphases on the federal election may also have been due to availability of resources and to the choice of difficult priorities in the face of simultaneous municipal elections.

In general, regardless of the perception of the campaign by the media, no local issues featured prominently in either constituency. Furthermore, there was very little analysis by candidates or media of the local implications of national issues. This calls to mind Irvine's claim that local candidates have inconsiderable impact on the outcome of elections. "The work that MPs do is never rewarded, nor is poor performance sanctioned, by our present electoral arrangements" (Irvine 1982, 782).

Perhaps changes to what candidates do during the election would change the work they do as members of Parliament in representing their constituencies. Current electoral arrangements don't focus on the local scene in any creative way. One change in the practice which we believe would make a difference involves developing a research base for constituency issue analysis. This could be accomplished by establishing a program of internships for university students in political science for the researching and compilation of a base of relevant information for constituencies. This data would be made available to candidates and their campaign organizations as well as to media organizations. The implications of this would be far-reaching in addressing the imbalance of resources available to both candidates and media which now constrains their research potential. It would provide a richer information environment for voters and change the work of MPs by enabling them to better represent their constituencies.

NOTES

This study was completed in June 1991.

1. This finding is somewhat paradoxical. The conventional wisdom among party strategists is that the local candidate is "worth" at most about 5 to 7 percent of the popular vote. This assumption has some support in the academic literature. Studies by Krashinsky and Milne (1983) and by Cunningham (1971) indicate a figure of about 10 percent for the electoral impact of the candidate. Irvine (1982) reproduces some election studies data on "importance" of the local candidate which range from a high of 30 percent in 1965 to a low of 21 percent in 1979, but suggests these responses are misleading and can more accurately be seen as a disguised reaction to the leader or the party. Clarke et al. (1991, 113), where figure 4.1 appears on page 115, insist two pages earlier that "in every instance the effect of local candidates is relatively small ... In general, the public reactions to local candidates do little to explain ... individual voting behaviour." This matter needs further careful study and analysis.

2. We also completed a content analysis of local newspaper articles about the campaign to determine the amount and extent of coverage of local candidates, and to analyse the prominence of issues and the context in which they were discussed. As we progressed with the collection and analysis of newspapers, we began to rethink our approach because of inconsistencies caused by the unavailability of back issues and missing microfilm and because of several difficulties in the coding itself. We completed our content analysis, yet we chose to report on findings obtained through a qualitative analysis instead. This involved a careful reading of newspaper clippings in conjunction with personal interviews conducted with members of the media. We found that we have been able to make solid conclusions based on this approach. No broadcast content analysis was conducted, although in-depth interviews were obtained from program and news directors of the radio and cable stations.

3. After his election, Bill Attewell successfully introduced a private members' bill changing the name of the riding to Markham–Whitchurch–Stouffville.

4. Liberal candidates had won every election in the riding from 1934 to 1979 except for Conservative victories in 1957 and 1958.

5. The *Financial Post* began daily publishing in February 1988, but by the fall its total circulation was only about 60 000–70 000. In the Toronto area, paid circulation in October was 30 945 daily and 36 960 on the weekend.

6. A U.S. presidential election was held the previous week.

7. In instances where media outlets had obligations to cover more than one municipality, these difficulties were multiplied. Classicomm in Richmond Hill faced the daunting prospect of attending to more than 150 candidates in their municipalities. This was also the case with Rogers Cable in Kitchener, which hosted debates for both mayoralty and federal candidates and provided live coverage of results on both election nights.

8. Although there is some question concerning the impact of the free trade issue on voting (see for example LeDuc 1991), its impact on the 1988 campaign is indisputable.

9. Cf. Clarke et al. (1991, 3). "In the first weeks of the campaign, the free trade issue did not immediately take off, as the parties' campaigns often dwelt on other matters." The Conservatives initially played down free trade, making the theme of their campaign "Managing Change." The NDP steered away from free trade because polling showed the public did not trust them on economic issues. Instead they stressed Broadbent's popularity. The Liberals' campaign began under a cloud of internal dissension and policy confusion.

10. The effect of free trade on marketing boards was such a crucial factor in the campaign that it prompted visits to the riding from Eugene Whelan, former minister of agriculture, and from Charlie Mayer, minister for the Canadian Wheat Board. Several local agricultural organizations hosted all-candidates meetings to discuss the issue. These visits and debates garnered much coverage in the press. It is interesting to note, however, that both the tone of discussion, and coverage in the media, portrayed the free trade issue largely in a national context, failing to assess its implication for agriculture in the local setting.

11. One candidate, whose campaign manager worked in the telephone industry, successfully used cellular phones and speed links to connect himself with his senior campaign workers. But we saw no use of telephone banks in these two constituencies.

12. This raises the ethical question of when a report to constituents should be considered a campaign document. It also highlights the advantage incumbent MPs have over challengers, especially when incumbents are from the government party. (Cf. comments on the Vancouver Centre campaign in Sayers 1991.)

13. Jeremy Wilson (1980–81) notes that "horse-race journalism" has become a permanent feature of the modern campaign in Canada but questions

whether so much of the media's energy need be applied to speculating on the contest.

14. Through contributions, Attewell raised nearly twice as much money as did his nearest rival, Bhaduria. He also had more than ten times as many workers, especially in the week after the municipal election.

15. Bill Attewell did co-sponsor a public forum on free trade. The *Thornhill Liberal* featured one editorial and several extensive letters to the editor on the subject.

16. The New Hamburg newspaper (located in Wilmot Township) reminded readers that because of the redistribution and the fact that the riding was new, technically there was no incumbent. But nearly every other newspaper regarded Brightwell as the incumbent and described him accordingly.

17. Several news editors complained of the difficulty in contacting alternative party candidates. This may have arisen from a different set of campaign priorities, a lack of personnel, or a newness to the process. Whatever the reason, some editors reported a closer rapport with the three major parties than with the alternative parties. In some instances, the latter were seen as not "courting" the media to the same extent as were the major parties.

18. Although not obliged to do so, Rogers Cable claimed the structuring of their campaign coverage followed the "equitable access" guidelines as set out by the CRTC. They had considered covering rallies and events but were concerned about giving candidates equal time. Coverage of these types of events would not have permitted all candidates the same access. The station found the best way of achieving fairness was through its candidate profiles and the all-candidates meeting, with its live phone-in segment. This meeting provided the public with an unbiased forum for evaluating the federal candidates. Rogers felt its strength in election coverage derived from its role as a public service, of not having to "create" news to sell air time.

19. The politics of ethnicity, a growing phenomenon in the Canadian electoral process, was the topic of an insightful study by Zajc (1990). This research is based on the experience of several ridings in southern Ontario during the 1988 federal election. While the riding of Markham was not specifically addressed, Zajc's study is relevant to Markham inasmuch as these events were part of a wider phenomenon.

20. While direct mail was first used by the Conservatives in the mid-1970s, other parties have been slower to realize the potential of this campaign tool. The use of direct mail is on the rise, however. In the 1988 election millions of pieces were sent out (Taras 1990, 186).

21. This contradicts the trend at the national leadership level, where televised debates and advertisements are increasing the status of electronic media in the electoral process (Barr 1991).

22. Many editors remarked that they would have liked to do more investigative reporting of both candidates and issues in the campaign. It is possible

this would have the effect of pulling out the local dimensions on general topics. In one example, the *Thornhill Liberal* on 16 November ran a background analysis on women's issues in a "local" perspective, relating the issue of women's shelters to a transition house in the riding. The NDP candidate Susan Krone was well equipped with information and statistics about the shelter. The availability of this type of information to candidates and members of the media would not only promote discussion of general issues in local contexts, it might also draw in topics which tend to be marginalized from campaigns and the press, such as women's issues. Candidates in both ridings spoke of daycare, for example (in particular in Perth–Wellington–Waterloo, where two debates on women's issues took place), but these discussions were largely in conceptual terms. They spoke of the government's role in daycare and the role of women in the family. Better information might lead to more informed discussion about issues rather than sterile debates over concepts.

23. Fletcher (1990) raised other concerns with respect to the way both the issues and public response are portrayed. Quite often, polls oversimplify complex issues and then present results in falsely derived categories which are supposedly reflections of "public preference." Polls reflect public feelings more than they do considered opinion. Indeed, the public is often poorly informed about issues, yet willingly expresses an opinion on them. Fletcher suggests this type of influence over the public agenda and framing of important issues dilutes the alternative channels of public input, especially from those having carefully considered the issues. The impact of polling practices on voters, election campaigns and the media is complex. It requires careful consideration as polls become increasingly entrenched in our electoral process.

INTERVIEWS

The interviews were conducted from October to December 1990.

Markham

Jag Bhaduria, Liberal candidate

Diarmuid O'Dea, campaign manager for Jag Bhaduria

Bill Attewell, Progressive Conservative candidate

Rob Anderson, campaign manager for Bill Attewell

Susan Krone, New Democratic Party candidate

Rob Saunders, campaign manager for Susan Krone

John Gamble, Independent candidate

Richard van Seters, campaign manager for John Gamble

Ian Hutchison, Libertarian candidate

John Andersen, news director, Classic Communications Ltd.

Jim Mason, editor, *Stouffville Sun*

Jo Ann Stevenson, editor-in-chief, *Markham Economist and Sun*

Marney Beck, editor, *Thornhill Liberal*

Perth–Wellington–Waterloo

Harry Brightwell, Progressive Conservative candidate

Mike Stinson, Liberal candidate

Mike Dunn, campaign manager for Linda Ham

Robert Boyce, campaign manager for Harry Brightwell

David May, publicity chairman for Harry Brightwell

Stan Puklicz, Christian Heritage party candidate

Paul Knowles, editor, *New Hamburg Independent*

Donald O'Connor, editor, St. Marys *Journal Argus*

Ronald C. Carson, editor, *Beacon Herald*

Doug Lester, program director, CJCS Radio

Marion Duke, editor, *Listowel Banner*

Robin Moore, program director, Trillium Cable Communications

Ivy Reeve, editor, *Milverton Sun*

Andy Bader, editor, *Mitchell Advocate*

John Juurinen, program director, Rogers Cable

Bill Beane, assignment editor, *Kitchener-Waterloo Record*

Fritz Roos, *Kitchener-Waterloo Record*

REFERENCES

Barr, Cathy Widdis. 1991. "The Importance and Potential of Leaders Debates." In *Media and Voters in Canadian Election Campaigns*, ed. Frederick J. Fletcher. Vol. 18 of the research studies of the Royal Commission on Electoral Reform and Party Financing. Ottawa and Toronto: RCERPF/Dundurn.

Beck, Marney. 1988. "Election Polls Reach the Saturation Point." *Thornhill Liberal*, 2 November.

Black, Jerome H. 1984. "Revisiting the Effects of Canvassing on Voting Behaviour." *Canadian Journal of Political Science* 17:351–74.

Canada. Elections Canada. 1988. *Report of the Chief Electoral Officer Respecting Election Expenses 1988*. Ottawa: Minister of Supply and Services Canada.

Clarke, Harold D., Lawrence LeDuc, Jane Jenson and Jon H. Pammett. 1991. *Absent Mandate: Interpreting Change in Canadian Elections*. 2d ed. Toronto: Gage.

Cunningham, Robert. 1971. "The Impact of the Local Candidate in Canadian Federal Elections." *Canadian Journal of Political Science* 4:287–90.

Davidson, W. 1988. "Bad Rap for Free Trade." *Markham Economist and Sun*, 9 November.

Eagles, Munroe, James P. Bickerton, A.G. Gagnon and Patrick J. Smith. 1991. *The Almanac of Canadian Politics*. Peterborough: Broadview Press.

Fletcher, Frederick J. 1987. "Mass Media and Parliamentary Elections in Canada." *Legislative Studies Quarterly* 12 (August): 341–72.

———. 1990. "Polling and Political Communication: The Canadian Case." Paper presented at the International Association for Mass Communication Research, Lake Bled, Yugoslavia.

Henrich, Arlonna. 1988a. "Little Local Election Controversy." *New Hamburg Independent*, 2 November.

———. 1988b. "Minister of Health Visits Morningside." *New Hamburg Independent*, 2 November.

———. 1988c. "Stan Puklicz: Christian Heritate Party Candidate." *New Hamburg Independent*, 2 November.

Irvine, William P. 1982. "Does the Candidate Make a Difference? The Macro-Politics and Micro-Politics of Getting Elected." *Canadian Journal of Political Science* 15:755–82.

Johnston, Richard, André Blais, Henry E. Brady and Jean Crête. 1989. "Free Trade in the 1988 Canadian General Election." Paper presented at the PIPES Seminar, University of Chicago, 1989.

Krashinsky, Michael, and William J. Milne. 1983. "Some Evidence on the Effect of Incumbency in Ontario Provincial Elections." *Canadian Journal of Political Science* 16:489–500.

LeDuc, Lawrence. 1991. "Voting for Free Trade? The Canadian Voter and the 1988 Federal Election." In *Politics: Canada*. 7th ed., ed. Paul W. Fox and Graham White. Toronto: McGraw-Hill Ryerson.

McNaught, Jana, and John Roe. 1988. "Revamped Riding Provides Opportunity for all Candidates." *Kitchener-Waterloo Record*, 20 October.

Markham Economist and Sun. 1988. "Free Trade – Ready or Not."
16 November.

Mason, Jim. 1988. "Attewell under Fire at Meeting." *Stouffville Sun,*
26 October.

Sayers, Anthony M. 1991. "Local Issue Space in National Elections:
Kootenay West–Revelstoke and Vancouver Centre." In *Reaching the
Voter: Constituency Campaigning in Canada,* ed. David V.J. Bell and
Frederick J. Fletcher. Vol. 20 of the research studies of the Royal
Commission on Electoral Reform and Party Financing. Ottawa and
Toronto: RCERPF/Dundurn.

Swarbrick, Anne. 1988. "Affordable Housing – A Voter's Concern." *Markham
Economist and Sun,* 2 November.

Taras, David. 1990. *The Newsmakers.* Scarborough: Nelson Canada.

Teetzel, David. 1988. "Smile, You're on Candidate Camera." *Thornhill Liberal,*
26 October.

Thornhill Liberal. 1988a. "Gamble Gets the Edge in Debate." 26 October.

———. 1988b. "PM Hosts Free Trade Rally in Thornhill." 22 October.

———. 1988c. "Don't Let Federal Vote Overshadow Ontario Vote."
12 October.

Webb-Proctor, Gary. 1988. "Markham Tories Pick Experience."
Globe and Mail, 2 June.

Wilson, R. Jeremy. 1980–81. "Horserace Journalism: The Media in Elections."
Journal of Canadian Studies 15 (4): 56–68.

Zajc, Lydia. 1990. "The Ethnicity and Competitiveness of Ethnic Minority
Nominees in the 1988 Federal Election." Montreal: McGill University,
Dept. of Political Science.

5

MEDIA COVERAGE OF LOCAL CAMPAIGNS

The 1988 Election in Outremont and Frontenac

Luc Bernier

IN THE CANADIAN political system, national results and local results are inseparable. According to our study, local candidates received little attention from the national media, but did not seem to be too concerned about it. Except for reports in weekly newspapers, which cover only regional news, coverage of local campaigns was relegated to the inside pages of major newspapers or the end of radio newscasts.

Local candidates received more attention from the local media; it is questionable, however, whether this attention had any impact on the vote. In general, the interviews conducted revealed that local campaigns targeted different voters or groups as each party concentrated on mobilizing its own potential supporters. In this context, the media are little used by local organizers because they are not seeking mass audiences.

The direct association often established in the public mind between election results and the personality of the leaders of the principal parties conceals a much more complex reality. The shift to the local level of national issues, which are often dealt with superficially, has an impact on election results. Local organizations have their say through such relatively inexpensive means as door-to-door canvassing and informal meetings. We talked to people with experience in local campaigns, whether through constituency organizations or the local media, to gain a better understanding of the impact of their activities and those of the national organizations.

The study focuses on two Quebec ridings. The first, Outremont, is in the heart of Montreal and the second, Frontenac, is relatively isolated from the major urban centres. We wanted to examine how the local campaign differed from the national campaign in these two ridings. The riding of Outremont is a microcosm of the demographic transformation taking place in Montreal, as in other large Canadian cities. In addition, Outremont was one of the few ridings in Quebec where all three major parties were well organized. In Frontenac, a more traditional Quebec riding, it is interesting to see how a candidate that had originally been parachuted in was able to be re-elected. Although Outremont had always been a Liberal riding, for the past 30 years Frontenac had experienced waves of Créditiste, Liberal and Conservative sentiment. The two ridings are well covered by local weeklies and "national" newspapers.

This study is the result of a series of 17 interviews conducted with candidates and organizers involved in the 1988 election campaign and reporters who covered the campaign for the local or national media. We asked each interviewee for other contact persons. We continued interviewing until the people we met stopped giving us new names. We also analysed advertising and articles that appeared on each of the candidates and the campaign in the two ridings.

Neither constituency seems to have received much attention from the national party organizations, though apparently for different reasons. In Frontenac, with the re-election of Marcel Masse almost certain, the national organizations did not feel obliged to devote much energy to the local campaign. In fact, Masse won a majority of the votes cast at every polling station (Sévigny 1988b). In Outremont, on the other hand, the Progressive Conservatives did not feel that they could win and, according to some organizers, decided not to expend too much effort on the riding. The Liberals felt that this was one of the few Quebec seats they had a good chance of winning. The national organization did not seem to be involved in this local campaign. In this context, Outremont and Frontenac in 1988 appeared to be constituencies where the local organizations and media could have played an important role.

Neither the media nor the local campaigns, however, had a major impact on the election results in these two ridings. Yet, in constituencies that have become too large for voters to have direct contact with candidates, the media can be a vital link, as they are at the national level.

The Progressive Conservative victories in both ridings suggest that factors other than local issues determined the outcome. In Outremont, for example, the campaign revolved around the issues of free trade and abortion. In Frontenac, the election could be described as a tacit understanding between the minister, who brings tangible benefits to his riding, and the voters, who guarantee him an overwhelming majority. The campaign revolved around free trade, but the election result was only slightly linked to that issue.

In both ridings only the Liberal and Progressive Conservative parties had well-structured political organizations. The New Democratic Party (NDP) played no real part in Frontenac but may have cost the Liberals their victory in Outremont. In Frontenac, journalists and organizers for the other parties were not sure that the NDP candidate had come to the riding at all.

Organizers generally deplored voters' lack of interest in federal party politics, unlike provincial politics, in which many of the organizers are or have been very active. Because of its lukewarm support for the Meech Lake Accord, the federal Liberal party lost much of its electoral support, support that could be attributed to the provincial Liberals. The provincial Liberals declared themselves neutral in the 1988 federal election campaign. In addition, the Liberals felt that relations with the national organization should be kept to a minimum given the unpopularity of the leader and lack of useful information coming from that organization. The Conservatives also felt that they did not need assistance from outside the riding, but did mention some cost savings from cooperative purchases made available by the national organization.

In the two constituencies described in this study, organizers emphasized the lack of substance in the debates, deplored the superficial knowledge of the issues and wished for a more serious discussion of the problems affecting the ridings.

THE RIDING OF OUTREMONT

Outremont is located in the centre of the island of Montreal. It includes the well-to-do residential neighbourhoods at the north end of Outremont and part of Westmount. The riding has a slight French-speaking majority (51.7 percent) that is clearly below the provincial average. It also includes a large Jewish community of approximately 10 000, as well as Portuguese, Greek and Italian communities. With more than one-third of its population born outside Canada, Outremont ranks third among all Quebec ridings in terms of number of immigrants.

The level of education is high: 23.6 percent of those over the age of 15 have a university degree, compared with 8.6 percent for Quebec as a whole. The average family income is $40 692. The average value of housing is $142 311. In general, these homes are of pre-1946 construction and are primarily tenant-occupied. The riding is mostly residential – a suburban-like community for those working in downtown Montreal.

Because of alterations in the riding map before the 1988 election campaign, Lucie Pépin, the incumbent, was campaigning in a riding whose boundaries had changed considerably. According to the 1986 census, there were 93 995 people living in Outremont, an increase of 17 000 over the 1984 constituency poll. Of this number, 72 840 were of voting age.

From the time the riding was established until the 1988 election, the people of Outremont had always elected Liberal representatives. In 1984, when Lucie Pépin succeeded Marc Lalonde as the member of Parliament for the riding, the Progressive Conservatives took only 29 percent of the vote – one of their worst showings in Quebec. Jean-Pierre Hogue, the Conservative candidate who defeated Lucie Pépin in 1988, was a newcomer to politics and to the Progressive Conservative party, although he had close ties with Jean Corbeil, the former mayor of Anjou and a Conservative candidate in that riding.

In addition to Jean-Pierre Hogue and Lucie Pépin, the other candidates were Louise O'Neill for the NDP, Harriett Fels (Green Party of Canada), Milenko Miljevik (Rhinoceros Party), Guy Huard (Party for the Commonwealth of Canada), Monique Marcotte (Communist Party) and Fernand Deschamps (Independent). The three larger parties all ran good campaigns.

The riding of Outremont covers not only the City of Outremont but also the central part of Montreal (Mile End) and the multi-ethnic neighbourhood of Côte-des-Neiges; it can thus be described as representative of Montreal as a whole. In Outremont, campaign material was distributed in Greek, Italian, Portuguese and Vietnamese, as well as through various ethnic publications such as *The Afro Canadian.*

According to Liberal candidate Lucie Pépin, Outremont can be divided into five sub-regions containing 41 different groups (Rivière 1988). With the revision of the electoral map, the riding was enlarged considerably, thereby diluting the Liberal vote that had existed previously. Outremont inherited constituents from the former riding of Laurier in which votes were more equally divided between the Liberals and the NDP.

The ethnic communities and the Côte-des-Neiges area were considered loyal to the Liberal party, while the NDP had the support of the eastern part of the riding around Park Avenue. The Conservative victory is attributable to the fact that the party was able to win the votes of the sector encompassing the City of Outremont. According to local political organizers, people in the wealthier areas voted for the Conservatives, while the NDP and Liberals shared the vote in the poorer neighbourhoods.

In the 1988 election, Outremont was considered a bell-wether constituency where the majority would probably vote for the party that formed the next government. As a result, the riding took on more importance for the media than it might otherwise have done. The major Montreal papers covered Outremont more than any other constituency in the city.

The Progressive Conservative candidate, Jean-Pierre Hogue, took the riding with 1 702 votes more than Lucie Pépin (see the results in appendix A). The NDP candidate, Louise O'Neill, claimed 20.5 percent of the vote, making Outremont one of only 10 Quebec ridings where the NDP gained more than 20 percent of the votes. None of the other parties really campaigned in the riding.

THE RIDING OF FRONTENAC

The constituency of Frontenac includes the municipalities of Thetford Mines, Black Lake and Plessisville and the neighbouring rural areas. It is 97.2 percent French-speaking. The average family income is $29 723, 14 percent less than the provincial average. The mining industry is becoming less and less important and is being replaced gradually by small contracting firms. Before the 1988 election, three municipalities and 4 919 voters were cut from the riding by redistribution. In 1988, 43 638 individuals were entitled to vote.

For the past 50 years, the riding has been held mainly by the Liberals. The Progressive Conservatives won this seat in 1958 and the Social Credit party held it on a few occasions in the 1960s. In 1984, Progressive Conservative Marcel Masse won the riding with a majority of 19 092 votes (71.3 percent of total votes), the largest margin by a Conservative candidate in the province. Following the campaign, Masse's election expenses were the object of an RCMP investigation that uncovered nothing illegal. However, the incident influenced the 1988 campaign.

Frontenac includes two distinct sub-regions: the asbestos region, located in the Appalachians, and the traditionally Liberal region of Plessisville in the St. Lawrence lowlands. Between the 1984 and 1988 elections, Masse's local organization was very active. To maintain his visibility in both regions, it organized meetings and factory visits and sent out some 238 000 letters over the four-year period.

The Liberal candidate in Frontenac was Réal Patry, an industrial commissioner and native of the riding who worked in Sherbrooke. The NDP candidate, Claude L'Heureux, was an NDP organizer living in Montreal. He was one of the last two candidates chosen in Quebec. Despite his promise to move to Frontenac, he made only a few brief appearances in the riding (Gruda 1988). The only other candidate, Jean Guernon of the Green Party of Canada, did almost no campaigning.

THE ELECTION CAMPAIGNS

The reporters and organizers interviewed generally felt that national election campaigns serve voters poorly because they become televised spectacles that overwhelm local campaigns. These spectacles are organized according to deadlines for news bulletins and major newspapers. National candidates no longer answer reporters' questions; they prepare 30-second spots for the television news. Despite the dominance of national campaigns, one organizer mentioned that local campaigns could be useful in reaching specific communities within a particular riding.

Party Platforms and National Issues

The organizers interviewed felt that, although national issues are viewed as the most important factors during election campaigns, voters in the two ridings were largely unfamiliar with the platforms of the federal parties.

In Frontenac, the Progressive Conservative and Liberal candidates centred their campaigns on the issue of free trade (Hébert 1988; Royer 1988b). In Outremont, in addition to free trade, abortion became a major issue (*La Semaine d'Outremont* 1988; Lavoie 1988). The Outremont candidates had clear-cut positions on the issue of abortion: the Liberal and NDP candidates favoured freedom of choice, while the Progressive Conservative candidate opposed it. The Conservatives even used a letter written by Liberal candidate Lucie Pépin in 1986, with a few additions of their own (see appendix B).

More generally, the 1988 election focused mainly on free trade and, to a lesser extent, on the Meech Lake Accord. Officially, the Meech Lake Accord did not separate the parties, all three national leaders having endorsed it. However, internal differences within the Liberal party over this issue may have had damaging effects.

By attacking the Free Trade Agreement and stating that he would scrap the agreement if elected, John Turner pushed the electoral debate onto slippery ground for Liberal candidates in Quebec. Free trade was the favourite topic of the Progressive Conservatives in Quebec, and the national Liberal leader gave them the opportunity to campaign on this issue at the expense of other issues, such as social problems, that could have helped the local Liberal candidates garner more votes. In Outremont, economic issues did not help the Liberal candidate.

Free trade thus put the Liberals in a difficult position in Quebec. If debate had focused on social policies, the Liberals and NDP would have had an advantage over the Progressive Conservatives. The Liberal candidate in Frontenac, Réal Patry, who made his living facilitating exports to the United States, denounced the defects of the Mulroney–

Reagan agreement. In Outremont, the Liberal candidate could not gain the support of the provincial MNA who preferred to remain neutral because of his stand on free trade. Although provincial Liberal MNAs were participating in the party's nomination meetings in some ridings, Liberal minister and provincial MNA Pierre Fortier stated that he intended to remain neutral and denied supporting the Conservative candidate (see appendix C) (Gruda 1988).[1] To Liberal organizers, this neutrality came as a hard blow to their campaign.

Local Issues

In Frontenac, the revitalization of the asbestos industry should have been a key issue, according to one reporter interviewed. This reporter, however, was the only one to mention this issue. The other reporters and organizers talked about the possibility of government grants if the riding re-elected the minister (Masse). Free trade was discussed only superficially; the issue of its impact on local small businesses was not raised.

In Frontenac, everyone agreed that the campaign was insipid. The majority of political organizers were working for Marcel Masse. The main question was whether he would win 65 percent or 75 percent of the vote.

In Outremont, there was no local issue as such; the issues were those that concerned the Montreal area generally. The Liberal and Conservative candidates both discussed securing the federally funded space agency for Montreal.

The Candidates

Do people vote for candidates or for parties? The candidates themselves feel that they play only a small role in voters' choices on election day. The Progressive Conservative candidate who eventually won in Outremont, for example, was a complete unknown at the start of the campaign.

According to one of the organizers working for this candidate, only a man could have won the election in Outremont in 1988. Organizers questioned whether female candidates are well received in the various cultural communities. However, one Conservative organizer believed that the Progressive Conservative candidate stood out from the NDP and Liberal candidates because of his distinguished career. It is difficult to believe that it was the candidate's personal characteristics that made the difference. He was able, however, to manipulate the abortion concerns of the riding's Hasidic community. It was largely by setting himself apart from the other candidates on this issue that he was able to win the riding.

Having been an MP did not seem to be enough to guarantee the re-election of Lucie Pépin in Outremont, even though she was well regarded (Reguin 1988). Pépin presented herself as a liberal-minded candidate. Her position on various issues was often similar to that of the NDP (Roy 1988; on the issue of Turkish immigrants see Rivière 1988; on childcare see *La Voce d'Italia* 1988). Thus the Conservative candidate was able to appeal to those voters who were further to the right. Moreover, with the transformation of the electoral map, Lucie Pépin inherited a riding with a large proportion of new voters who had little awareness of her work as their MP.

In Frontenac, those interviewed felt that nothing could have prevented Marcel Masse from being re-elected in 1988. Both reporters and organizers felt that the minister's promise to distribute benefits in the riding if he were re-elected tipped the scale in his favour.

Masse was able to show that a prominent candidate, even though parachuted in, could be successful if he had a good chance of being appointed to the Cabinet. It was the first time that the riding of Frontenac had been represented by a minister with such an important cabinet post, enabling him to direct subsidies and job creation to the riding. He was able, for example, to secure monies from the Laprade fund[2] for the riding of Frontenac, which was not originally an intended beneficiary of this fund. To mitigate the problem of frequent absences from the riding because of his ministerial duties, Masse records a series of television programs once a month. The series is broadcast on Sunday mornings on a local television station.

In short, in Outremont and Frontenac, the benefits of being the incumbent MP differed significantly. In terms of visibility and media attention, there are obvious advantages for a member of the party in power. Even a relatively well-known opposition member like Pépin did not have the visibility of a cabinet minister. Pépin faced the additional difficulty of achieving visibility in an urban riding, and one with boundary changes, and was thus at a distinct disadvantage in comparison to Masse and his position in Frontenac.

Organizers in both Frontenac and Outremont mentioned that it was possible for particularly strong local candidates to resist a national trend but that such cases were rare. They added that the winning candidates could also be swept away in the next election, regardless of their previous majority.

Finally, campaigns certainly do not have to be based on attacks on the other candidates. On the evening of the defeat in Outremont, Louise O'Neill stated, "If I had known that Ms. Pépin was so weak, I would not have run against her" (Desnoyers 1988). One organizer explained that, in the long term, personal attacks do nothing but discredit the political institutions. In both ridings, the Progressive Conservatives chose to ignore the other candidates. Both campaigns were very civilized on the whole, with the exception of the demagogic use of the issue of access to abortion in Outremont.

Candidates Debates

It is not in the best interests of candidates who are ahead in the polls to take part in debates that may cause them to lose votes. Organizers are wary of these debates as they have no control over them. The Progressive Conservative candidat in Outremont, who needed to raise his profile in the riding, nevertheless avoided debates. He took part in only one, which was not broadcast on television or radio.[3]

There were no candidates debates in the Frontenac campaign. The Union of Agricultural Producers (UAP) tried without success to organize a debate on the impact of free trade (which the UAP assumed would be negative) on the agricultural sector.

People watched the televised debates between the national party leaders. These debates had a direct impact on both voters and local party organizations. The latter tend to gain or lose motivation after these debates, depending on the leader's performance. For example, John Turner became an asset for the Liberals in the two ridings following the televised French-language debate, even though he had been seen as a negative factor earlier.

Local Organizations, National Parties and Leaders

The local party organizations in Outremont seem to have had very little contact with the national organizations, largely because of their different priorities and concerns.

Local organizers, both Liberal and Conservative, felt that they were left to themselves during the campaign. In Frontenac, it was also felt that national organizers knew nothing about the riding's problems and needs.[4] People in both ridings wondered whether their national organizations were really interested in the election of the local candidates.

No party leader visited Outremont or Frontenac.[5] For the Liberals, John Turner was viewed as a negative factor in their campaign. The Liberal organization in Outremont was also part of the revolt that sought to replace John Turner as leader. The mood changed after the leadership debates, when most thought that Turner had performed well.

Although a certain nostalgia for the Trudeau era created rifts within the Liberal party, other Liberals felt that Trudeau loomed like an ominous shadow over the campaign. One of the factors underlying the

Conservative win in both Outremont and Frontenac was the belief of many voters that the Liberals had held onto power too long. According to some of the organizers interviewed, the voters felt that the Liberal team had not yet been sufficiently revitalized.

Among the Progressive Conservatives, it was felt that the leader's performance contributed to the party's victory in 1988. For example, the Conservative candidate in Outremont used a photograph of himself with Brian Mulroney for several of his advertisements in the weekly newspapers. The Liberal candidate, Lucie Pépin, appears alone in her campaign photo.

Political parties spend huge sums of money to establish national organizations whose sole purpose is to win elections. Organizers in the ridings say, however, that the national organizations do little to help them once the election has been launched. Does this mean that local organizers like to present their work as the most important? What do national organizers say when questioned about the importance of their work during election campaigns?

According to local organizers, the national organizations target selected ridings in which they become involved more actively. Others see a division of responsibilities that leaves the two organizational levels barely linked at all. From their national organizations, local organizers receive material under a group purchase arrangement, which results in considerable savings. As a result of this arrangement, the unit price of large signs or flyers distributed door-to-door is greatly reduced. The Conservative candidate in Frontenac received the most help from the national party organization of all the candidates and was the most successful in taking advantage of this assistance.

In Quebec, the power of the unbeatable Liberal machine has been legendary. The situation seems to be different now. While Pierre Trudeau guided the destiny of the Liberal party, victory was almost a foregone conclusion. In Frontenac, everyone agreed that Trudeau's influence was the major factor in the repeated victories of the former federal Liberal MP.

The NDP remains largely non-existent in Quebec, except in ridings where more charismatic candidates achieve personal victories from time to time. According to their opponents, the Progressive Conservatives, who were virtually absent from the Quebec scene 10 years ago, had the best organization during the past two federal general elections. They were able to recruit members of the Parti québécois, provincial Liberals, members of the Union nationale, and former Créditistes (in Frontenac) as organizers.

According to one Liberal organizer, "During the by-election in

Laurier-Sainte-Marie, we had the best organization imaginable, yet we stood no chance of winning." One defeated candidate said that the local organization's work was only a small factor in the election results. Nevertheless, several organizers still believe that local organization is essential to reach ethnic communities, which are often less interested in national issues than in matters of integration and immigration.

Local party organizations are also important on election day in getting out the vote. Getting the right people to the polls calls for an effective local organization. It involves being able to keep track of how the vote is developing, which the Conservatives did successfully in Outremont and Frontenac, while the Liberals and NDP did not.

Volunteers and Nomination Meetings

Local party organizations sometimes rely on volunteers to make up for a lack of funds or paid workers. Although the NDP in Outremont had little money, it did have a strong team of grassroots supporters, particularly in the eastern part of the riding. The Progressive Conservatives, relative newcomers to Quebec, initially lacked the organizational base needed to conduct an effective campaign in the riding. For their part, the Liberals had the resources and tradition but suffered from poor motivation.

There are many reasons why people volunteer during election campaigns, including ideological conviction, the hope of tangible benefits in the future and also the pleasure of being involved in a collective social organization. For example, some party workers participate in campaigns at all levels, municipal, provincial and federal. Nomination meetings often serve to mobilize a core of volunteers for the campaign.

None of those interviewed could remember precise details about the evening the riding nomination meeting took place – as though the event was a legal formality with little inherent importance. Marcel Masse, for example, was nominated by acclamation in 1984 and 1988 (Royer 1988a). A newspaper article discussing the nomination of the Liberal candidate in Frontenac does not even mention anyone running against Réal Patry (*Courrier Frontenac* 1988). For the Liberals in Outremont the big event was not the nomination meeting, which was held long before the election campaign began, but Jean Chrétien's visit on 27 October (a meeting that was in effect the second launching of the campaign). Nevertheless, successful nomination meetings can bring together a core of 200 or 300 members needed to organize the campaign. However, such volunteers are becoming harder to mobilize.

Election organizations also rely on another type of volunteer. Some candidates can call on friends working in communications companies or companies that conduct surveys to provide their services free of charge at election time. It is possible that, with the first type of volunteer becoming increasingly scarce, the second type may soon become more important. This decrease in the number of grassroots volunteers may be attributable in part to feelings of weariness and cynicism toward politics in the electorate generally.

Financing and Election Expenses

According to those interviewed, national campaigns are becoming increasingly expensive. The cost of local campaigns has also risen with the introduction of more sophisticated electronic equipment. The equipment – computers, camcorders, faxes, etc. – is expensive to rent and often not very well used by local organizations.

Those interviewed agreed that the *Canada Elections Act* complicates the work of party constituency organizations. Countless examples were raised:

- If a party distributes a flyer two days before the campaign, as the Liberals did in Outremont, the cost is not reported as an election expense, even though the flyer benefits the campaign.
- In urban areas, it is very difficult to find space for a campaign office that is both suitably located[6] and relatively inexpensive. This is a major expense and an excellent example of the limitations of the law. Because money spent before the election is called is not counted under the spending limit, it is preferable to rent campaign facilities for $1 000 a month for six months than it is to pay $2 000 per month for the two months of the campaign. Although the total cost is greater, only $2 000 must be declared as election expenses ($1 000 for each month of the campaign).
- In a large riding such as Frontenac, travel expenses can be considerable. If a person "volunteers" to drive a car for the campaign period, is this an election expense? Similarly, a communications consulting firm that normally charges $200 an hour for its services might charge $25 an hour during the election campaign. Which rate should be used for determining election expenses?
- According to the interpretation of some of the organizers interviewed, expenditures of less than $20 do not have to be recorded as election expenses. For example, if an individual delivering flyers door-to-door is paid $20 when starting out in the morning and another $20 after lunch, this cost does not have to be reported as an election expense.

All the candidates felt that the limits on election expenses were too low and should be raised. However, limits on expenses are necessary, they emphasized. One organizer pointed out that doubling expenditure ceilings would not necessarily ensure that campaigns were better managed. It is possible, for example, that more people would ask to be paid instead of volunteering, and a situation similar to the current one would result even though more money was being spent.

On the other hand, losing an election can be very costly for the defeated candidate. Some defeated candidates interviewed mentioned that they had had to spend several thousand dollars of their savings. All candidates interviewed, winners and losers, felt that the minimum number of votes needed for candidates to be eligible to recover their deposits should be more flexible.

To ensure fairness, should election expenses be paid out of public funds more directly? Should businesses be involved in party financing? Perhaps election campaigns should be financed differently if expenses cannot be reported more effectively.

Those interviewed agreed that the current *Canada Elections Act* is full of loopholes and that the calculation of eligible expenses is inadequate. In addition, concerns were expressed, even by winning organizations, about the impact on local campaigns of independent spending by various groups.

The Use of Opinion Polls during Election Campaigns
Although there were few comments on this issue and polls are seldom used in local campaigns, organizers felt that national polls do have a significant effect on the motivation of local organizers, depending on whether the poll is positive or negative. Excessive numbers of polls, however, as there were in the 1988 election, may diminish their impact.

The organizers interviewed said that most voters are interested in poll results. Many people like to vote for a winner, so that a poll published a few days before the vote tends to help the party thought to be in the lead. For this reason several of the organizers thought the publication of polls should be banned in the last week of the campaign. National party organizations could still make use of polling but could not make the results public – a solution that is not considered realistic in the present context. The information would tend to leak out in any case.

Campaign Coverage by the Media

Media Presence
Coverage of constituency-level election campaigns occurs primarily through local newspapers. In Frontenac and Outremont, these papers resemble advertising circulars in which small teams of reporters publish

a limited number of articles. These teams are too small to cover more than one event at a time. As well, some political activities may not be covered owing to a shortage of space. The limited size of the teams also explains why news releases issued by the political parties are often published in full, with no analysis.

In both ridings, campaign coverage dealt primarily with the Progressive Conservatives and Liberals. As one reporter covering the election in Frontenac said, "Because of time constraints, I have to apply positive discrimination by choosing to cover those individuals who stand a chance of winning." If the number of parties that stand a real chance of electing their candidates increases in the future, it is difficult to see how local papers will be able to cover campaigns adequately, particularly with limited budgets.

During the 1988 election campaign, Outremont was covered by one weekly paper, *La Semaine d'Outremont*, which closed down during the campaign, and a monthly paper, *Le Journal d'Outremont*. In *Le Journal d'Outremont*, the federal and provincial members write a column in each issue. In fact, it was in this column that the Liberal MNA declared his neutrality (see appendix C). The neighbourhoods of Côte-des-Neiges and Saint-Louis, which are part of the riding, also have weekly papers. One other weekly, the *Super-Hebdo*, which is distributed free, also covered the Outremont campaign.

Outremont is also covered by the principal Montreal media, including television (CTV, CBC, Radio-Canada, Télé-Métropole, Quatre-Saisons and Radio-Québec), newspapers (*La Presse, Le Devoir, Le Journal de Montréal*, the *Gazette*) and numerous radio stations. Local cable television channels, community radio stations and student papers also make campaign information available.

Frontenac is covered by two weekly papers, the *Courrier Frontenac*,[7] and the Plessisville paper, *La Feuille d'érable*. The riding also has a community television channel, a cable channel and radio stations in the Réseau des Appalaches. Sherbrooke's *La Tribune* and Quebec City's *Le Soleil* have resident reporters in the region. The reporters interviewed told us that they themselves originate the news they report; none used news from the wire services.

Campaign Coverage

On the local scene, organizers rely more heavily on direct distribution of material to voters than they do on media coverage. Political organizers interviewed did not seem to attach much importance to media relations, except for the smaller parties that lack organization and funds. These parties must make the most of media coverage to become known.

According to the local organizers interviewed, material delivered right to voters' mailboxes plays an important role in an effective campaign. In the words of one organizer, "You have to bypass the media." It is not a matter of burying voters under a heap of flyers, but of ensuring that they have seen a picture of the candidate and remember his or her name on election day. This requires one or two flyers[8] during the campaign and one within 48 hours of election day, as well as large signs placed strategically throughout the riding.

In each organization, one or two people at the most were responsible for such duties as writing news releases. In both ridings, the fact that reporters had no time to do in-depth analyses was criticized. The reporters explained that this was partly the result of budgetary constraints but also added that there was not enough newsworthy material to cover in the local campaigns.

In Frontenac, the organizations and reporters agreed to hold a weekly news conference at which important announcements would be made. These weekly news conferences were enough for the local papers and, presumably, for the organizations, which did not really have time to prepare additional material.

The organizers view the print media as a publicity vehicle that is too expensive and should be used sparingly since its benefits during elections remain uncertain. Some organizers told us that they placed advertisements in weekly newspapers solely to maintain good relations with their management. Yet no one complained about unfair treatment from local papers. Some candidates believed that coverage was generally mediocre but not biased in favour of one party or another.

Television coverage of local campaigns occurs only incidentally. For example, the Liberal candidate in Outremont was given several opportunities for television appearances because she was the party's spokesperson on several national issues. Similarly, Marcel Masse's participation in a television debate on Radio-Canada soon after the election was called, his most important media appearance of the campaign, stemmed from his ministerial role. In addition, from time to time, local candidates may also appear on camera, when a national figure visits the region.

Television is too costly for local publicity, and radio listeners are too few in number to make radio an effective advertising medium for election campaigns in most areas. In Frontenac, one organizer told us that he aired messages on the local radio station immediately preceding the obituaries, the program with the highest number of listeners.

In Outremont, local organizations preferred to hold meetings of small groups of voters with their candidate. These meetings, during which voters were invited to make financial contributions to the campaign, made it possible to reach a part of the electorate that would otherwise be difficult to target. Although it is not possible to reach large numbers of voters with this communications approach, it does enable the organizations to meet with specific groups they have chosen to target.

If local organizers had the time and resources to develop more discussion material and to provide input to the media, the media might take more interest in local campaigns.

Coverage of election campaigns could be improved through greater attention to regional news. Furthermore, election campaigns should be covered by teams, because few individual reporters can do both coverage and analysis. Columnists find it easier to do their job if someone else has done the coverage.

Media reporters and campaign organizers hold each other responsible for the poor quality of local campaign coverage. On one hand, organizers complain that media coverage is superficial. On the other hand, reporters complain that there is far too little to cover in local election campaigns.

Coverage will not likely improve in the long term since the media – local as well as national – are facing tighter budgets. The media are increasingly covering campaigning that takes place between nine and five on weekdays, overtime costs having become prohibitive. It seems unrealistic to think that in the foreseeable future, the media will have greater resources to cover election campaigns. The shortage of media resources to cover local campaigns means coverage is limited to the superficial. Media treatment has shifted from systematic coverage of all ridings to more selective coverage, to coverage of just a few important ridings.

Some journalists believe that their coverage is not critical enough of politicians; some even feel that they are being used as vehicles for candidates' publicity. One reporter explained that campaigns are organized as a spectacle that leaves little room for in-depth debate of issues. As a result, people vote without knowing the impact that major national issues such as free trade and the Meech Lake Accord will have on their lives.

Limited resources also mean that reporters can cover only the larger parties. In this sense, they help make the principal parties better known, leaving the smaller parties on the sidelines. In Frontenac, only the community channel, whose mission involves alternative television, covered the campaign of the Green Party of Canada.[9]

One reporter interviewed in Montreal explained that, during election campaigns, parties are very accommodating to reporters, sometimes even on the evening they are defeated. The reporters also felt that their relations with political parties were very professional and that the parties respect the autonomy of the media.

CONCLUSION

What are the geographical factors that influence the vote? Are there different reasons for the way the people of Quebec voted in Frontenac and in Outremont? Did national or local issues make the difference? Did local candidates win on their own, or were people voting through them for their party leaders? Have local issues become less important over the years? Such questions illustrate the complexity of the reasons for the Progressive Conservatives' re-election in 1988 (see Clarke et al. 1991).

There is disagreement about whether the 1988 election was a typical case because free trade was such a dominant issue.[10] In Outremont, the emotionally charged issue of abortion took on unexpected importance. In Frontenac, it is possible that the impact of other factors was minimal, since nothing could have prevented the re-election of Marcel Masse. He increased his percentage of the vote from 71.3 percent to 73.6 percent – the third highest result for the Progressive Conservatives in all of Canada during that election.

Provincial Liberal politicians and strategists were generally in favour of free trade with the United States and ratification of the Meech Lake Accord – two issues that divided the federal Liberals between those who looked back to the Trudeau era and those who stood behind John Turner. In Outremont, Lucie Pépin was in favour of the Accord, as was Réal Patry in Frontenac. The neutrality of the provincial Liberals and tensions within the federal Liberals damaged the party's image and ultimately contributed to its defeat.

We chose to study two constituencies representing different trends in Quebec today. Outremont is representative of the demographic changes that are gradually transforming the city of Montreal. Frontenac represents the aging population of rural Quebec. In both constituencies voters did not vote on the basis of local issues or candidates; they voted instead for the Free Trade Agreement, little understood as it was. Organizers agreed that people voted on issues they knew little about, in part because of the shortage of high-quality information on such issues. Local organizations had neither the time nor the resources to explain the local impact of national issues to voters. At the same time, journalists said there was a shortage of interesting local material to cover. Local campaigns must escape this vicious circle if they are to regain the interest and importance that both journalists and organizers deem necessary to constructive democratic debate.

In both ridings, the people elected the Progressive Conservatives because the party had been able to win the Quebec nationalist vote through its promise regarding the Meech Lake Accord. This nationalist vote had escaped them since the hanging of Louis Riel and may slip away from them again at the next general election. The distinction between national, regional and local issues is not always clear. For example, the battle over abortion in Outremont was clearly local, but similar confrontations took place elsewhere in Canada.

The Outremont seat won by the Progressive Conservative candidate in 1988 was no longer the one that had been a Liberal stronghold since its creation. Its demographic composition had changed. Lucie Pépin did not lose to a local hero; she lost in a riding that was not really any different from the rest of Montreal, to an unknown who took advantage of both the Conservative wave that swept the Liberals out and his opponent's position on abortion.

Marcel Masse won a resounding victory in Frontenac because he was able to show the benefits he could bring to the riding. The Progressive Conservatives won the election in these two ridings by promising tangible benefits to the voters, by avoiding detailed debate on free trade, and by forging a majority made up of the most conservative elements of the electorate, the nationalist vote, and that of the business community. The Conservatives were well enough organized to spread their message without recourse to the media and to secure the funds they needed to finance their campaign operations.

In Frontenac, the Liberal organization could not measure up to that of the Conservatives. In Outremont, the Liberals were well organized, but this was not enough. The Conservatives were able to attract certain provincial Liberal, PQ and Union nationale organizers to make up for their recent appearance on the Quebec political scene. This coalition is fragile, however, and may not remain intact for any length of time. In the next election, the Bloc québécois, even with no platform, no organization and no money, could win 40 to 50 seats in Quebec if the current situation prevails, according to the individuals we interviewed.

RECOMMENDATIONS

1. Reduce the length of election campaigns to promote fairness among candidates and parties.
2. Establish a permanent system for enumerating voters to permit shorter election campaigns.

3. Finance election campaigns primarily from public funds to promote fairness among candidates and make the expenses reimbursement system more flexible.
4. Improve the system for accounting for election spending.
5. Improve the quality of information available during a campaign by publicly funding the work of analysts in each region who would develop complete and detailed information on policy issues. Such workers would help to compensate for the shrinking number of volunteers that constituency organizations can count on.

APPENDIX A

Table 5.A1
Election results – Frontenac

	Votes received 1988	Percentage of votes received*		
		1988	1984	Variance
Conservative party		73.6	71.3	2.3
Marcel Masse	25 872			
Liberal party		19.9	22.8	-2.9
Réal Patry	6 978			
NDP		5.1	2.8	2.3
Claude L'Heureux	1 785			
Other		1.5	3.0	-1.5
Jean Guernon	511			

Margin of victory:	53.8%
Votes:	35 464
Participation:	80%
Urban polling stations:	84
Rural polling stations:	84

Election expenses	Number of contributions	Total amount ($)	Expenses ($)	% of limit
Conservative party	314	42 877	38 818	92.8
Liberal party	66	24 975	23 100	56.1
NDP	1	45	0	0.0
Other	0	0	0	0.0

*Percentage totals do not equal 100 due to rounding.

Table 5.A2
Election results – Outremont

	Votes received 1988	Percentage of votes received		
		1988	1984	Variance
Conservative party Jean-Pierre Hogue	17 597	38.4	29.0	9.4
Liberal party Lucie Pépin	15 895	34.7	41.3	-6.6
NDP Louise O'Neill	9 379	20.5	18.3	2.2
Other	2 919	6.4	11.4	-5.0

Margin of victory:	3.7%
Votes:	46 381
Participation:	76%
Urban polling stations:	183
Rural polling stations:	0

Election expenses	Number of contributions	Total amount ($)	Expenses ($)	% of limit
Conservative party	120	32 225	38 046	86.6
Liberal party	84	66 706	40 083	91.2
NDP	263	23 317	27 516	62.6
Other	9	558	449	—

APPENDIX B
TRANSLATION OF LETTER CIRCULATED BY THE PROGRESSIVE
CONSERVATIVES IN OUTREMONT AT THE TIME OF THE
1988 ELECTION CAMPAIGN

COALITION Pour la Vie QUÉBEC
For Life

C.P. 104   BEACONSFIELD, Qué., H9W 5I6

INFORMATION AUX ELECTEURS D'OUTREMONT

VOICI COMMENT VOTRE DEPUTEE TRAVAILLAIT POUR VOUS EN 1986

CI-DESSOUS, EXTRAITS D'UNE DE SES LETTRES.

Liberté de choix
Freedom of Choice

Association canadienne pour le droit à l'avortement (ACDA)
Canadian Abortion Rights Action League (CARAL)

July 1986

Dear Friends,

I would like to introduce you to the Canadian Abortion Rights Action League (CARAL), an organization in favour of freedom of choice for Canadian woman with respect to family planning.

Please join me in supporting CARAL in its fight to obtain freedom of choice for all Canadian women.

Neither I nor CARAL believe that people will vote for a particular candidate on the basis of his or her stand on a single issue; however, I know that freedom of choice with respect to the voluntary termination of a pregnancy is certainly one of the issues that people will be discussing with their MPs. CARAL survives on contributions from people who are in favour of this option. Please join me in supporting CARAL today. Your contribution of $25, $35, $50 or $100 or more will help us win the battle. Thank you.

Sincerely yours,

Lucie Pépin
Honourary Director

ELECTION-VIE '88

PS: If you share my views and are in favour of freedom of choice, join me and send your contribution to CARAL today. Our adversaries have many resources, but together we can win.

POUR QUI VOTEREZ-VOUS?
ON NE VOTE NI BLEU NI ROUGE NI CAILLE   **VOTONS JEAN PIERRE HOGUE**
ON VOTE POUR LA VIE

APPENDIX C
POSITION OF THE PROVINCIAL LIBERAL MNA
FOR OUTREMONT IN 1988

A word from your MNA, Pierre Fortier   *Journal d'Outremont*
September 1988

Title: **The upcoming federal election campaign
         and the Free Trade Agreement**

Clearly, one of the topics that will be at the centre of the upcoming election campaign will be the Free Trade Agreement between Canada and the United States. Given the importance of this issue for the economic health of Quebec, I feel compelled to clearly state the reasons why I support this agreement.

Of course, as the Member for Outremont since November 1980, I have always observed an objective neutrality during municipal and federal elections. In fact, working at the provincial level within a political entity that is completely independent of any other authority, whether federal or municipal, I have always respected the point of view of my electorate.

However, within our federal system, the two levels of government must cooperate to promote policies that foster the economic development of Quebec, particularly when it is a policy as fundamental as that supported by the Free Trade Agreement.

What you should know about the expected impact of free trade is that all the serious macro-economic models (Economic Council of Canada, Conference Board, federal Department of Finance, Informetrica and so on) predict positive effects as far as revenues for Quebec residents are concerned. Moreover, public figures in Quebec with various political affiliations are joining together to support the Free Trade Agreement. The names of these leaders include Robert Bourassa and Jacques Parizeau.

I would like to have had enough time and space to comment on a document recently published by the Liberal Party of Canada on this topic. Suffice it to say that I in no way support the view expressed by the Official Opposition in the House of Commons on this issue. Certainly, everyone agrees on the need for Canada (and Quebec) to diversify its markets. This was the concern that in 1971 led then federal Liberal minister Mitchell Sharp to propose the "third option." In 1971 the U.S. market represented 86.5 percent of our exports of finished goods; 15 years later, in 1986, this figure was 90.5 percent.

Let's be realistic. For better or for worse, the U.S. is our immediate neighbour and the Free Trade Agreement will allow us to promote and harmonize our trade relations with this important client.

PIERRE FORTIER

[Translated for publication]

NOTES

This study was completed in March 1991.

The author would like to thank Johanne Poulin for her assistance in preparing this study.

In this study, quoted material that originated in French has been translated into English.

1. In Ontario, Premier David Peterson came back from a trip abroad to campaign with John Turner (Gauthier 1988; Gagnon 1988).

2. A fund set up when the federal government decided not to complete the Laprade heavy water plant at Bécancour (Sévigny 1988a).

3. This was an information session on apartheid that took place on 6 November 1988. It was the only time that the three major candidates were together at the same debate (*Journal d'Outremont* 1988).

4. One national organizer replied that certain local organizers take themselves too seriously!

5. One of the reporters interviewed thought that Brian Mulroney had passed through Frontenac in 1984 or 1988. In any case, his visit had been covered by a reporter assigned to the neighbouring region.

6. Suitably located facilities are easily accessible by public transportation to facilitate access by volunteers.

7. According to a poll published in the *Courrier Frontenac*, it has a readership of 35 000 (see Baker 1988).

8. Organizers explained that to be effective flyers had to contain as many photographs as possible, with prominent party figures supporting the candidates, large type and as little text as possible.

9. The community channel aims to be the voice of those who do not normally have a chance to be heard. The expression used was: "The Green Party was supported by the community television channel." The Green Party candidate was also interviewed with the other candidates in the local weekly.

10. It may be that the 1988 election was no different from any other (see Brodie 1989).

REFERENCES

Baker, Bruno. 1988. "35 000 lecteurs assidus au Courrier Frontenac." *Courrier Frontenac* (12 September).

Brodie, Janine. 1989. "The Free Trade Election." *Studies in Political Economy* 28 (Spring): 175–82.

Canada. *Canada Elections Act*, R.S.C. 1985, c. E-2.

Clarke, Harold D., Jane Jenson, Lawrence LeDuc and Jon H. Pammett. 1991. *Absent Mandate: Interpreting Change in Canadian Elections.* 2d ed. Toronto: Gage.

Courrier Frontenac. 1988. "Réal Patry mise sur ses racines." (31 May).

Desnoyers, André. 1988. "Jean-Pierre Hogue s'installe comme député progressiste-conservateur d'Outremont." *Journal d'Outremont* (December).

Gagnon, Lysiane. 1988. "Sur la vague." *La Presse* (22 October).

Gauthier, Gille. 1988. "Peterson finira la campagne avec Turner." *La Presse* (12 November).

Gruda, Agnès. 1988. "Électogrammes." *La Presse* (22 October).

Hébert, Pierre. 1988. "Libre-échange au centre du débat." *Courrier Frontenac* (10 October).

Journal d'Outremont. 1988. "Trois des huit candidats visent la victoire." (15 November).

Lavoie, Gilbert. 1988. "Pas facile de faire campagne chez les soeurs Marie-Réparatrice." *La Presse* (18 October).

Reguin, Olivier. 1988. "Des députés tous ministrables." *Liaison Saint-Louis* (30 October).

Rivière, Daniel. 1988. "Outremont devenu société des nations." *Journal d'Outremont* (July).

Roy, Tristan. 1988. "L'ABC des élections dans le quartier." *Liaison Saint-Louis* (16 October).

Royer, Mario. 1988a. "Marcel Masse candidat dans Frontenac." *Courrier Frontenac* (6 June).

———. 1988b. "Marcel Masse vante les mérites du libre-échange." *Courrier Frontenac* (24 October).

La Semaine d'Outremont. 1988. "Avortement: Louise O'Neill défend la position du NPD." (2 August).

Sévigny, Pierre. 1988a. "Le ministre Masse affirme: 'La région de Plessisville a été bien servie en argent.'" *La Tribune* (4 November).

———. 1988b. "Majorité dans tous les bureaux de scrutin." *La Tribune* (23 November).

La Voce d'Italia. 1988. (13 August).

6

RIDING THE WAVES
Parties, the Media and the 1988 Federal Election in Nova Scotia

Leonard Preyra

THE 1988 FEDERAL GENERAL ELECTION, which resulted in Brian Mulroney's Conservative party capturing 169 of 295 seats in the House of Commons, was perhaps the most tumultuous Canadian election ever. In a *Maclean's*/Decima poll taken immediately after the 21 November election, 3 out of 5 respondents said they made up their minds during the campaign, and 27 percent said they changed their minds at least once during the campaign. Half those surveyed maintained that media coverage helped them make their decision (*Maclean's*/Decima 1988, 19). According to the 1988 Canadian National Election Study, 27 percent of voters cited their local candidate as the most important factor in their voting decision.[1] Among the other major factors that governed how people voted, 53 percent of those polled claimed to have voted for "the party as a whole," and 20 percent based their assessments on national party leaders (Frizzell et al. 1989, 118). A vast majority of those surveyed for the Study said that the policy stands of leaders and local candidates – especially on the Free Trade Agreement – were most influential in shaping their voting behaviour (ibid., 123).

While a great deal of work has been done on the national aspects of the 1988 election – national leaders, national issues and national media coverage – very little has been written about local candidates, local issues and the local media. This lacuna is surprising given the fact that so many voters claim to vote primarily on the basis of local candidate attributes. Besides, in Canada each voter has one ballot and can vote for only a local candidate.

The information flow to voters from candidates and the media is deeply affected by the communication strategies in use during election campaigns. These include the traditional "three waves" of campaign literature, as well as canvassing, mailings, news coverage and commentary (Fletcher 1990, 4–5). In addition, new technologies such as fax machines, cellular phones and computers have profoundly altered the nature of campaign communication for parties and the media, affecting how stories are researched, written, edited and filed (Abramson et al. 1988; Desbarats 1990).

Campaign communication is also characterized by different levels of mediation. Messages can be unmediated, such as in free-time broadcasts and spots; or partially mediated, as in broadcast interviews and leaders debates; or they can be heavily mediated, as in newspapers and magazines and television news (Fletcher 1990, 5).

To help conceptualize the context in which local campaigns unfold, Sayers (1991) has developed the notion of "issue space." Issue space represents the local information environment in which voters make their voting decisions. Local issue space is defined by the "interpenetration" of local, provincial and national politics as well as political and media organizations. According to Sayers, the definition of issues and the importance ascribed to them are likely to vary vertically within media and the parties – that is, across the hierarchy of parties and the media from local to national.

This study examines the communication strategies employed by political parties and the media in the Nova Scotia ridings of Annapolis Valley–Hants and Halifax during the 1988 federal election. Its objective is to determine the extent to which voters were able to make informed choices in selecting their local candidate based on the flow of information that was available to them in their constituencies. In terms of media coverage and campaign strategies, was the local contest significantly different from the national? Were different issues debated at the riding level? What was the balance between national, regional, and riding issues in the campaign literature, advertisements, public discourse and media coverage during the campaign? Were national issues made salient to local voters by being examined from regional and local points of view?

Through a content analysis of newspaper coverage of the campaign and from interviews conducted with candidates, their campaign managers and key figures in the local media, an analysis is presented of how the local candidates attempted to "reach" voters and how the media covered the campaign.

RIDING PROFILE

As far as Nova Scotia and Atlantic Canada are concerned, Halifax is a bell-wether riding. Except for the 1980 campaign, in every election since the Second World War, the party that captured Halifax also won a majority of Nova Scotia (see table 6.1) and Atlantic Canada seats in the new Parliament. Except for the Stanfield years and the 1988 election, the party that took Halifax also formed the government. These aggregate results not only tell us something about the riding, but they also serve as a cautionary reminder that, at least in Nova Scotia, local campaigns followed national or provincial trends long before new communications technologies and electioneering tactics came into existence.

Nevertheless, the Halifax data also offer convincing evidence that even seemingly overwhelming national tides can be resisted by certain

Table 6.1
Federal election results in Halifax and Annapolis Valley–Hants, 1945–88
(percentage of popular vote)

Year	Former Gov't	Won/Nova Scotia	Halifax			Annapolis Valley–Hants		
			Lib.	PC	NDP	Lib.	PC	NDP
1945	Lib.	Lib.	47.6	34.5	16.9	55.7	38.1	4.8
1949	Lib.	Lib.	57.1	32.5	10.4	50.0	50.0	0.0
1953	Lib.	Lib.	55.3	40.8	3.9	48.4	51.6	0.0
1957	PC	PC	47.2	50.6	2.2	42.0	58.0	0.0
1958	PC	PC	37.6	59.9	2.6	41.8	58.2	0.0
1962	PC	PC	45.4	46.9	6.7	43.6	52.6	2.4
1963	Lib.	Lib.	50.0	46.0	4.0	48.5	49.8	1.7
1965	Lib.	PC	42.6	47.4	9.5	43.7	53.2	3.1
1968	Lib.	PC	35.6	60.3	4.1	40.1	56.6	3.3
1972	Lib.	PC	31.4	56.2	12.3	35.7	58.5	5.0
1974	Lib.	PC	40.7	49.3	9.3	43.0	52.5	3.7
1979	PC	PC	40.4	40.5	18.5	29.9	50.1	20.0
1980	Lib.	PC	41.6	38.6	19.7	31.3	42.0	25.3
1984	PC	PC	34.4	44.8	20.4	28.5	53.8	16.0
1988	PC	Lib.	43.0	38.0	17.7	40.1	44.2	12.5

Source: Compiled from Feigert (1989).

types of "local" candidates. Liberal support in Halifax actually fell by over 10 percent during the wave of "Trudeaumania" which supposedly swept the country. "Stanfieldmania" best describes the Nova Scotia drift during those years when Robert Stanfield held Halifax and the leadership of the Conservative party. Halifax is also a swing riding. The last four federal elections have seen an alternation in power between the Liberals and the Progressive Conservatives, with margins of victory averaging about 4.6 percent of the popular vote. Annapolis Valley–Hants, on the other hand, has been a Progressive Conservative and Nowlan family fiefdom for over four decades. George Nowlan won the riding for the Tories in 1948, and his son Pat inherited it upon his father's death in 1965.

Electoral results are not all that distinguish the two ridings. Annapolis Valley–Hants, covering 5 433 square kilometres, with a population density of 16.5 people per square kilometre, is primarily a rural and agricultural riding. It is best known for its orchards, fertile farmlands and the highest tides in the world, recorded in the neighbouring Bay of Fundy. Halifax, on the other hand, is a typical urban riding. It covers a mere 250 square kilometres but boasts a population density of 364.5 per square kilometre (Eagles et al. 1991). Its populace is cosmopolitan and its economy relatively diversified. It is also the regional heartland of Atlantic Canada.

In addition to urban–rural differences and contrasts in the extent of competitiveness in the two ridings, there were also significant differences between the contending candidates. Stewart McInnes entered the Halifax contest as a high-profile government and "political" cabinet minister for the region. McInnes faced a powerful challenge from Mary Clancy, a well-connected and colourful left-leaning Liberal lawyer and media personality. Ray Larkin, the NDP candidate, a bright and articulate lawyer and passionate defender of regional concerns, represented one of the best hopes for his party in Atlantic Canada. With this cast of characters, a three-way race, and the possibility that a senior government minister might go down to defeat, the Halifax riding was guaranteed both national and local media and party attention. Pat Nowlan, the Tory candidate in Annapolis Valley–Hants, undefeated in seven consecutive elections, entered his eighth campaign as a party rebel who several times publicly threatened to leave his party over the Meech Lake Accord, official bilingualism and the GST. (In fact, shortly after the 1988 election, he was disowned by his riding association for leaving the Tory caucus and declaring himself an Independent Conservative.) Nowlan is a charismatic and well-organized campaigner who knows his riding intimately. His Liberal opponent, John Murphy, a high-profile community service activist went into the campaign with the knowledge that his predecessor fell short by a 25 percent margin in the previous election; his party had not won the riding since 1945. Keith Collins, an economist and Rhodes scholar with deep roots in the community, carried the NDP banner facing certain defeat. Apart from Nowlan's reputation as a maverick, the Annapolis Valley–Hants contest promised to generate little excitement. The Conservative party felt it was a safe seat, and the media saw no real contest shaping up (interviews with Bill Spur and Al Kingsbury).

One would expect from this brief comparison of Halifax and Annapolis Valley–Hants that their dissimilarity would be reflected in campaign themes and media strategies pursued at the riding level. This was not the case. Despite obvious differences between the ridings, electoral communication strategies and media coverage were not only strikingly similar but also revolved largely around national themes and national leaders. Furthermore, in neither riding were national themes and issues made salient to local voters by being translated into the regional or local "vernacular": the discourse remained national in focus and content. How do we explain this resemblance?

To begin, it should be recognized that general elections in Canada are national elections and are primarily devices for re-electing or ejecting federal governments. Therefore, it should not surprise us to find that campaigns revolve around a discussion of national leaders and the national issues. The process begins with a bias in favour of nation-focused perspectives.

The predominance of a national perspective in election coverage has emerged through various studies. Content analysis of recent election coverage found that coverage has a decidedly national focus, and that stories often emphasize the leader's behaviour (Clarke et al. 1991, 88). Studies by Fletcher (1987, 1990) suggest that the media's preoccupation with national leaders, parties and issues often neglects the local candidate. Furthermore, the national campaigns of the parties are oriented primarily to the national media and must rely on a "a trickle-down effect" to reach the regions. Local coverage is often left to smaller radio stations and community weeklies. The quality of election coverage by local media, however, is generally low, with very poor analysis or explanation of issues (Bell et al. 1991).

In addition, national economic trends in the gross national product, trade balances, the deficit, and inflation, interest and unemployment rates have local effects and inevitably influence local campaign appeals and electoral outcomes. Certainly, more work needs to be done on possible relationships between the state of the national economy and the campaign appeals and electoral prospects of parties, leaders and local candidates.

Apart from these "macro" considerations, however, this study suggests that the conduct, style and content of electoral communication at the constituency level was primarily shaped by three sets of relationships: the intra-party integration of national and local campaigns; the core–periphery news-gathering affiliations of the national and local media; and riding-specific factors.

This study found that no single factor (i.e., television or the Free Trade Agreement) fully accounts for the national focus of local party campaigns and media coverage. It proposes that forces not unique to the 1988 election made it difficult for local candidates and reporters to fashion or act on independent campaign communication strategies.

THE INTRA-PARTY DIMENSION

Much has been made in the established literature of the sovereignty of riding associations, their right to choose their standard bearers, and the means by which they will conduct local electoral campaigns (see Carty and Erickson 1991). While this study found no evidence of direct national party intervention in the selection of local candidates, or even binding directions from national to local party organizations regarding the conduct of the campaign, it did find that, in general, the vertical integration of national campaign organizations greatly influenced the conduct, style and content of electoral communications in Halifax and Annapolis Valley–Hants.

How did the national party shape local campaign strategy? The argument below is supported by reference to pre-election spending, letters of endorsement, provincial campaign coordinators, regional cooperation, party polling, national campaign themes, platform declarations, riding services packages, national and regional media advertising, debate strategies, leader tours and national party media contacts. Each of these influenced the campaign strategies of local candidates and affected the way in which the local media covered the election.

Pre-election Spending

The 1988 election campaign began long before the writs were issued. Some may even argue that the 1988 campaign started the day the Mulroney government was sworn in in 1984. More certainly, however, the Conservatives commenced organizing for the election in 1986 with the establishment of a campaign coordination team under the direction of Norman Atkins (Lee 1989, 247–48). By May 1988, the national campaign organization was in place and likely campaign themes and tactics were discussed. At that point, the Conservatives began announcing new government projects and initiatives – a sure sign that an election was pending. According to *Maclean's*, between 20 May and late September, the Tories announced more than 70 federal projects worth approximately $8 billion (1988, 14). Included in this pre-election package of promises was $3.2 billion for Hibernia and additional funds for the Atlantic Canada Opportunities Agency. Prior to this period, the government, among other things, had announced a $40 billion defence procurement plan which included $8 billion for nuclear submarines and $9.6 billion for new frigate construction. The health of the Canadian navy is of particular concern to Haligonians. The navy's main base in Halifax employs 13 000 personnel, has a yearly payroll of $484 million, and spends a further $121 million on local services (Caplan et al. 1989, 43).

This distribution of federal government largesse in the pre-election phase figured prominently in the campaign appeals of Tory candidates throughout Nova Scotia, but particularly in that of Stewart McInnes, the Conservative candidate in Halifax and minister of public works who was widely seen as the minister responsible for ensuring that his riding and Nova Scotia got its share of government spending. (The national Liberal party outlined its 40-point platform before the election, and the federal NDP also made pre-election pledges; however, not being in government, they had neither the resources nor the organization to make as much political hay of projects targeted at Atlantic Canada.) In short, the pre-election announcement of new government ventures and promises attracted not only favourable media attention, it also permitted the national parties (especially the party in government) to "position" themselves (and by extension their local candidates) for the coming campaign. In particular, it enabled the national parties to tailor their promises to suit targeted ridings and regions and provided local candidates with the pattern for campaign communiqués (Caplan et al. 1989, 23–52).

Letters of Endorsement
Just as the spending of money in the riding or region signified that the local or regional campaign had the attention of the national party, so too did letters of endorsement signed by party leaders indicate that the local candidate had the blessing of the national party. Ordinarily, approval is automatic; however, when the local candidate is a renegade like Pat Nowlan, endorsement was by no means a foregone conclusion. The requirement of endorsement imposes a discipline on local

candidates and ensures that the policy postures of local campaigns will be in harmony with the broader national goals articulated by party leaders (interview with Clara Jefferson). Other aspects of electoral legislation and party practices in Canada ensure that independent or nonconformist local candidates like Pat Nowlan often pay a high price for straying too far from the party line.

Provincial Campaign Organizations

Not to be underestimated in the pre-election shaping of local campaign communication strategies are the provincial campaign organizers who were responsible for "carrying out the national campaign as it affected their particular area and to oversee the proper functioning of the local constituency campaigns" (Courtney 1981, quoted in Frizzell et al. 1989, 18). Early in the campaign, the Nova Scotia campaign committees (which generally mirrored national committees) served as liaisons with their national counterparts and helped in the coordination of local campaigns. Halifax, as a marginal riding, got a great deal of attention, and coordinators sought to ensure that their candidates had the people and resources to fight effective campaigns. (In the case of the Halifax NDP, there was a great deal of hostility over the national party's failed attempt to "parachute" a campaign manager into the riding who allegedly had national sympathies (interview with Ray Larkin).)

In any case, all three provincial organizers made sure that all candidates and/or their agents were aware of the legal and party requirements for electoral campaigns. In addition, facilitators for all three parties organized special or provincial seminars for campaign managers and candidates where information was exchanged and coordinated. The Conservative party, for example, had one major regional meeting of Nova Scotia Tory MPs and constituency executives before the election. At these meetings, ridings were encouraged to search for and nominate candidates if they had not already done so. Five other regional meetings for campaign managers were also arranged during the pre-election phase. At these "election readiness" workshops, candidates and/or their campaign managers discussed campaign organization and management, media relations and communication strategies, canvassing, polling, town hall debate tactics and sample answers to frequently asked questions. Organizational manuals, videotapes, reference materials and other aids supporting these technical aspects of electioneering were subsequently made available to candidates in the precampaign phase and were used extensively at the outset.

The Liberal party and the NDP in Atlantic Canada held their "election readiness" workshops later but essentially used seminars in much the same way. Robert Lee characterizes the atmosphere at these workshops well: "The Tories ran three-day candidate colleges in Ottawa, hosted by Norman Atkins and known as Norm's Boot Camp. The school gave candidates the motivational boost of an evangelical retreat, the self-confidence of a Dale Carnegie course, and the sales enthusiasm of an Amway convention; all conducted with the forced bonhomie of a gathering of the Moose Lodge. It must have been hell but it was thorough" (Lee 1989, 39). One striking result of all this coordination was that campaign structures and management processes at the local level, both within parties and between parties, were virtually identical. Campaign organizations in Halifax and Annapolis Valley–Hants (for all three parties) consisted of the candidate, campaign manager, a policy advisory committee of 12–15 people, two or three media liaison people, and a number of volunteer, part-time (foot, phone and flyer) canvassers determined by the number of polling stations in the riding and/or the strength of the riding association.

In addition to promoting organizational symmetry, provincial facilitators, by holding regional policy conventions, also attempted to encourage policy coherence and consistency, both with the national party platform and within the region itself. Early in the campaign, Liberal and NDP activists in both the Annapolis Valley–Hants and Halifax ridings complained at their respective Nova Scotia and/or Atlantic Canada caucus meetings that national party strategists were out of touch with the political climate in their region – particularly with regard to free trade. The relationship between the Halifax and federal NDP organization was particularly tense and hostile in this regard (interview with Jim Gill). Nevertheless, candidates for all three parties were much more aggressive and successful in coordinating regional policy positions, and, in these attempts, provincial coordinators and Halifax candidates played a leading role. Should it surprise us to find that this drive for organizational and policy coherence, consistency and coordination would lead to the creation of similar campaign communication strategies?

National Polling

Still in the pre-election phase, national party polling played an integral part in precampaign efforts to forge a consistent communication strategy in the 1988 election. The Conservative party's polls done by Decima six months before and three weeks into the campaign, supplemented by tracking polls and focus groups, undeniably influenced national party campaign strategy. Data from these polls were made available to all affected ridings, including Halifax. Even though the local samples were too small, national polling data and subsequent assessments of them were used by Halifax candidates to corroborate the wisdom of initial plans and the broad outlines of local campaign communiqués.

Published party and media polls during the campaign similarly influenced riding-level politics. According to all campaign managers interviewed, polling results had palpable effects on strategic voters, on the number and morale of volunteers and contributors who wanted to go with the winners, and on those who were interested in patronage.[2] Most important though, local campaigns had to react publicly and tactically to the national polls which brought more national waves to local shores and forced candidates to ride the crests and troughs they created. Pat Nowlan, for example, responded to a post-debate drop in the polls by setting up 14 "town hall" meetings in 12 days to stem what seemed like a Liberal tide.

National Campaign Slogans

Once the election was announced, national party campaign slogans began to play an important role in setting the communications agenda of local candidates. The Conservative rallying cry "the party and the leader capable of managing change" was taken up by local campaigns and the media in both Halifax and Annapolis Valley–Hants. It immediately set the early focus of the campaign on leadership and competence. (In Annapolis Valley–Hants, there was less emphasis on the former.) In any event, local candidates did not really have much of a choice in this regard; after all, almost all party literature generated at the national level would include that message and the media sustained this agenda by focusing on John Turner and his incompetent management of his own party.

The Liberals, much to the chagrin of local candidates in Nova Scotia, chose to begin the campaign with a defence of their 40-point policy program which was announced days before the campaign opened. Apart from the sheer unwieldiness of the platform, the initial confusion over the cost of particular initiatives (especially daycare), and the discord within the Liberal national campaign organization over John Turner's leadership, local candidates felt frustrated at the reluctance of the national party to concentrate on the single issue of free trade (interview with Mary Clancy and John Murphy). At the outset, this lack of focus within the national campaign had an adverse impact on the ability of Liberal candidates to attract volunteers and contributions and diverted media and public attention from the free trade "spin" that local candidates were trying to impose on the campaign.

The NDP in Nova Scotia found itself in a similar dilemma. The national party chose to focus its campaign on Ed Broadbent and the theme "A Fair Deal for Average Canadians" (replaced later by "Main Street and not Wall Street or Bay Street values"). New Democrats in Nova Scotia, long used to seeing popular provincial and federal leaders plummet at the polls, were frustrated at this tactic and at the seeming "embourgeoisement" of the national party. Like its local Liberal counterparts, the NDP wanted to make it a free trade election (with core-periphery, rich-poor, dependence-independence themes), but the national party, in an attempt to distance itself from the charge of being pacifist, socialist and captured by organized labour, concentrated instead on issues like health care, the environment, unfair taxation, pension reform, child care and the overall theme of "fairness." In short, local campaign messages, even when they were unique, were superseded by national ones. Even though the local New Democrat and Liberal candidates railed against the Free Trade Agreement at the outset, the local media did not cover it as a "free trade election" until it became the main issue at the national level. Up to that point, the focus remained on national leadership and competence.

Policy Manuals

Overall campaign themes and slogans were buttressed by loose-leaf policy briefing manuals outlining the latest official party positions on a wide range of issues. As one observer described these guidebooks: "Each party instructed its candidates on the accepted line on any policy issue; this task fell to the national campaign committee known as 'communications.' The committee's purpose was to ensure that candidates would all be 'singing from the same hymn book,' thereby assisting the leader in the delivery of his message to the public. This approach enabled the parties to send forth a homogenized brigade of candidates, or, as the Book of Common Prayer puts it, a 'noble army of martyrs' " (Lee 1989, 39).

On the basis of our content analysis of media election coverage, it appears that most platform issues were barely discussed or not raised at all during the local campaign. Nevertheless, these policy manuals were used as their "main reference point" by local campaigners, especially for secondary issues. Typically, manuals were used by candidates and their agents in responding to questions posed by the media and by the general public or in local debates. Even locally produced campaign literature (mostly emphasizing free trade or local candidate credentials) usually took the national party position and applied it to local conditions and concerns. Annapolis Valley–Hants Liberal and

New Democrat candidates made more direct use of these policy manuals than their urban counterparts. Stewart McInnes, because of conventions of party discipline, cabinet solidarity and ministerial responsibility, found it next to impossible to adopt distinct positions on issues. When national party stands seemed inappropriate for local conditions, incumbents tried to ignore or soft-sell those positions. In 1988, however, many Tory candidates, given the aggressive promotion of the Free Trade Agreement by their national leaders, felt compelled to include and defend free trade as part of their communication strategy. Policy directives (both implicit and explicit) from national party sources, in other words, served to harmonize national and local platform agendas.

Riding Services Packages

Complementing these "policy directives" were "riding services" or "candidate services" packages which were made available to all local campaigns. These facilities were used by all local candidates in a variety of ways. All three parties, especially the Conservatives, wanted consistent use of party signs, colours, logos, buttons, etc. and made these campaign materials available to local candidates at minimal cost in order to tempt them into using these services – an offer candidates couldn't refuse. One candidate likened it to "catalogue shopping" – everything from coffee cups with the party logo to campaign literature was available. Local campaign teams, facing pecuniary, personnel and time pressures, did not feel it was advisable to "reinvent the wheel" as far as these communication services were concerned.

Local candidates for all three parties, even those that insisted on using locally produced literature, used these "canned" signs, advertisements, letterheads, pamphlets, flyers, brochures, newsletters, press releases, statements and speeches, answers to interest-group questionnaires and other prepackaged material as part of their overall communication campaigns. Most merely added their own names and messages to national publications. Even Pat Nowlan, the candidate who tried to put the most distance between himself and his party, used glossy brochures from the national party with his name on them.

The fax machine (the only evidence of new technology in these local campaigns) also brought a virtual deluge of similar but more up-to-date material from national and provincial campaign coordinators. When all else failed, candidates or campaign managers used "crisis hot lines." In most cases, hot lines were used to ask how speedily riding services materials (or policy clarifications) would arrive at local campaign headquarters. Again, even though there was no national party compulsion involved, local candidates were almost driven to using these cost-saving materials. The effect of this was to homogenize campaign literature across the various ridings and to ensure that both national and local campaigns presented one consistent and coherent image to voters.

National Advertising Strategies

Similar effects and incentives were experienced by local candidates as a result of the advertising strategies of the national parties. According to *Maclean's*, during the pre-election phase, the Conservatives spent $24 million dollars promoting free trade through government mailings and advertising (1988, 24). For the election itself, the Conservatives budgeted $8.1 million: $2.4 million for provincial campaigns and $5.7 million for national advertising, tour and operations (Frizzell et al. 1989, 15). In the last week of the campaign alone, two million Tory advertising dollars were spent. The Liberals and the New Democrats spent $3 million each in advertising (*Maclean's*/Decima 1988, 24; Frizzell et al. 1989, 45). Clearly this massive national advertising (and free-time broadcasting) could not help but have an enormous "spillover" effect on local campaign communications. In a poll taken immediately after the election, 26 percent of those surveyed claimed that these television advertisements helped them make their decision (*Maclean's*/Decima 1988, 19).

Furthermore, all three candidates in Halifax, either in conjunction with the national party or with neighbouring campaigns, either "tagged on" to these regional ads or produced their own regional ads based on the national model(s). This concerted media advertising effort was a cost-effective way of producing and delivering advertisements (local candidates usually paid a flat fee to the national organization or signed over a part of their post-election reimbursement); however, national or regional media buys also required campaign integration and allowed the national organization an entrée into shaping the style and content of media messages at the local level.

Televised Debates

All campaign managers interviewed agreed that debate strategies employed by the national leaders and the perceived outcome of the debates themselves also had a terrific impact on the campaign in the trenches. Issues discussed during the debates, especially free trade, were fixed on the campaign agenda and John Turner, the leader who seemingly "won" the debates, found himself back in the race. Ed Broadbent was a double loser. He not only emerged from the debate with his personal competence in question, but he also ceded championing of the anti–free trade cause to John Turner.

The debates had a ripple effect on local campaigns in Nova Scotia. To New Democrats in Halifax and Annapolis Valley–Hants, the debates were a disaster. Not only did they lose the "Broadbent advantage," but they also "lost" the free trade issue (and strategic voters) to the Liberals. In addition, during the debate, Turner was able to successfully accuse the NDP of wanting to withdraw from NATO and NORAD, a charge which did not sit well with electors in the garrison town of Halifax. The Halifax NDP tried desperately to argue that Atlantic Canadians should not trust the Liberals or the Conservatives, that Ray Larkin and the NDP were the true defenders of the region. It was all in vain. They could not distance themselves from the national campaign.

The Halifax and Annapolis Valley–Hants Liberals felt the opposite effect. The debates reinforced their commitment to the free trade issue, resurrected their leader and energized their activists. When post-debate polls showed that the Liberals were "still in the game," it led to a "400 percent" overnight increase in the number of volunteers and a dramatic increase in donations to the cause (interview with Mary Clancy).

To local Conservatives, the free trade issue became unavoidable. Both McInnes and Nowlan had to modify their campaign plans to neutralize the anti–free trade and pro-Turner momentum. Nowlan, for example, who prior to the debate had sought to avoid any discussion of the Free Trade Agreement, immediately (and very publicly) set about attacking Liberal and New Democrat "myths and lies" about free trade (interview with Clara Jefferson).

In short, regardless of whether or not one agrees that the debates had an impact on voting behaviour, they undoubtedly served to support or undermine local communication efforts and influenced the behaviour of candidates, activists and supporters (interviews with Jim Gill, Ross Stinson, Dan Campbell, Clara Jefferson, Steve Mattson and Norman Watt).

Campaign Tours

Campaign tours by leaders and party stalwarts were another way by which the national party was able to influence the local campaign. (According to the same Maclean's/Decima poll quoted above, 24 percent of those asked said that tours helped them make their voting decision.) The tour stops were carefully chosen. Each region was allotted a specific amount of time. "The specific constituency locales within the province were selected because they gave local meaning to the day's theme and/or because the local party's election fortunes were considered particularly important in attaining the objective of a majority government" (Frizzell et al. 1989, 20).

Halifax, as a "marginal" riding and the regional metropole, did receive a significant degree of attention from luminaries of all three parties. Brian Mulroney, Michael Wilson and John Crosbie showed the flag for the Tory party in Halifax. John Turner, Sheila Copps, Eugene Whelan and Vince Maclean (Nova Scotia Liberal party leader) visited both Halifax and Annapolis Valley–Hants for the Liberals. During one of his visits to Halifax, Turner appeared at a press conference with almost all 32 of the party's Atlantic Canada candidates and unveiled an "Atlantic Canada Charter," a 12-point Liberal election platform for Atlantic Canada which addressed regional concerns like highways, government procurement, tourism, decentralization of government departments and support for fisheries and energy. The NDP spent $1.5 million on its tour arrangements and Ed Broadbent visited Halifax twice (interview with Jim Gill).

One of Broadbent's visits illustrates well the importance that local candidates place on tours by party dignitaries, the kinds of tensions that can arise when national and local priorities clash, and the reality that through "sins" of commission or omission the national party can have significant effects on constituency campaigns. Throughout the campaign, the Halifax NDP tried to get special messages and statements from Ed Broadbent on two of the more controversial issues at the riding level – Canada's acquisition of nuclear submarines and East–West Coast pay equity for dockyard workers. After much jockeying behind the scenes, it was agreed that Broadbent, at a well-attended press conference, would declare his support for the 2 500 Halifax dockyard workers who were fighting to close a $3.46-per-hour wage gap with their West Coast counterparts. Unfortunately, at the appointed time, no such declaration was made because the national organization did not want Broadbent or the party to be too publicly associated with organized labour. The local candidate bitterly accused the party of being less interested in principles and local concerns and more concerned about providing photo opportunities for the national press with Halifax as a backdrop. After an angry behind the scenes dispute with party insiders, Broadbent later declared himself in favour of dockyard equity at a sparsely attended news conference far from the glare of national cameras (interview with Ray Larkin). By then, however, the damage had been done, and the local NDP campaign became estranged not only from national organizers but also from local union supporters. In short, leader tours not only provide photo opportunities for local candidates, but they also organizationally and symbolically join local and national campaigns and issues – sometimes with negative repercussions for local candidates.

Precisely because of this explicit coupling of national and local candidates, especially on the free trade issue, the Conservative candidate in Annapolis Valley–Hants did not ask Mulroney, national cabinet ministers, or any other strong defenders of the Free Trade Agreement to visit the riding (interview with Clara Jefferson). Whether they would have done so is another matter. Both the Conservatives and the New Democrats considered Annapolis Valley–Hants a "safe" Conservative seat, and national undertakings to include it on "the tour" would have been unlikely. (As noted above, a number of Liberal noteworthies did visit Annapolis Valley–Hants during the campaign, suggesting that, despite their party's poor showing in previous elections, the party brass had not written off Annapolis Valley–Hants or John Murphy.)

Each of the national parties was also able to direct some Nova Scotia print-media attention to particular campaigns by each identifying one meeting per day they would like to have covered. The Halifax *Chronicle-Herald*, for example, guaranteed all three major parties that a reporter would be at each of the daily party-designated events, although it did not guarantee what would be written or even that reportage would make it to print.

In short, while we found no direct intervention or binding instructions from the national party in the selection of local candidates or their campaign communication strategies, we also found little evidence that suggests that ridings are sovereign and autonomous in the conduct of their media campaigns. Although one can argue that the national party did not tell local candidates what issues to talk about or how to address national issues, the vertical integration and spillover effects of national party strategies ensured that local candidates would merely ride the waves created by national leaders and issues. Even local campaigns (like the Halifax NDP effort) that energetically attempted to distance themselves from national forces could not avoid the crests and troughs created by national party activity. Despite the existence of differing objectives, distinct personalities and dissimilar conditions, local campaigns could not escape the electoral "spins" shaped by their parent organizations. Whether local campaigners liked it or not, there were both strong incentives for them to coordinate their communication strategies with the national, and powerful disincentives against being out of step with the national campaign. In other words, if local campaign organizations, policies and electioneering techniques were miniature replicas of those pursued at the national level, the responsibility lay in no small part with the concerted efforts of national party organizations to fashion consistent, coherent and winning media campaigns and corporate identities.

THE INTRA-MEDIA DIMENSION

To argue that factors relating to the vertical integration of party campaigns made it possible for national parties to influence local strategies, issues and candidate images does not deny that the media also played a considerable role in transforming the election into a referendum on national leaders and single issues. In fact, much the same argument can be made about the relationship between national and local media outlets. Just as economies of scale and specialization and the vertical integration of campaign organizations enabled national parties to control local campaign communication strategies, so too did the relationship between national media establishments and their local clients or affiliates ensure that national stories would figure more prominently than local ones in the local media. Consequently, local voters were poorly informed about the local implications of national issues and had little opportunity to learn how these issues would affect them directly or even how their local candidate viewed these issues.

Media Profile

All the major TV stations in Halifax, CBC, ATV and MITV, are affiliated with or owned by national media conglomerates – CBC, CTV and Global respectively. (Annapolis Valley–Hants does not have local TV stations but picks up most relays from Halifax.) For election coverage, they all essentially used the same news-gathering techniques. To begin with, the time devoted to local election coverage was determined within an informal industry-wide formula which proposes that a standard period be allotted for international, national, provincial, sports, weather and entertainment news. According to some media and most party sources, the local CBC station, because of its superior resources, offered the best coverage of the Halifax and Annapolis Valley–Hants electoral campaigns. During the course of the election, it offered its viewers 11 news or public affairs items dealing mainly with the contest in Halifax and 4 in Annapolis Valley–Hants (confidential interview with CBC employee). Most TV attention was directed to the campaign during the closing week(s) of the campaign. Local coverage was further limited by the fact that reporters did not specialize in politics or even work full-time on election stories. Most important, though, for a vast majority of news stories, national feeds or national leads from "parent" companies were used either directly or with local reactions. In other words, local TV election coverage was driven by national stories emanating from national sources.

The dominant radio stations in Halifax and Annapolis Valley–Hants have similar working relationships with national conglomerates. CJCH Radio is a division of Toronto-based CHUM Limited. For election coverage it used Broadcast News, Canadian Press and CHUM. Because CJCH is housed in the same building as ATV (which is also owned by CHUM), it uses CTV material as well. CHNS Radio is a division of Maclean-Hunter Limited. It used Broadcast News and Newsradio for election coverage. Annapolis Valley Radio (AVR) is affiliated with Broadcast News. It got 90 percent of its audio coverage from Broadcast News Audio Service and generated about 10 percent of its news locally. As the AVR news editor described it, "the local ridings do not generate enough interesting news. National sends us their best feeds and we concentrate on the best of these and use them for leads. We usually follow this up with local spinoffs or local candidate reactions." As with television, no radio reporters were devoted specifically to the local campaign(s), and the actual time devoted to "politics" (let alone elections) in any given six-minute newscast was very rarely more than a minute. Given that AVR's team of seven reporters represented the largest private radio news-gathering contingent in the region, the amount of time devoted to local coverage by others was not likely any greater.

All local campaigners seemed to agree that newspaper coverage of the election was superior to that of television and radio, and most political observers in Atlantic Canada agree that the Halifax *Chronicle-Herald* (HCH) is the newspaper of record in the region. It is one of the few independently owned media outlets in Canada, and it dominates the Halifax market. According to the Government of Nova Scotia, Department of Industry, Trade and Technology statistics, an average of 88 730 copies are bought daily, and, if one includes its afternoon version, the *Mail-Star*, that number climbs to 146 619. By contrast, its only rival, the *Daily News*, has a paid circulation of 28 000 (Nova Scotia, Dept. of ITT 1990b, 58). The HCH, with bureaus in Ottawa and Toronto and numerous others throughout Atlantic Canada, employed about 45 reporters in November of 1988. It even had a bureau in Annapolis Valley–Hants. We decided to analyse the HCH's election coverage to determine in what measure national and local candidates, issues and perceptions figured in its reportage.

We also wished to compare it to its country cousins in Annapolis Valley–Hants – the *Advertiser* (circulation 9 992), the *Hants Journal* (circulation 5 266) and the Berwick *Register* (circulation 2 747) (Nova Scotia, Dept of ITT 1990a, 59). These top three weekly Annapolis Valley–Hants newspapers are all owned and operated by Cameron Publishing. So concentrated is the ownership that the three major Annapolis Valley–Hants newspapers share reporters, run each other's advertisements and do not compete with each other for stories. Unlike the HCH, local papers in Annapolis Valley–Hants also do not use wire services, nor do they carry national stories unless they can find local angles to them or get local reactions. As one reporter (Brent Fox from the *Advertiser*) put it, "we look at the election through the other end of the microscope." Nevertheless, despite the local emphasis of these weeklies, the resources devoted to local election coverage were minuscule. One or two reporters covered the campaign part time depending on who was available and whether or not other interesting things were happening. For the most part, reporters felt that the Annapolis Valley–Hants campaign was too "boring," "low key" and "uncompetitive" to generate coverage. Most of the reporters assigned to the campaign were generalists and juniors and, judging from the difficulty we had in finding them, turned to greener pastures at a high rate.

The HCH's national election coverage strategy was fairly straightforward. During the first two weeks, the newspaper virtually ignored the national campaign. During the next few weeks of the election, it relied on CP wire services and its central Canadian bureaus. Unlike other major national newspapers, the HCH did not "follow the leaders" on tour throughout the election. It did "pick up" the party leaders whenever they were in the region; however, it was not until the last two weeks of the election that it sent two reporters to follow the Liberal and PC leaders on their cross-country tours and joined the Ed Broadbent tour a week later. As the HCH saw it, the leader tours, tailored as they were to the requirements of the electronic media, were not all that useful for print purposes. The editor of the HCH also felt that the media covered too many stage-managed (made-for-television) events in 1984 and was determined not to let it happen again. The newspaper had a "game plan" and stuck to it. In terms of priorities, the HCH decided it would concentrate first on events within the province, followed by regional and then national stories: by all accounts, a newspaper not given to riding national waves.

Newspaper Content Analysis

In order to assess systematically the pattern of print campaigns, a content analysis was undertaken of several Nova Scotia newspapers. (See the Appendix for a discussion of the methodology.) As we can see from table 6.3, in terms of total number of articles, national actors and sources apparently got marginally more coverage than local actors and sources in local newspapers. For example, 51.6 percent of the articles coded featured national actors while 48.4 percent publicized local ones (see also table 6.7). However, once we consider the prominence given to national and local actors and sources – the placement of articles in the paper, their length and forms of coverage – national concerns were overwhelmingly emphasized. National sources and actors monopolized front page, editorial, and columnist/commentary pages, while local campaigns were relegated to local/provincial, special election and other (usually advertising) sections (see table 6.2).

We found a familiar pattern when "length of item" was compared. Approximately three-quarters of coverage under eight paragraphs focused on local matters. Only 31 percent of the lengthier articles referred to local sources or local actors. This is even more remarkable given the fact that almost 62 percent of all items coded were eight or more paragraphs long. Similarly, national sources and actors were predominant in news stories, background articles, commentaries, photographs and cartoons, while local campaigns tended to be items coded as features, candidate profiles, advertisements and electoral information.

In comparing the Halifax and Annapolis Valley–Hants newspaper coverage of national and local campaigns, we noted a stark difference

Table 6.2
Placement of articles devoted to national and local sources of information and actors by Halifax and Annapolis Valley–Hants newspapers

Prominence	National sources		Local sources		National actors		Local actors	
	N	%	N	%	N	%	N	%
Front page	179	85.2*	31	14.8*	195	80.9*	46	19.1*
Local page	3	12.0	22	88.0	9	31.0	20	69.0
Provincial page	3	21.4	11	78.6	3	42.9	4	57.1
Editorial	27	100.0	1	0.0	19	81.8	5	18.2
Columnist/commentary	8	88.9	1	11.1	13	92.9	1	7.1
Election section	164	42.2	225	57.8	157	37.8	258	62.2
Other/advertising	8	16.7	40	83.3	3	6.8	41	93.2
Total	392	54.2	331	45.8	399	51.6	375	48.4

N = actual number of items.

% = % of items appearing on text page.

*Read horizontally, the two sources columns or two actors columns total 100.0%.

that confirms the media strategies described above (see table 6.3). The HCH devoted almost 60 percent of its coverage to national sources and actors, while 75–100 percent of Annapolis Valley–Hants newspaper articles were exclusively locally oriented. One should not conclude from these "balance of coverage" figures, however, that rural electors are less influenced by national actors or issues. In Annapolis Valley–Hants a majority of weekly newspaper readers also read the HCH and watch Halifax-based television stations. The differences may merely reflect the fact that the media sources are complementary and occupy different news and public affairs niches. The data (table 6.4) also confirm that, as it was at the national level, free trade was the dominant issue as far as media coverage in both Halifax and Annapolis Valley–Hants was concerned. (In fact, if anything, our figures understate the case. We did not include in our coding data articles on free trade that did not mention parties or the election.)

The evidence also suggests that party strategies were almost equally important. In fact, while free trade dominated the front and editorial pages, party strategy-related issues pushed free trade into second place on the local, provincial, columnist and special election sections. Party strategy was also more likely to be the subject of shorter news items. While free trade dominated the news story category, party strategy was more likely to be discussed in background and commentaries. Again, one should explain this finding. Included in the "party strategy"

Table 6.3
Attention devoted to national and local sources of information and actors by Halifax and Annapolis Valley–Hants newspapers

Newspaper	National sources		Local sources		National actors		Local actors	
	N	%	N	%	N	%	N	%
Chronicle-Herald	384	58.7	270	41.3	381	56.1	298	43.9
Kentville Advertiser*	8	22.2	28	77.8	15	31.3	33	68.8
Hants Journal	0	0.0	17	100.0	2	8.0	23	92.0
Berwick Register	0	0.0	16	100.0	1	4.5	21	95.5
Total	392	54.2	331	45.8	399	51.6	375	48.4

N = number of items.

% = % of items appearing in that paper.

*Includes Friday Advertiser.

Table 6.4
Attention devoted to election issues by Halifax and Annapolis Valley–Hants newspapers

Issues	Chronicle-Herald		Kentville Advertiser		Hants Journal		Berwick Register		Total[a]	
	N	%	N	%	N	%	N	%	N	%
Government management	29	5.4	2	4.3	1	5.0	0	0.0	32	5.1
Free trade/ economy	201	37.2	20	42.6	6	30.0	6	33.3	233	37.2
Socio-cultural	37	6.8	3	6.4	0	0.0	0	0.0	40	6.4
Environment	13	2.4	3	6.4	0	0.0	0	0.0	16	2.6
Foreign policy	17	3.1	0	0.0	1	5.0	0	0.0	18	2.9
Women's issues	13	2.4	4	8.5	0	0.0	0	0.0	17	2.7
Federal-provincial	2	0.4	3	6.4	0	0.0	0	0.0	5	0.8
Regionalism	2	0.4	0	0.0	0	0.0	0	0.0	2	0.3
Labour- management	6	1.1	0	0.0	0	0.0	0	0.0	6	1.0
Party strategies	191	35.3	11	23.4	0	0.0	0	0.0	202	32.3
Miscellaneous/ advertising	30	5.5	1	2.1	12	60.0	12	66.7	55	8.8
Total[b]	541	86.4	47	7.5	20	3.2	18	2.9	626	100

Total [a] gives the number and percentage of items dealing with each issue.

Total [b] gives the number and percentage of items from each newspaper.

category was "horse-race" coverage of debates and polls. (See the Appendix for methodology.) Note also the tremendous gap in coverage between the top two "issues" and the rest. For example, the "federal-provincial" category included such concerns as national unity and the Meech Lake Accord, yet less than one percent of total coverage mentioned them. As table 6.5 shows, not only did local media coverage focus on national leaders and issues, but the "level of analysis" or the perspective adopted by the larger local newspapers was also largely national. One could perhaps argue that there is an inverse relationship between newspaper size and perspective.

Furthermore, when one breaks these numbers down with prominence as a primary consideration, 83.2 percent of front page news items, almost 100 percent of editorial and columnist commentaries, and

Table 6.5
Perspectives of Halifax and Annapolis Valley–Hants newspapers on election issues

	Chronicle-Herald		Kentville Advertiser		Hants Journal		Berwick Register		Total[a]	
Perspective	N	%	N	%	N	%	N	%	N	%
National	373	69.6	27	62.8	8	40.0	6	33.3	414	67.1
Local	82	15.3	16	37.2	12	60.0	12	66.7	122	19.8
Regional	80	14.9	0	0.0	0	0.0	0	0.0	80	13.0
International	1	0.2	0	0.0	0	0.0	0	0.0	1	0.2
Total[b]	536	86.9	43	7.0	20	3.2	18	2.9	617	100.0

Total [a] gives the number and percentage of items adopting each perspective.

Total [b] gives the number and percentage of items from each newspaper.

59.3 percent of election section material adopted national perspectives. Local and regional points of view, as expected, were more likely to appear on local or provincial pages as riding features or candidate profiles. National perspectives were overwhelmingly favoured (78.2 percent) in items over eight paragraphs, while local/regional perspectives appeared more significant in shorter items.

Finally, with regard to actor traits emphasized, table 6.6 shows that over 75 percent of all items coded focused on the policy stands of leaders and local candidates rather than personal background or character. This pattern generally held across newspapers, type of content, length of item and section of newspaper. This finding is surprising, given the conventional wisdom that the media are overly preoccupied with political personalities and colourful or trivial aspects of the campaign. (Perhaps a similar study of television coverage might yield different results.) Table 6.6 also parallels the 1988 Canadian National Election Study findings that the policy stands of candidates figured most prominently in influencing voting decisions.[3]

To a large extent, our content analysis of local newspaper coverage confirms that local media coverage in the 1988 federal election was primarily nationally oriented. Not only did most electoral coverage focus on national leaders, issues and perspectives, but even those stories judged to be "local" in content were inspired by national developments. Just as local parties, despite their best efforts, ended up putting local "spins" on national party communiqués, so too did the local media devote most of their attention to getting local angles into national stories.

Table 6.6
Actor traits emphasized by Halifax and Annapolis Valley–Hants newspapers

	Chronicle-Herald		Kentville Advertiser		Hants Journal		Berwick Register		Total	
Actor traits	N	%	N	%	N	%	N	%	N	%
Personal background	69	12.7	6	16.2	1	5.3	2	11.1	78	12.6
Policy stands	429	78.7	29	78.4	14	73.7	15	83.3	487	78.7
Character	47	8.6	2	5.4	4	21.1	1	5.6	54	8.7

Total gives the number and percentage of items emphasizing each trait.

Not only were national reports considered more newsworthy, but they were also cheaper to reproduce and use than locally generated news items.

Note that we are not concerned here with the impact of party and media conglomerates on the range of choice offered. As Anthony Downs pointed out decades ago in his *Economic Theory of Democracy* (1957), over time political competitors tend to move toward the centre of the issue spectrum and peddle similar issue "products." All we are arguing here is that the local press, largely because of media integration and the resulting economies of scale and specialization, came to the same conclusions as local parties – there was no need to "reinvent the wheel" as far as campaign communications were concerned; all one needed to do was tailor national material to meet local conditions.

THE INTRA-RIDING DIMENSION

Local Candidates and the Media

Given this overwhelming reliance on nationally inspired material, the local media did very little proactive or original-issue analysis of the election or local campaigns. When they were not using national feeds with local angles, most local media reports relied on reportage generated from all-candidate encounters. One Halifax TV station, for example, held a weekly panel session where local candidates discussed issues. Coincidentally, Mary Clancy and Pat Nowlan represented their parties often on this show. Cable TV had "meet the candidate" interviews and televised parts of some local debates. Radio stations held open-line talk shows (or debates) with candidates either as a group or singly. Newspapers did riding or candidate profiles and published answers to questionnaires completed by candidates.

Television coverage of the campaign was unanimously condemned by the candidates. Local campaigners felt that the format of news and public affairs programming allowed little room for analysis and channelled reporting into coverage of gaffes, trivia and dramatic confrontations. Halifax campaign managers also felt it was hard to get local TV news exposure because events had to be arranged after the supper hour in order to attract a crowd. By then, however, the five or six o'clock (local) news was over, and local election coverage was unlikely to make the nightly national-oriented network news. By the next day, it was old news.

Print media coverage was viewed in more favourable terms, but it too was usually complimented in a back-handed way: it was not as bad as TV, and it was unbiased in the sense that all campaigns received the same substandard coverage. Campaigners felt that there were local issues deserving media attention. These included the funding for a housing development which was withdrawn by the Canada Mortgage and Housing Corporation and the attempts by dockworkers to attain wage parity with their western counterparts. There was also the larger regional issue of overfishing in Grand Banks, off the coast of Newfoundland. It was felt, however, that issues such as these were ignored because they did not fit the media's nationally driven agenda, and those that were covered were superficially explained and researched.

Some complained about "pack journalism."[4] Many lamented the media's understanding of "balanced coverage."[5] Others felt that the media were unfair in that they treated hardworking and lazy campaigns equally by ensuring that other candidates all got equal time and space to respond to claims made and campaign events initiated by active candidates. Some (usually challengers) argued that rather than merely providing equal time or space, the local media should have played a more interpretative role by reporting their own impressions of campaign strengths and weaknesses and by declaring winners and losers. In Annapolis Valley–Hants, activists felt that the media were intimidated by the incumbent and avoided controversial matters. On the other hand, incumbents in both ridings felt that the media were biased against them because they saw themselves as "the opposition" or were opposed to free trade.

Media reporters had their own litany of complaints about the local campaign. Because the 1988 election in Nova Scotia was held almost concurrently with provincial and municipal elections, several reporters felt that they, party activists and voters were "electioned out." Furthermore, even though there was a dramatic increase in the number of media events during the campaign(s), no extra staff was added. The three elections put a great strain on financial and human resources, leaving very little time, energy or inclination for electoral analysis.

The tremendous size of the riding was also a problem for Annapolis Valley–Hants reporters. Events were held too far away and were therefore not only difficult to cover but also less interesting to local subscribers. Many journalists also complained about the candidates themselves. One reporter contended: "local candidates are boring, and their campaigns unimaginative. They avoid issues, cover very little of substance, and all sound the same. All they want is free advertising." In Annapolis Valley–Hants reporters felt "competition gets coverage and there was no real contest." (In Annapolis Valley–Hants, a surprising number of reporters admitted that they ignored the NDP candidate's campaign initiatives because he stood no chance of winning.) According to some Halifax reporters, they were driven to looking for unusual or entertaining aspects in order to interest readers and appear different from the competition. The local candidates did not provide them with any variety or interesting material.

The prevalence of television in the campaign strategies at the national level, such as leaders debates and advertising campaigns, has not yet found its way to the riding level. While all campaigners lamented the lack and quality of TV coverage, for example, no special attempts were made by local candidates to secure spots on the six or ten o'clock news, in 30-second sound bites or in photo opportunities, or to make attractive visuals and other material which are more suitable to the medium. The principal means of engaging the local media seemed to be via faxed press releases and public service announcements. The Halifax NDP was ranked ahead of the other parties (by the Halifax media) in its ability to attract broadcast media attention; however, even its campaign was considered amateurish by national standards. In part, one can argue that many of the communication strategies of political organizations at the constituency level, such as press releases, are incompatible with the nature of the broadcast media with its emphasis on visuals and sound clips. This may explain, in turn, the lack of interest by local radio and television in the local campaign.

Many reporters questioned whether it was their role to drive the local campaign agenda or to be judgemental. Almost all press people acknowledged and defended the convention among journalists that major party candidates should get equal time, be asked similar questions, and be given the opportunity to respond to statements from other candidates. The only "bias" reporters would admit to was in the amount of attention devoted to incumbents. Reporters acknowledged that the incumbent usually got more attention because she or he was more widely known, had more to say, had more to lose and attracted more attention from other candidates. Government incumbents had a greater edge. As Al Kingsbury, local reporter for HCH, stated, "the government incumbent has a huge advantage. Money is distributed, jobs and projects are announced. We sometimes worry about appearing partisan, but the government is the government."

We found little supporting evidence in our content analysis of the alleged imbalances of coverage and the "incumbency advantage" (see table 6.7). At the national level, Prime Minister Mulroney was the primary actor mentioned more often than Turner or Broadbent. Locally, however, Liberal candidates Murphy and Clancy got more attention than their incumbent rivals. As sources of election reports, or organizers of campaign events, Mulroney and Turner got equal coverage,

Table 6.7
Attention devoted to national and local candidates as primary actors and sources of coverage

	Primary actor		Primary source	
	N	%	N	%
Broadbent	63	7.6	70	9.4
Mulroney	140	16.8	108	14.4
Turner	130	15.6	108	14.4
Clancy	23	2.8	18	2.4
Larkin	19	2.3	17	2.3
McInnes	21	2.5	20	2.7
Collins	19	2.3	15	2.0
Murphy	24	2.9	20	2.7
Nowlan	22	2.6	13	1.7
Other national	124	14.9	128	17.1
Other local/provincial	248	29.8	231	30.9
Total	833	100.0	748	100.0

Note: Primary actor refers to the principal subject of the news item. Primary source refers to origin of the information contained in the news item. Other national and/or other local actors and sources refers to other national and/or local organizations and/or individuals featured in a news item.

while the incumbent got more in Halifax and less in Annapolis Valley–Hants. With one exception in Annapolis Valley–Hants, NDP candidates got less attention at both the national and local level as both principal actors mentioned and sources of campaign coverage. Overall, as shown in table 6.7, national leaders generally got over four times as much coverage as their local candidates.

Regardless of whether or not incumbents got more or less coverage, we found that many reporters are extremely cynical about politicians in general, particularly government party incumbents, and see themselves as "watchdogs." More coverage does not necessarily mean favourable publicity to incumbents. In short, the media–candidate interface at the riding level was surprisingly antagonistic. Even in Annapolis Valley–Hants, where the general tone of the campaign was far more neighbourly, only a thin veneer of civility covered the real antipathy that reporters and politicians had for each other.

Local Candidates and their Financial and Human Resources

While the substantive aspects of campaigning in Annapolis Valley–Hants and Halifax were similar, there were significant differences in the amounts of revenue raised and expended during the contest. On the "contributions" side, as table 6.8 shows, major party candidates in Halifax raised well over twice as much as their country cousins ($156 952 versus $71 688). As far as expenditures go, in general, Halifax candidates used over twice as much as their rural counterparts on media advertising ($83 670 versus $38 766). In Halifax, all three candidates neared their spending limits, while in Annapolis Valley–Hants, the biggest spenders used only two-thirds of their allotment, and the NDP used 26 percent.

Note also that, with the exception of the NDP candidate in Annapolis Valley–Hants (who lost his deposit), all candidates came out of the campaigns with sizable surpluses in their war chests. The 1988 election was a bitter-sweet loss for Stewart McInnes who found himself with $65 340 left over for future party activities. In large part, these disparities are explained by differences in the competitiveness of the two ridings, the cost of available media, and the pool of potential contributors.

While there were stark differences in the volume of funds raised and spent to fight the election in Halifax and Annapolis Valley–Hants, electioneering techniques were not as dramatically different in the two ridings. In both areas, local candidate tactics for reaching constituents showed a definite bias against using television and radio. As table 6.8 shows, with one exception, the broadcast media were hardly used by local campaigns (particularly incumbents) to communicate with voters

Table 6.8
1988 campaign expenses and finances in Annapolis Valley–Hants and Halifax
(dollars)

	Annapolis Valley–Hants			Halifax		
	Liberal	PC	NDP	Liberal	PC	NDP
Expenses						
Radio	1 637	1 205	2 155	7 769	0	2 000
Television	0	0	0	0	0	0
Newspapers	5 055	1 568	2 142	6 601	7 230	539
National buy	2 950	0	0	7 290	0	1 937
Other media	10 198	7 775	4 081	13 656	20 067	16 587
Total media	19 840	10 548	8 378	35 310	27 297	21 063
Salaries	2 000	6 970	770	0	0	18 936
Office	6 427	10 114	2 919	7 663	14 310	7 244
Travel	812	910	0	782	0	0
Other	2 033	2 370	10	1 386	2 621	105
Total expense	31 112	30 912	12 077	45 147	44 228	47 348
% of limit spent	66.9%	66.4%	26.0%	94.3%	92.4%	98.9%
Income						
Reimbursement	16 296	15 292	0	22 574	22 475	23 593
Contributions	35 673	25 048	10 967	36 367	87 093	33 492
Total income	51 969	40 340	10 967	58 941	109 568	57 085
Surplus (Deficit)	20 857	9 428	(1 110)	13 794	65 340	9 737

Source: 1988 campaign contributions and expenditures reports submitted to the chief electoral officer.

via paid advertising. TV was not used because desired spots were costly, TV productions are expensive and time consuming, and TV broadcast areas do not neatly fit riding boundaries. Despite the fact that cable TV provided a better "fit" of riding boundaries and viewing areas and was easily and freely available, it was virtually ignored by local candidates because "nobody watches it." Cable TV coverage of the election in Annapolis Valley–Hants and Halifax was largely restricted to delayed broadcasts of parts of all-candidates debates held at local universities (Acadia and Saint Mary's respectively). Radio was used very little, primarily by challengers who wished to develop "name recognition." (Mary Clancy, the Liberal candidate in Halifax, spent over three times as much as rivals on radio advertising because, as one of her advisers put it, "she has a voice and personality that goes over very well on radio.") For news coverage and advertising, the newspaper was a much more accessible and popular vehicle. Nevertheless, by far the largest proportion of local campaign expenditures and human resources was devoted to producing and disseminating other media – lawn signs, flyers and other printed material.

Interviews with candidates and their advisers confirmed this preference for print (or face-to-face) modes of electoral communication. When asked to rank various campaign techniques for reaching voters, incumbents placed "identifying and getting out the vote" at the top of their list, followed by literature drops and all-candidate meetings. Challengers for the most part had similar priorities, except that getting out the vote was not as highly rated. In neither case, however, was advertising or media coverage generally ranked at the top.

The Halifax New Democrats seemed most divided about which communication tactics were best. The provincial coordinator felt that one was "not going to shape fundamental values during the campaign; therefore, the priority should be on identifying your vote and getting it out." The candidate felt it important that "the voter makes contact with the candidate and talks about issues." The campaign manager believed the key lay in "developing the candidate's profile and shooting for news coverage." Even though they disagreed over the rating of news coverage, all agreed that canvassing and all-candidate encounters were most important overall.

All-candidate encounters were highly ranked by parties because of the publicity they generated. Just as they were at the national level, debates were *de rigueur* at the riding level and were scrupulously attended by the local media. Incumbents sought to avoid them or at least limit potential damage. Most complained that media (particularly radio and television) coverage of local debates was superficial and tended to focus on "highlights" or sensational and trivial moments. National themes predominated. There, the similarity with national debates ends, however. With one exception, debates were not televised. (In 1988 the Halifax candidates did engage in an experimental CBC-televised debate which was broadcast throughout the region; however, according to one campaigner, it was done largely because the Halifax campaign simultaneously mirrored both the national and regional contest (interview with Dale Godsoe).) Thematic debates organized by local occupational groups or educational institutions proliferated. There were nine issue-specific debates held in Halifax and four in Annapolis Valley–Hants during the campaign. Some candidates complained about the stage-managed atmosphere with "packed" meetings and planted questions. Most (usually challengers) felt that the debates were useful because they were community events which attracted a lot of attention (even though they were not always well attended) and forced candidates to address substantive and specific concerns of the organizing agency.

In addition to all-candidates or meet-the-candidate gatherings, canvassing played an important tactical role in campaigning at the riding level. While canvassing may be a means by which voters and candidates educate each other about salient issues, canvassing at the riding level was used first and foremost to help identify and get out the vote. Any discussion of issues was mere foreplay; any educating of those canvassed was largely incidental. Unlike at the national level, canvass (or poll) results were not used to engage the local media or even to assess the effectiveness of campaign communication tactics.

In short, with the exception of the telephone and fax machine, campaign communication strategies at the riding level focus on print (brochures, billboards, lawn signs), canvassing and town hall meetings. The newer technologies in campaign communication such as television advertising, public opinion polls, videotaped messages, telemarketing and computerized information management are not nearly as prominent at the constituency level (if they are used at all) as are the more traditional methods.

Local Candidates and Pressure-Group Campaigning

Probably the most significant new development at the riding level in 1988 was the direct and very public involvement of pressure groups in the electoral process. As is well known, nationally, the business community saturated the market with pro–free trade ads. The "Canadian Alliance for Free Trade and Job Opportunities," representing 35 companies and business associations, spent an estimated $1.3 million on its own campaign. The "Pro Canada Network" spent $750 000 to fight the Free Trade Agreement (*Maclean's*/Decima 1988, 26). These advertising campaigns got a great deal of attention in Nova Scotia, as they did everywhere else. However, not nearly as much was done by way of local pressure-group "advertising" in Halifax and Annapolis Valley–Hants. Instead, the local media were inundated with press releases and public statements from major regional corporations like Sobeys, National Sea and Clearwater, singing the praises of free trade or threatening job losses and plant closures if the agreement was rejected. Conversely, local federations of labour, agriculture and poultry producers, McCain Foods and some small businesses publicly predicted unemployment, deindustrialization, and a loss of social and political security if the trade deal was adopted. According to most media interviewees, pressuregroup "advertising" in this form, involving job losses and job creation or plant openings and closings, was hard to ignore, even though most journalists thought they were being used for partisan purposes.

In addition to pressure-group activity on the free trade question, the Public Service Alliance of Canada (PSAC) had also targeted 17 ridings across Canada. Halifax was one of them. The PSAC and Dockyard Trades Council picketed Stewart McInnes' campaign headquarters throughout the campaign and did attract some unfavourable attention to the Conservative candidate's campaign. Local branches of the Canadian Labour Congress and the Canadian Auto Workers staffed phone banks and did some in-house canvassing and agitating among their members. While "orchestrated" may be too strong a term to use in this context, members of all campaign teams confessed to either distributing interest-group literature or being "consulted" prior to action being taken.

As with debates and polls, whether or not "third-party" advertising had a significant impact on voters or local media coverage was hotly disputed. Most local candidates did express concern, however, about pressure-group advertising going unregulated, while political parties themselves had to work within strictly enforced limits. Late in the campaign, when all their funds had been expended, candidates also felt helpless at their inability to respond to interest-group challenges. Once again, however, apart from its implications for electoral laws, national pressure-group advertising presented the recurring image of local "advertisers," like their party and media counterparts, caught in the eddies of a national wave.

FINDINGS AND RECOMMENDATIONS

To summarize, this study found that party communications and media coverage in Annapolis Valley–Hants and Halifax mirrored the national campaign insofar as they focused on, or reacted to, national leaders, issues and perspectives. In large part, this pattern can be attributed to the party and media desire for campaign integration, economic rationalization and "profit" maximization. In order to realize economies of scale and specialization and to forge consistent corporate identities, local parties and the media made themselves more dependent on their parent organizations. These considerations were not unique to the 1988 election and will therefore continue to have a nationalizing effect on federal campaigns. (If anything, newer campaign technologies, corporate restructuring and national pressure-group involvement will probably lead to greater centralization.)

Whether or not this narrowing of focus or nationalization is acceptable depends very much on the biases one brings to the question. Should the onus for producing and widely disseminating alternative information be on parties and the media, or should parties merely have information available for the interested public? Clearly, the voting public was offered a torrent of information dealing with national leaders, issues and perspectives during the 1988 election through media coverage of the campaign.

However, there were other channels for those wishing to swim against the tide and to consider local candidates and other issues and perspectives. These channels included material by interest groups and unions and campaign literature by parties which in many cases was not distributed because of a lack of human resources. Those voters seeking policy details or discussion of lesser-debated local and national issues and perspectives had to be more enterprising and energetic. Despite the lack of focus on local issues such as fishing, housing and employment parity, it was also felt that several national issues such as tax reform and Meech Lake were absent from discussion and debate. Even though these "other" matters were not widely discussed or advertised, a wealth of detailed and alternative information was available to members of the interested public upon request. The fact remains, however, that much of this material was prepared by the central organizations and carried a national perspective.

While the substance of local and national campaigning was similar, the style was definitely different. Local campaigns in Annapolis Valley–Hants and, to a lesser extent, Halifax remain very traditional. Candidates engage the media and voters principally through the use of the printed medium, canvassing and town hall debates. In part, the lack of attention devoted to local campaigns can be attributed to the "branch-plant" inability or unwillingness of local party and media outlets to develop original story lines or to present their material in different packages. (Given the constraints on resources available to the local media, this tendency is quite understandable.)

While we found a few differences between the Halifax and Annapolis Valley–Hants campaigns, it would be premature to attribute these differences totally to urban or rural factors. For example, there was a deeper sense of alienation from national parties in Annapolis Valley–Hants. One could just as easily explain this alienation by examining the structures of competition, the personality of candidates, the economic situation of the riding, and so on. One should also note that despite the similarity in campaign themes both at the national and riding level, the outcome was different in each riding. Halifax defeated the Conservative incumbent and returned a Liberal, while Annapolis Valley–Hants retained its four-decade loyalty to the Tories and the Nowlan name.

Finally, getting back to normative questions, one is presented with a dilemma. On one hand, we all wish to elect independent members of Parliament, people who will not sacrifice their principles or the interests of their ridings in the quest for party or individual advancement; on the other, we lament the lack of leaders who "show leadership" and speak and act decisively on behalf of their parties. Many of us believe that parties should act as agents of national integration and present and defend consistent and coherent platforms across the country. We assert that parties should translate platform promises into policy outputs. How does one reconcile these seemingly contradictory desires for unity and diversity in electoral campaigns? Party organizations that were too strong would make candidates and members of Parliament irrelevant. Parliamentarians who were too independent or dogmatic would make governing difficult.

Recommendations for reform should steer a middle course between the Scylla and Charybdis of excessive nationalization and localization. Clearly, restructuring party and media conglomerations is beyond the mandate of this Commission. Perhaps the answer lies not in changing the national focus of electoral activity, but in improving the ability of the riding and local media to put local issues onto the national election agenda, to better analyse the implications of national developments from a local point of view, and to discuss a broader range of national issues at the riding level. To this end, a number of possible suggestions can be considered.

For example, the local information environment for voters can be much improved by the provision of clear and concise "mission statements" by local candidates which outline their credentials, objectives and stands on local and national issues they consider important. This material could be produced by local candidates and disseminated via broadcast, print, mail and other electronic means by Elections Canada to every registered voter.

The quality of public debate could also be enhanced by a better use of community channels on cable television. While it would be tempting to recommend that cable television be required to provide free or other air time to local candidates or election coverage, it is questionable that such a resource would be widely used. According to program directors in the area, a great deal of time was available to candidates in 1988 but not used. The limited resources of community programming make it difficult for cable outlets to "create" their own stories; therefore, election coverage on these stations is usually a result of specific requests by political organizations. This Commission should consider providing both candidates and cable television stations with incentives, perhaps in the form of subsidies, to make better use of this medium for electoral purposes.

The calibre of local electoral communications could also be improved by strengthening the abilities of local reporters and campaign personnel. The Commission should encourage colleges, universities and schools of journalism to offer cross-disciplinary courses or graduate internships (to media and party activists) with a view to advancing their knowledge of the role of elections and the techniques of electioneering. Alternatively, the Commission may wish to consider recommending that local media be partially reimbursed for every new reporter (hired for the election period) devoted exclusively to election coverage.

The Commission may also wish to consider the impact of nationally publicized polls on candidates and party supporters and activists at the riding level. While the impact of polls on voters is debatable, we found a high degree of consensus among campaign managers that polls have a profound impact on the number and enthusiasm of volunteers. There appears to be an emerging consensus among party activists that polls be restricted during certain phases of the election and that essential background information be made available every time poll data are publicly cited. Perhaps "front-page" poll reports should be subjected to some type of "peer review" before publication, or, at least, "offended" parties could be given the opportunity to respond when the polling results are first released.

As with polling, campaign managers expressed a great deal of concern about the unchecked involvement of pressure groups in the electoral process. It is unfortunate that the activities of political parties, the leading vehicles for freedoms of association and expression in liberal democracies, are controlled by electoral laws, while those of narrower interests are not. "Third-party" involvement appears particularly undemocratic where the resources of local candidates are restricted and the full brunt of pressure-group activity is brought to bear during the closing weeks of the election on particular candidates.

With regard to interest-group activity in campaigns, we came across a number of "grey areas" the Commission may wish to investigate further. In both Annapolis Valley–Hants and Halifax, local campaigners admitted to working in concert with pressure groups. In one case, a local candidate was consulted by a business interest group before it placed an advertisement in the paper. In another, a third party produced an anti–free trade brochure and a local candidate distributed it. While this type of third-party involvement is not widespread, it has the potential to allow parties to escape electoral laws aimed at controlling candidate revenues and expenditures. It also opens up the possibility that these interests may serve as silent partners in party enterprises or otherwise use parties to subvert the democratic process.

Another instance of interest-group involvement concerns the local cablevision company in Annapolis Valley–Hants, Kings Cable, which made sizable contributions to the Liberal and Conservative (but not the New Democratic) party campaigns. Donations such as these give the appearance of a conflict of interest and raise questions about balanced coverage.

We also heard allegations that in Halifax it is a common practice for leading law firms to "second" lawyers to work as local campaign managers, with the expectation that the firm will be appropriately rewarded after the election. (Table 6.8, for example, shows that the Halifax NDP campaign claimed almost $19 000 on salaries, while the Liberals and Conservatives declared nothing.) Advertising agencies are also alleged to be developing a similar relationship with local campaigns. If these allegations are true, they make a mockery of campaign contributions and expenses declarations made to the chief electoral officer.

In short, it is beyond the mandate of the Commission to recommend structural changes to the electoral system, political parties or media conglomerates; however, much can be done in establishing and enforcing fair "rules of the game" for parties, media and other interest groups. This Commission could also make significant recommendations for improving the quality of electoral debate, by broadening the range of information offered and the communications instruments used, as well as strengthening the abilities of local candidates and media personnel to more skilfully chart and navigate a course that would preserve local diversity without seriously undermining party and national unity.

APPENDIX
NOTES ON CONTENT ANALYSIS METHODOLOGY

This content analysis consists of a coding of all (626) election-related items which appeared in the Halifax *Chronicle-Herald*, Kentville *Advertiser, Hants Journal* and Berwick *Register* between 1 October, the day the election was called, and 21 November, election day. These four newspapers were selected because they are the largest circulating newspapers in Halifax and Annapolis Valley–Hants.

Items were coded according to the section of the newspaper they appeared in, length, type of content, source(s) of information, principal actor(s) mentioned, actor traits emphasized, most prominent issue(s) and perception of issue(s).

For a sample listing of newspaper sections and types of content coded, see table 6.2.

"National sources" and "Local sources" identify where the information contained in a coded item originated (see tables 6.2, 6.3 and 6.8). "National sources" and "National actors" include party leaders, business, labour, polling, media and other interest groups and prominent individuals acting at the national level. "Local sources" and "Local actors" include any organization or group working within the region, province or riding.

Eleven "prominent issues" were coded at the outset (see table 6.4). However, only two stood out – "free trade" and "party strategies." "Free trade" included items which explicitly associated that issue with party stands or the election. Other issues like unemployment, inflation, tax reform and interest rates are subsumed under this heading; however, the number of references to these in 1988 were negligible. Under "party strategies," we included newspaper descriptions and assessments of national and local party and candidate electioneering strategies and tactics.

In the "Perspective" category of table 6.5, we asked "Does this item adopt a national, regional/provincial, local or international perspective on the issue being dealt with?"

With regard to the "Actor traits emphasized" category of table 6.6, "personal background" includes references to individual credentials, experience or occupation. "Policy stands" refers to the actors' statements on or knowledge of an issue. "Character" means competence, integrity, reliability, compassion, et cetera.

A number of people are partly responsible for the content analysis used in this study. David Bell, Gail Chamberlain and Fred Fletcher helped put the code book together. Gail Chamberlain, my research assistant, also did the tedious job of coding approximately 626 newspaper items from the four newspapers. Donald Naulls introduced me to the world of content analysis and helped me analyse the data. I could not have done a content analysis without their assistance.

NOTES

This study was completed in August 1991.

1. Various party strategists suggest that the importance of the local candidate is much more complex. Many party officials feel that the local candidate is usually "worth" 5–7 percent of the vote. This view has some support in the literature. See Clarke et al. (1991, 113–15) and Bell and Fletcher (1991).

2. The impact of polls appears to be more complex than was presumed by local strategists. Johnston et al. (1991) suggested that polling in the 1988 election interacted with televised leaders debates to produce both strategic voting and bandwagon phenomena. Polls are also proliferating at the local level, boosting the profile of many local races (Fletcher 1990, 17). The dynamic effects on the national and local campaigns created by polls will undoubtedly be a focus of future studies.

3. When survey respondents ranked parties, leaders, and candidates as influences on their vote decisions, 70 percent of those designating leaders and nearly 60 percent of those referring to parties or local candidates said there was an issue basis to their choice (Clarke et al. 1991, 114).

4. Taras (1990, 89) claims that the phenomenon of pack journalism is rooted in the coverage of a major event, such as an election campaign, in which a group of journalists who cover the same news stories, hear the same speeches and read the same press releases eventually come to subscribe to the same theories and rumours and write the same stories. Many believe this "collective mentality" among journalists largely sets the media's agenda.

5. Fletcher (1990, 24) lists several impediments to equitable coverage in the print media: the narrow focus on leaders, the limited range of issues given significant coverage, the negative tone of much coverage, the proliferation of media polls and the lack of accountability (broadcasters are accountable to the CRTC in the event of complaints).

INTERVIEWS

The interviews were conducted in January and February 1991.

Clancy, Mary, Liberal party candidate, Halifax.
Campbell, Dan, Liberal party campaign manager, Halifax.
Godsoe, Dale, Liberal party riding president, Halifax.
Young, Carole, Liberal party, Nova Scotia campaign chair.
Murphy, John, Liberal party candidate, Annapolis Valley–Hants.
Watt, Norman, Liberal party campaign manager, Annapolis Valley–Hants.
de Mont, Patricia, Liberal party riding president, Annapolis Valley–Hants.

McInnes, Stewart, PC party candidate, Halifax.
Stinson, Ross, PC party campaign manager and riding president, Halifax.
Smith, Dora Lee, PC party Nova Scotia, director of operations.
Nowlan, Patrick, PC party candidate, Annapolis Valley–Hants.
Jefferson, Clara, PC party campaign manager, Annapolis Valley–Hants.
Gullon, Ron, PC party riding president, Annapolis Valley–Hants.

Larkin, Ray, NDP candidate, Halifax.
Gill, Jim, NDP campaign manager, Halifax.
Williams, Rick, NDP media relations, Halifax.
Beach, Deana, NDP Atlantic Canada coordinator.
White, Mary Jane, NDP Nova Scotia director of organization.
O'Connor, Dan, NDP Nova Scotia federal liaison and media adviser.
Collins, Keith, NDP candidate, Annapolis Valley–Hants.
Mattson, Steve, NDP campaign manager, Annapolis Valley–Hants.
Hortie, Hector, NDP riding president, Annapolis Valley–Hants.

Fleming, Michael, news director, Halifax *Chronicle-Herald* (HCH).
Meek, Jim, reporter/columnist, HCH.
Stevenson, Marila, reporter, HCH.
Crichton, Jim, news director, 96 CHNS and FM-101 Radio.
Howe, Rick, assignment editor, 92 CJCH-C100 FM.
Pratt, Dick, news director, Atlantic Television System (ATV).
Soosar, John, assignment editor, ATV.
Campbell, Mark, assignment editor, ATV.
Ryan, Kelly, reporter, Maritime Independent Television (MITV).
Smith, Brett, director of programming, Halifax Cablevision.
Kingsbury, Al, reporter, HCH, Kentville.
Brown, Teresa, reporter, Kentville *Advertiser.*
Fox, Brent, reporter, Kentville *Advertiser.*
Christie, Kim, reporter, *Hants Journal.*
Spur, Bill, news director, Atlantic Valley Radio.
Fisher, Elizabeth, program director, Kings Cable.

BIBLIOGRAPHY

Abramson, Jeffrey B., F. Christopher Arterton and Gary R. Orren. 1988. *The Electronic Commonwealth.* New York: Basic Books.

Bell, David V.J., and Frederick J. Fletcher, eds. 1991. *Reaching the Voter: Constituency Campaigning in Canada.* Vol. 20 of the research studies of the Royal Commission on Electoral Reform and Party Financing. Ottawa and Toronto: RCERPF/Dundurn.

Bell, David V.J., Frederick J. Fletcher and Catherine M. Bolan. 1991. "Electoral Communication at the Constituency Level: Summary and Conclusion." In *Reaching the Voter: Constituency Campaigning in Canada,* ed. David V.J. Bell and Frederick J. Fletcher. Vol. 20 of the research studies of the Royal Commission on Electoral Reform and Party Financing. Ottawa and Toronto: RCERPF/Dundurn.

Canada. Statistics Canada. 1988. *Federal Electoral Districts – 1987 Representation Order: Part 1, Profiles.* Ottawa: Minister of Supply and Services Canada.

Caplan, Gerald, Michael Kirby and Hugh Segal. 1989. *Election: The Issues, the Strategies, the Aftermath.* Scarborough: Prentice-Hall.

Carty, R.K., and Lynda Erickson. 1991. "Candidate Nomination in Canada's National Political Parties." In *Canadian Political Parties: Leaders, Candidates and Organization,* ed. Herman Bakvis. Vol. 13 of the research studies of the Royal Commission on Electoral Reform and Party Financing. Ottawa and Toronto: RCERPF/Dundurn.

Clarke, Harold, Jane Jenson, Lawrence LeDuc and Jon Pammett. 1991. *Absent Mandate: Interpreting Change in Canadian Elections.* 2d ed. Toronto: Gage Publications.

Courtney, John C. 1981. "Campaign Strategy and Electoral Victory: The Progressive Conservatives and the 1979 Election." In *Canada at the Polls, 1979 and 1980: A Study of the General Elections,* ed. H.R. Penniman. Washington, DC: American Enterprise Institute for Public Policy Research.

Desbarats, Peter. 1990. *Guide to Canadian News Media.* Toronto: Harcourt Brace Jovanovich, Canada.

Downs, Anthony. 1957. *An Economic Theory of Democracy.* New York: Harper.

Eagles, D. Munroe, James P. Bickerton, Alain G. Gagnon and Patrick J. Smith. 1991. *Almanac of Canadian Politics.* Peterborough: Broadview.

Feigert, Frank. 1989. *Canada Votes: 1935–1988.* Durham: Duke University Press.

Fletcher, Frederick J. 1987. "Mass Media and Parliamentary Elections in Canada." *Legislative Studies Quarterly* 12:341–72.

———. 1990. "The Media and Elections in Canada: An Overview." Issue paper prepared for the Royal Commission on Electoral Reform and Party Financing. Ottawa.

Frizzell, Alan, Jon Pammett and Anthony Westell. 1989. *The Canadian General Election of 1988.* Ottawa: Carleton University Press.

Johnston, Richard, André Blais, Henry E. Brady and Jean Crête. 1991. "Letting the People Decide: Dynamics of a Canadian Election." Typescript of a forthcoming volume based on the 1988 Canadian National Election Study. With permission of the authors.

Lee, Robert Mason. 1989. *One Hundred Monkeys.* Toronto: Macfarlane Walter and Ross.

Maclean's/Decima. 1988. "The Voters Reflect." 5 December.

Nova Scotia. Department of Industry, Trade and Technology. 1990a. *Annapolis Valley Region: Statistical Profile.* Halifax: Statistics and Research Services.

———. 1990b. *Halifax County Region: Statistical Profile.* Halifax: Statistics and Research Services.

Sayers, Anthony M. 1991. "Local Issue Space in National Elections: Kootenay West–Revelstoke and Vancouver Centre." In *Reaching the Voter: Constituency Campaigning in Canada,* ed. David V.J. Bell and Frederick J. Fletcher. Vol. 20 of the research studies of the Royal Commission on Electoral Reform and Party Financing. Ottawa and Toronto: RCERPF/Dundurn.

Taras, David. 1990. *The Newsmakers: The Media's Influence on Canadian Politics.* Scarborough: Nelson Canada.

7

ELECTORAL COMMUNICATION AT THE CONSTITUENCY LEVEL
Summary and Conclusion

David V.J. Bell
Frederick J. Fletcher
Catherine M. Bolan

CANADIAN DEMOCRACY IS in crisis. Overwhelmingly, and in some instances dramatically, public attention has been focused on constitutional aspects of the crisis: Quebec's position in Canada and its implication for other priorities on the national agenda; concerns over regional representation in Ottawa; and the claims of Canada's Aboriginal peoples for self-government. The work of the Royal Commission on Electoral Reform and Party Financing will have little impact on the first of these pressing national problems. Its recommendations, however, will touch the other two and can affect profoundly another, perhaps less visible, aspect of our political malaise: the crisis of democratic participation.

A recent study of citizen's attitudes in the United States by the Kettering Foundation (1991) examined growing concerns among the American public about the political process. Many felt that important public issues are usually discussed by policy and opinion leaders, the media and others in a way that neither connects with their concerns nor makes any sense to them. Ultimately, the public feels disconnected from political debate (ibid., 4). Feeling "squeezed out" of the political system, they believe that their connection to politics, through their elected and appointed officials, has been severed.

Many people are unable to see themselves reflected in the way issues are currently discussed during election campaigns (and at other times), especially with respect to national institutions. They feel they have no say in national decisions. As the Kettering study found, however, there is a greater sense of being heard when public discussion reflects issues closer to home (Kettering 1991, 44). It was felt that if the bigger issues – such as education, homelessness and health care – were localized, the public would see their concerns reflected in the way current issues are discussed. The essential element in electoral democracy – public dialogue – is felt to have shifted out of the hands of the electorate.

In a recent speech, Pierre Lortie, Chair of the Royal Commission on Electoral Reform and Party Financing, placed the concerns about the current and future status of our electoral democracy into an analytical framework for electoral reform. The points raised by Mr. Lortie can serve as a blueprint for a healthier democracy that would provide Canadians with higher standards of responsiveness and greater input into their electoral system. The first task in reforming the electoral process is to secure and strengthen the democratic rights of citizens as electors. Second, we must encourage effective representation within parliamentary government through greater citizen accountability, by improving regional representation, and by broadening the fabric of representation to integrate the various linguistic, ethnic and religious groups into Canadian politics (and into the public debate in the media). Third, we must strengthen the capacities of political parties as the primary political organizations. This is especially the case given the proliferation of special-interest groups and their pursuit of single-policy positions outside party organizations and given changes in the media that have altered the relationship of the party organization with the grass roots. Fourth, electoral regulations must establish fairness among parties and candidates in terms of spending limits, free and paid broadcast time and coverage of the campaign by the media. Finally, Canadian democracy must enhance public confidence in the integrity of the electoral process and representative government. Mr. Lortie also expressed the view that informed discussion of electoral reform must recognize the importance and influence of the media in modern election campaigns. In his words, the responsiveness of the electoral system and public confidence in it are influenced at least as much by the practices of the media as by those of other participants in the process. The responsibility for delivering the information upon which voters hold their representatives accountable rests with the media; its coverage must be timely, accurate and supportive of quality public debate.

The role of the media in election campaigns is the subject of debate within the industry itself, where considerable discussion on the issue of public accountability has resulted in some instances in codes of ethics and industry guidelines. Some initiatives at the national level include the "Statement of Principles" of the Canadian Daily Newspaper Association (CDNA). In addition, most provinces now have press councils which act as complaint mechanisms. (There have been recent suggestions that press councils are the most obvious body to establish a national set of ethics for the Canadian newspaper industry.) As well, smaller dailies such as the *Kitchener-Waterloo Record* have developed codes of ethics for their employees. Most of these codes, however, do not contain guidelines dealing directly with election coverage. An exception is the Canadian Press (CP). Among other things, CP's *Stylebook* provides guidance to journalists on the methodological aspects of interpreting and reporting polls, such as the margin of error, accuracy of the results, sample size and response rate. Many newspapers, as well as the CBC, have appointed ombudsmen as liaisons to the public. More recently, the Canadian Broadcast Standards Council and the Cable Television Standards Council have developed codes of ethics.

The desirable characteristics of a more responsive electoral democracy are particularly salient for an analysis of the campaign at the local level, for the constituency-level campaign embodies in microcosm virtually all of the issues and concerns expressed in Mr. Lortie's five points. Accordingly, the findings and conclusions presented here, although based on our research on campaign communication at the local level, address the crisis of participatory democracy in a national context.

THE CASE STUDIES

Each of the case studies reported in this volume has focused on different aspects of the research protocol and therefore each approaches the problem of studying local campaigns and the mass media from a slightly different angle. This variation in design results in a rich exploration of themes and issues. Although the studies address similar questions, each makes a distinctive contribution. The differences among the studies make it desirable to begin by outlining the contributions of each before attempting general observations.

British Columbia (Anthony Sayers)

Local issue space represents the local information on which voters make their voting decisions. The size and quality of local issue space are directly affected by several factors, the most significant of which are the number and quality of available media, the demography of the constituency, the resources available to the candidate and the relative independence of the candidate from regional or national party strategists and demands.

Sayers found that a major difference in the information environment of the two BC ridings was the extent to which issues were presented in the media. In Vancouver Centre (VC), there was a wider range of local issues, and they were targeted to specific groups, such as women, lesbian and gay, and "ethnic" voters. In Kootenay West–Revelstoke (KW-R), the free trade issue was effectively localized, yet this process was also restricted to some extent by the available resources of the media. Sayers argues that the more localized interpretation of the free trade issue by the media in KW-R was due to the lesser extent to which local, regional and national issues "melded" as they did in VC.

Sayers did not observe the degree of integration between national and local party and media organizations found by Leonard Preyra in Nova Scotia. In VC, he found virtually no relationship between the national and local Conservative campaigns, noting very little input by the local organization into the national party's substantial advertising campaign in the region. Rather, the local Conservatives were closer to the provincial arm of the party. Similarly, the major VC dailies placed more value on a good British Columbia story than a national story of equal significance.

In general, considerable campaign information was available for electors in both British Columbia constituencies. Both national campaign themes and local concerns were articulated to some degree by the campaigns. However, the information was often presented in terms not directly salient to local voters, and local issue coverage often gave way to national "horse-race" coverage.

Ontario (David V.J. Bell and Catherine M. Bolan)

Free trade dominated the campaign agendas and the media coverage in both Ontario constituencies. When the focus shifted away from free trade, the discourse of the local campaign echoed national themes and arguments. While many of these national issues had important local implications (such as free trade in the agriculture-based riding of Perth–Wellington–Waterloo), neither the candidates nor the media explored them in local terms.

Bell and Bolan also raised several issues regarding campaign financing and expenditure regulations, including possible controls on expenses for seeking the nomination; possible tax deductions for individuals contributing to nomination campaigns; free-time requirements on community cable channels (especially given the rising prominence of that medium in election campaigns and the desirability of avoiding large-scale paid television advertising at the local level); and simplification of regulations concerning financing and expenditures.

As in British Columbia, electors in Ontario received considerable campaign information. Even more than in BC, however, national issues predominated, and there was no real attempt, by the media or most candidates, to explain the local implications of national issues.

Alberta (Andrew Beh and Roger Gibbins)

In Calgary, it was found that newspapers generally concentrated on "personalities" and conflicts rather than on the policies and platforms that were expressed at staged events such as press conferences. When stories were initiated by party organizations, they were more likely to involve policies and platforms, although the final press stories still tended to focus on personalities and conflicts. Local candidates were lost in a "jungle" of stories pertaining to free trade and to the national campaigns, leaders, parties and issues. Local coverage in Macleod, as in Calgary, meant in reality increased coverage of the national campaign, leaders and/or issues as viewed through the prism of the constituency campaign. Even in the rural riding of Macleod, where the community weeklies gave relatively greater coverage to the local campaign, local coverage had a very national flavour.

Without a national campaign, it appears that the Reform Party did not receive as much coverage as its strength in these ridings would suggest. Nevertheless, it was by no means ignored. In general, voters in the Alberta ridings were provided with national and regional information sufficient to make a reasoned voting decision, but local campaign information was more difficult to find.

Quebec (Luc Bernier)

Both Outremont and Frontenac were very fertile media environments during the 1988 campaign, yet they produced largely superficial coverage and little issue-based analysis. Outremont and Frontenac differed from the other constituencies in these studies, where the free trade issue dominated the political and media agendas. Bernier reports that Meech Lake and abortion were both major and emotional issues.

In general, both candidates and media felt that local candidates have very little impact on the outcome of elections. In these ridings, covering local election campaigns was not a priority for the local media. There were no all-candidates debates.

Regulations regarding financing and expenditures were seen as being too permeable, particularly in the calculation of admissible expenses. There were numerous instances where campaign expenditures had occurred before the accountable time period. As well, candidates and organizers felt that limits on election expenses were too low for effective campaigning and should be raised.

Bernier found a considerable lack of alignment among the federal, provincial and local branches of the Conservative and Liberal parties. The regional issue of Meech Lake seems to have played a prominent role, drawing various factions of provincial Liberals, Parti québécois and the Union nationale into the local Conservative organizations. This, Bernier argues, upholds the view expressed by media and political organizers that the local campaign and traditional party organization generally have a minimal impact on electoral results in Quebec. Apparently, the "nationalist vote" secured the Conservative victory in both ridings.

The campaigns in these Quebec constituencies appear to have been sufficiently differentiated from the national campaigns to suggest that electors received considerable information to assist them in their vote decisions. Nevertheless, purely local information was not readily available.

Atlantic Region (Leonard Preyra)

Leonard Preyra explored three main themes involving the "vertical integration" into a national context of local issues and practices among political or media organizations: first, the relationship between national and local branches of parties; second, the relationship between local and national media; and third, the local campaign team and the local media. Preyra concluded that the local party communications and media coverage "mirrored the national campaign," and both the parties and the local media made themselves "dependent on their parent organizations" in order to realize "economies of scale." The capacity of the local campaigns to make national issues relevant to their electors was limited by resources and degree of integration of national and local organizations.

GENERAL FINDINGS

In examining the findings of the case studies, our main objective has been to assess the extent to which the communication needs of parties and the information needs of voters during election campaigns are met at the level of constituency campaigns. While the 10 constituencies cannot be considered representative, they provide a range of experiences from which some conclusions can be drawn. We can also compare some of our findings with those of a recent survey of constituency association executives.[1]

In general, our researchers found that local campaigns are "miniature replicas of the national race" (Bell and Bolan). Similarly, Beh and Gibbins note that "while the local candidates and campaigns did not vanish without a trace, they were clearly overwhelmed and all but submerged by the national campaign." Nevertheless, local campaigns did have some capacity to differentiate themselves from the national campaigns of their parties. We found two instances among the major parties in which candidates worked hard to distance themselves from their leaders and others where campaign materials generated by the national party organizations were dismissed as "useless."

As far as issues are concerned, the extent to which local issues were articulated or national issues explained in local terms varied considerably among the constituencies. Free trade was both a local and a national issue, although it was more localized in ridings such as Kootenay West–Revelstoke. The media localized national issue stories (or used national wire stories with local angles), but lack of resources limited this process. In larger urban ridings such as Vancouver Centre, a wider range of media resulted in a broader mix of issues from local, regional and national perspectives. In Alberta, few purely local issues were evident, though local perspectives on national issues were present in some news coverage. Even where the focus was on the local candidate, the issues were national. In Ontario, while many national issues had important local implications, neither the media nor candidates presented them in that way.

The content analysis conducted in Nova Scotia showed that national leaders got four times the press coverage of local candidates. The focus there was overwhelmingly national. Even local stories tended to be inspired by national developments.

In the Quebec ridings, according to Bernier, organizers felt that national issues were the most important factors in voting; however, voters in Outremont and Frontenac were unfamiliar with the platforms of the federal parties. Talk about free trade in many ridings was vague, and its impact on small business was not discussed.

The extent to which local campaigns relied upon national and provincial parties for campaign themes, materials and campaign literature varied. Bell and Bolan concluded that "local candidates assume their task is to 'speak the party line' " and that "the discourse of the local campaign mirrored national themes and arguments." In many ridings, local organizations received material under a group purchase arrangement that provided "considerable economies of scale" where the unit price of large posters or flyers for door-to-door distribution was greatly reduced. How local campaigns made use of party materials differed. Bernier noted that the Conservative candidate in Outremont used a photo of Mulroney for several ads in weekly papers; the Liberal candidate's ads featured a photo of the candidate alone.

Some organizations felt that national organizations did little to help local campaigns once the election was called. Others relied extensively on press releases from head office, adding "spins" on local candidates before using them to communicate with media organizations. The same applied to radio advertising where the local candidates would "tag" their names onto the end of standard "spots." Preyra noted that the availability of "campaign packages" from the national parties had a "nationalizing" effect on the local campaign. However, Sayers noted that the campaign literature in the British Columbia ridings had a definite local emphasis, giving local campaigns a clear impact on local issue space. The campaign process leaves room for at least some local emphasis in most ridings, but it is not always used.

Constituency-level campaigns still rely extensively on "traditional" methods of campaign communication, with particular emphasis on canvassing and literature drops. Other traditional activities, such as all-candidates debates, seemed to be shifting from the town hall to the TV studio, primarily on cable channels and especially in urban areas. While the print media were preferred for advertising, they were used sparingly because of cost and undetermined impact on voters. Some organizations placed advertisements in the weekly papers solely to maintain good relations with management. Television was generally not used for local publicity because of cost and lack of fit between riding and broadcast areas. Radio was used quite sparingly, except in rural areas. Candidates communicated with the media regularly through faxed press releases. In some ridings, news coverage was more important to campaigns where advertising was seen as lacking in credibility. According to Beh and Gibbins, local campaign organizations in Alberta did little more than "inform reporters about scheduled, formal events."

The balance among local, national and regional issues varied. Our qualitative and quantitative analysis of newspaper content revealed a predominance of national issues (or local stories that echoed national themes and arguments). In urban Calgary West, for example, only 13 percent of election coverage was oriented toward the local campaign. In the rural riding of Macleod, local candidates and campaigns received more than twice the space devoted to the national campaign, and in some cases the ratio of local to national was greater than four to one. Our interviews with media and party organizations, however, revealed a perception that, in general, coverage was balanced. This sentiment was echoed by party strategists responding to the national survey of constituency associations, of whom 50 percent felt that the principal media in their ridings provided balanced coverage of both local and national campaigns. Opinion was evenly split on whether the media focused more on the national campaign and ignored local contests (25 percent) or focused primarily on the local candidates and campaign (25 percent) (Carty 1991). Obviously, perceptions differ widely on this issue. (This may be due, in part, to competing definitions of a local issue.)

Coverage in local news media clearly reflected both the priorities of the news organizations and the campaign effort and skill of the candidates and their workers. However, at least some journalists approach local campaigns with the conviction that they are inherently boring, an attitude that limits attention to even the most creative local campaign. Nevertheless, it seems clear that the failure to articulate local issues in many ridings was at least as much the responsibility of the candidates as of the news media.

"Bell-wether" ridings, perceived as predicting the national outcome, are followed more extensively by the media. One such riding, Outremont, received more coverage in the major Montreal newspapers than any other riding in the city. The same pattern held for the ridings in Vancouver and Halifax. These ridings, unlike most others, also received coverage outside the area.

Lack of resources was a major impediment to more extensive coverage and to more in-depth analysis of the issues and stories of the campaign. Many media personnel lamented the lack of time, space and staff to undertake more investigative reporting. Some campaign organizations took advantage of the lack of staff at news organizations by providing "ready-to-publish" materials. Some reporters felt they were being "used" as publicity vehicles. Others claimed that "the campaign is organized as a show which leaves no room for detailed questions." Journalists in Calgary argued that the shortage of local emphasis was a result of the "lack of freshness and excitement in local constituency politics."

Stories in the local press tended to focus on rallies, events (mostly staged) and visits to the ridings by touring party notables. As with the national campaign, much of the coverage featured hecklers, moments of confrontation between candidates, and personalities. News coverage of local candidates often decreased as the candidates' positions became known. They were seen by journalists as "rehashing the same information." This is typical of campaign coverage and reflects standard news values. It is, however, unfortunate in terms of voter information needs. Journalists and attentive voters become "saturated" with campaign information long before most voters begin to pay attention. The availability of substantive campaign information declines just when less attentive voters need it most. Campaign advertising peaks later. It fills the gap to a degree but tends to focus on the national campaign.

The overlap of the municipal and federal campaigns in several provinces, along with the limited resources in the case of the smaller papers, forced several media organizations to focus on one campaign at the expense of the other. The local media were also found to have played a major role in shaping the local political debate by compiling candidate profiles around a specific set of topics, mostly national issues.

There was some evidence of the "incumbent advantage" noted in previous studies, but the content analysis in Nova Scotia did not demonstrate measurable media bias. However, incumbent members, especially on the government side, were able to use announcements of grants or policies as a source of publicity. In Ontario, Bill Attewell's status as MP enabled him to distribute newsletters to the newly drawn riding before the election was called. In one case, journalists were somewhat intimidated by the incumbent and avoided reporting anything that might provoke him. Despite some advantages, incumbents often felt targeted by an oppositional media. Journalists noted that incumbents are more widely known and often have more credible campaigns. Whatever advantage incumbents might have, Canada's relatively high rate of turnover among MPs indicates that challengers are often successful.

Even with a small sample of 10 constituencies, we found that local campaign strategies differed significantly by riding. First, ridings varied along urban and rural lines. In rural ridings, there was more emphasis on "traditional" methods of campaigning, where voters held high expectations of personal contact and might get "offended" if the candidate did not call personally. Media environments differed extensively in the two settings. In rural ridings, there was more local media attention to the constituency campaign, as well as a higher level of campaign activities, such as all-candidates debates. News coverage, however, tended to ignore substantive issues.

Second, riding size is also a factor. Large ridings (which also tend to be rural) place considerable stress on the financial and human resources of party organizers as a result of the need for extensive travel and multiple campaign offices. Media coverage was similarly impeded by lack of time and personnel to cover events in large ridings. Perhaps, as a result, radio played a more prominent role.

The findings of the Royal Commission's survey of constituency associations support our conclusion that media use differed significantly between rural and urban ridings. While the print media were regarded as having some importance to the local campaign in most ridings, they were perceived as very important in 63 percent of rural ridings in contrast with 45 percent in urban ridings. The results for radio were similar: 78 percent of strategists in rural ridings regarded it as somewhat to very important, compared to 56 percent in urban ridings. There were no significant urban–rural differences on the importance of television, which ranked behind newspapers overall.

Targeting by the national parties was a significant factor in some local campaigns. This was certainly the case in the Ontario riding of Perth–Wellington–Waterloo, which was a close contest between the Conservative and Liberal candidates. The local campaign featured a steady stream of high-profile visitors, including several ministers and the prime minister. Campaign organizations devoted considerable resources to preparing for and trying to exploit these visits. The Conservatives recaptured the riding by a very close margin, less than one percent. In contrast, the riding of Markham, where the Conservative candidate won by the biggest plurality in Ontario, hosted very few visits. Across the country, key ridings received considerable attention, including targeted national advertising, while others received minimal assistance or, indeed, tried to distance themselves from the national campaigns.

In 1988, a program by the Progressive Conservative party involved the targeting of competitive ridings through new technologies such as direct mail and phone bank systems. Entitled "Target '88," approximately 200 000 potentially "switchable" voters were contacted through a series of letters and phone calls from the national party in an attempt to identify voters' concerns, recruit volunteers and mobilize the vote. The information was also used for local material to insert into Prime Minister Mulroney's speeches in particular ridings (Lee 1989, 261–65). The program was deemed successful by the party organizers and will likely be used in the next campaign. It may well be emulated by other parties. In 1988, local associations could opt in at a price: $5 000 and 10 volunteers. Despite the local involvement and the probable gain in voter support for the candidate, control of the message remained national. The focus was on support for the party. In informational terms, the program did not strengthen local campaigns. Moreover, Robert Mason Lee (ibid., 263) noted that the tactic shifts "message development from the broad band of television to the narrow band of the computer."

With respect to the local campaigns themselves, there were considerable differences in media use patterns. For example, the willingness of party organizers to use cable community channels varied. In the Ontario ridings, all-candidates debates on the community channel were an important feature of the campaigns. Many of these featured phone-in segments in which viewers questioned candidates on a wide range of issues. This forum for elector-candidate interaction appears to be of increasing importance in larger urban centres, where attendance at "town hall" style meetings is in decline. In contrast, local strategists in the Nova Scotia ridings did not use a good deal of the community channel time they were offered, claiming that "nobody watches it." Communication researchers, noting developments in the United States, argue that failure to use this channel is short-sighted, and that cable companies and party organizations can build audiences for such programming (Desbarats 1991).

News coverage was limited in most ridings. Potentially important local issues were ignored because they did not fit the narrative line on the campaign taken by the national media. This agenda was set by the national parties and the national media and made it difficult for local candidates or regional parties to become part of the discourse. Minor parties often felt that no matter how "newsworthy" their statements or activities, they were given little attention (Hackett 1991). Media access is, of course, extremely important to many minor parties that run candidates with little chance of winning in the hope of injecting into the campaign discourse issues that they feel strongly about. The proliferation of parties with a reasonable chance to win will challenge the campaign coverage practices of the media.

CONCERNS AND ISSUES

The case studies raised a series of concerns that apply to local campaigns in general, especially to their efforts to get their messages out to voters and to compete for election in a context of fairness.

Campaign Volunteers

At the local level, interpersonal communication through canvassing remains an important part of the campaign process. The researchers noted that a considerable number of the campaign organizations studied suffered from a shortage of volunteers. A national survey of local party strategists confirms these findings. Party organizations required an average of 231 volunteers to run an effective local campaign, according to local organizers; in 1988, each campaign had an average of 170 volunteers (Carty 1991). Recruiting for campaign activities appears to be an increasing problem. Perhaps, as noted by Bell and Bolan, this is a reflection of changing social conditions with both spouses working outside the home and the increasing numbers of single-parent families. Fewer people have time for outside activities. The general trend is compounded by increasing job-related time pressures and, in some jurisdictions, overlapping election campaigns that deplete the energies of activists.

Many organizations also reported that worker morale was heavily influenced by poll results. As Luc Bernier found, the impact was especially critical near the end of the campaign where, even though numbers of volunteers had stabilized, a favourable poll that boosted worker morale could have a considerable impact on the local campaign. Bernier also reported that leaders debates had a direct effect on volunteer morale.

Low numbers of volunteers kept the distribution of campaign literature below optimum levels in some cases. This is a problem for local strategists, given that the distribution of campaign literature is one of the most important campaign strategies, with 86 percent claiming it to be very important or somewhat important in their campaigns. This tactic ranked third after canvassing (93 percent) and getting material in local newspapers (91 percent) (Carty 1991). Sayers also noted that volunteers are seen as giving the local candidate credibility.

Published Polls

News reports of polls are becoming major components of election campaign coverage in the national, regional and local media. As a result, both urban and rural ridings experienced the impact of polls in 1988. Seventy-seven percent of local party strategists reported that polls made a difference to the local contest in 1988. Increasingly, polls are an important aspect of local party strategy. Over one-third of ridings did their own polling in 1988; the same number thought the information changed their campaign (Carty 1991).

Sayers noted that the reportage of national poll results in the community papers in his rural riding reduced local issue space. Even some journalists and editors are concerned about possible bandwagon effects and the "crowding out" of local stories by poll reports. The appeal of polls to the news media is explained by David Taras: "Polls are irresistible to the media. They create dramatic headline stories where winners and losers are declared, and they allow news organizations to demonstrate that they are on top of the latest information" (Taras 1990, 180).

Advocacy Groups

The campaign activities of advocacy groups in 1988, especially single-issue groups, were of considerable concern to many local party organizations. Campaign managers, restricted by spending limits and other regulations, resented the fact that advocacy groups were not subject to electoral laws. Leonard Preyra reported that the Halifax riding was one of those targeted by national interest groups, resulting in an unfair advantage or disadvantage for particular candidates. Such targeting can have a strong impact on the local campaigns. Such was the case in the riding of Outremont, where Lucie Pépin's pro-choice platform was subjected to extensive third-party intervention by the national pro-life network. The impact of advocacy groups on local issue space varied considerably. In some, there was little activity or advocacy group efforts had limited impact, as Sayers found in the two BC ridings. In others, their influence on the local campaign was significant. Half of all local party executives who responded to the Carty survey reported that a "single issue interest group" played an active role in the local campaign in an attempt to support or oppose their candidate. Of the groups identified, 51.2 percent were pro-life and 26.4 percent mobilized around the issue of free trade.

DISCUSSION

In designing their research, the contributors to this volume had to confront a conceptual problem that proved more difficult than it first appeared: what is a local issue? To a considerable degree, their approach to this question determined their conclusions. Those who defined the concept "local issue" narrowly, as in effect issues unique to a particular constituency or community, found that local issues played almost no role in federal election campaigns. Those who defined the concept as issues with a distinct local impact or focus – as, for example, the threat to or opportunities for a local industry posed by the Free Trade Agreement – found that local issues had a larger role. Even with that definition, however, the local element in campaigns was limited in most ridings. Nevertheless, we believe that the latter formulation is the more appropriate, especially in the light of citizen concerns about the relevance of politics to their lives. While distinct local issues may well emerge in federal election campaigns, the effectiveness of campaign communication as a factor in political legitimacy may be assessed more appropriately in terms of the extent to which local campaigns bring out the local significance of the major issues of the national campaign.

Sayers has demonstrated that the character of the riding, the relationship of the local, provincial and national party organizations, and the structure of the media are all influential in determining the extent of local issue space. Regional factors remain important in voting (Irvine 1981), and the major parties are increasingly targeting their appeals to specific competitive ridings and groups. Although campaign themes tend to be national, sometimes with differences between English and French, they are often given a regional or even local "spin" by campaign strategists.

It would appear that candidates, media and voters all see federal elections as national events that should focus on national issues rather than local concerns. "There are no local issues in federal elections," one campaign manager said. "The ... party could have elected a poodle in this riding," complained one unsuccessful candidate. People do not care who the candidate is, according to many of those interviewed. They vote for the party and the leader. Local campaigns are of marginal significance. These views appear to be widely accepted by party strategists and observers, though many local candidates still "run scared" because even a few votes could make the difference.

If there is public demand for effective local campaigns and the translation of national issues into local concerns, will political competition not force the parties to meet those needs? While there is an incentive in the process of electoral competition for parties to meet voter needs, their primary concern is with winning enough seats to form a government. Therefore, they will focus their campaigns on two major objectives: (1) consolidating and mobilizing their core voters and (2) reaching those voters they identify as possible converts to their cause. Their focus during campaigns is short-term. This orientation may lead to effective local campaigns in some ridings, but it will not promote effective linkage between citizens and candidates overall. It is important, therefore, to consider other means to promote effective local campaign communication.

Local campaign communication has been profoundly altered by new telecommunications technologies. In the pretechnology era, political dialogue occurred predominantly at the local level, through the constituency associations of political parties. According to one observer, voters had a clearer perception of the local candidate than of the national leader (Lee 1989, 29). While new technologies such as polling, advertising and especially television have transformed political campaigning at the national level, their impact in the constituencies has also been considerable. The emphasis of campaigning has shifted from the local candidate to the national leader, and the leader's emphasis has shifted from regional concerns to national ones. New technologies such as television have not eliminated parties as the primary political organizations but have transformed the party from a bottom-up to a top-down organization (ibid., 28–37).

As the Canadian National Election Survey data show, fully 27 percent of those surveyed in 1988 say they voted on the basis of the local candidate (including, however, his or her party affiliation). While this figure is an accurate representation of what voters tell interviewers and has held over several elections, party strategists and analysts do not believe it gives a true indication of voter motivations and behaviour. Nevertheless, it may be an indicator of an increasingly widespread popular desire for a greater role for and accountability of local MPs. The "crisis in Canadian democracy" has many facets, one of which features a sense of frustration that members always seem to vote the party line and fail to represent the views of their constituents.[2] An appeal to this malaise is one of the strengths of the Reform Party.

Observers have noted a strong desire to restore the integrity, vitality and scope of the public dialogue, beginning with the way the public joins in the discussion of major policy issues. Public dialogue is seen as pivotal because it is the "natural home for democratic politics ... People depend on the dialogue to provide opportunities for the public to hold counsel with itself and give public definition to the public's interest" (Kettering 1991, vi). Perhaps rather than a need for more information in order to make political choices, the real need is for different kinds of information. From this perspective, too much political discourse involves politicians – and media pundits – talking rather than listening.

Reconnecting the public to the political process – specifically, the policy issues that are considered – would involve rethinking the way the political agenda is set to more clearly reflect the concerns of the public in current political debate (Kettering 1991). It would also involve providing the public with a clearer sense of where they fit into various policy issues and their connection to them by localizing policy issues. Despite the strong national focus of politics in the United States and Canada, most citizens want to know how national policies affect their communities. In addition, as the Kettering respondents complained, much political reporting is incomprehensible. Issues tend to be debated in language and concepts, using specialized jargon and "professional speak," that obscure their importance to individuals and communities. This makes clear the need for local campaigns and local members to have an important role in connecting citizens to the political process and reinforcing its legitimacy.

Journalist Robert Mason Lee, having looked at the 1988 federal election campaign in his book *One Hundred Monkeys*, concluded that changes in the nature of campaign communication have resulted in a similar feeling of alienation among voters in Canada. In particular, he noted that the conduct of campaigns no longer responded to, or reflected, regional and local concerns (Lee 1989, 39). This, he claims, is directly related to advances in new telecommunications technologies:

> Although Canadians were able to observe the political process as never before, ... they found the distance between themselves and the political process increasing. Rather than enjoying a more intimate political dialogue, they found themselves confronted with a hot line to strangers. The technologies did not create an actual dialogue, such as that between a community and its riding association, but the illusion of a dialogue, between everyman and the disconnected electrons of a television image. (Lee 1989, 40)

It has also been argued that the news media are partly responsible for the alienation of many Americans from politics. News coverage of politics is frustrating for many voters because it fails to provide timely information on issues of concern to them and often does not present sufficient background to make current events comprehensible. The coverage tends to focus on the more sensational aspects of politics – disasters, scandals and politicians' personal lives – rather than on matters of substance, respondents said. The Kettering respondents were also alienated by the negativism of campaigns, in both advertising and news coverage. As one respondent put it: "We talk more about the 'horserace' aspects of elections and campaigns than we do about the candidates' positions on issues" (Kettering 1991, 55).

Leonard Preyra is quite right to refer to the normative problem as a "dilemma." In order to reconcile the public demand and need for effective representation of local concerns with the need for strong national leadership, suggested reform must indeed "steer a middle course between the Scylla and Charybdis of excessive nationalization and localization." Without restructuring our parliamentary system and abandoning party discipline, some minor reforms would permit more "free" votes and greater autonomy for Canadian backbenchers to vote according to their conscience or constituency preference. (The British Parliament could provide lessons in this regard. Canadian party discipline is viewed by some as more rigid than in the Soviet bloc prior to perestroika!) A move to greater autonomy from the party, however, raises the possibility that many members might reduce their constituency service work, which is now their major link with their constituents, in favour of more policy-oriented work in committees or the House of Commons. Such a shift could actually reduce links with constituents, especially if the policy work was not highly visible at home (Price and Mancuso 1991, 217).

In parliamentary systems based on single-member district electoral systems, there is an inevitable tension between the assumptions underlying the doctrine of responsible government and those related to territorial representation. Responsible government requires party discipline, not only for stability, but also so that the governing party can be held collectively accountable for the actions of the government it supports. Party discipline, however, weakens the link between the individual MPs and their constituents. Even when regional caucuses within the government party demonstrate considerable influence, that influence is often invisible because caucus secrecy is jealously guarded and claims of influence may be met with scepticism. We have noted, above, that Canadians appear to want more effective regional and local representation. It is possible, however, that the way in which election campaigns are presented to them is one factor in persuading them that their representatives are unimportant. Indeed, when MPs owe their elections to the party leader and the national campaign, their influence is likely to be weakened (Fletcher 1987, 367).

How, then, do we "reconnect" the public with politics? One way would be to make elected and appointed officials more accountable for their actions, such as through campaign finance reform, codes of ethics and so on. These actions, while well-intentioned, will improve the situation only marginally. More significant reforms might aim at creating a more constructive and dynamic relationship among citizens, public officials, the media and interest groups. The task is to create more room for citizens and community groups in a public discourse that tends to be dominated by politicians and large organizations. The institutions of direct democracy, operative in some American states, focus more on policy decisions than dialogue, and those processes tend also to be dominated by large organizations and professionals (Kettering 1991, 7–8). The need in a parliamentary system appears to be for more interaction between representatives and citizens and more accessible forums at the community and constituency level for free and open discussion.

It is possible that the local campaign would achieve more importance if the level of political debate were higher. The tendency for the national campaign to become a television spectacle of 10-second "sound bites" and expensive negative advertisements need not be repeated at the constituency level. On the contrary, local candidates could help raise the level of debate if they had more resources and incentives to relate national issues to the local constituency or region. Substantive campaigns at the local level might well gain greater media attention. This conclusion was supported by all of the authors engaged in this project.

POSSIBLE REFORMS

Although there is debate among our contributors regarding the appropriate balance among local, regional and national campaigns, it seems clear that more effective local campaigns would benefit voters and reinforce the legitimacy of the electoral system. There is, however, little scope for direct state intervention. Perhaps the most useful directions for reform involve increasing the opportunities and incentives for better local campaigns and improved campaign coverage.

Parliamentary reform that provides greater scope for MPs might make the role of constituency representation more visible. This, in turn, would increase the importance of local campaigns. Incumbents already have ample subsidies for constituency communication between elections. Incumbents, however, must also confront challengers and respond to public concerns in forums that promote open, accessible, public dialogue.

Candidates must remain free to run their own campaigns, but access for local candidates to the media could be improved. Financial resources and problems of "fit" between constituency boundaries and media service areas limit advertising opportunities, but more use could be made of local radio stations and cable community channels for all-candidates debates, phone-in shows and the like. Access is now legally provided for the registered parties through both paid- and free-time provisions, but not for candidates, whether representing parties or running as Independents. Provision of free time and sale of paid time are optional at the local level. Access to legally mandated broadcast time is controlled by the national organizations of registered parties. One possible reform would be to require local radio stations and cable community channels to provide time for local candidates and/or organize debates and phone-in programs.

Many working journalists at the local level felt poorly prepared for federal election coverage. They lacked information on the constituencies they were covering and on the electoral process itself. Elections Canada could assist here by assembling materials that could be used as background. Another suggestion for improving the public discourse during election campaigns is to provide workshops for local media. These workshops could deal with the practical problems of campaign reporting as well as the ethical problems in providing "fair" coverage. Workshops could also explore likely issues in a forthcoming election and, more important, examine ways to bring out their local implications. Such workshops could deal with such obvious matters as how to gain access to the substantial data banks held by the Canadian Press and major media. The workshops could also deal with establishing guidelines for coverage and informing local journalists about existing guidelines. Workshops along these lines could encourage coverage that would strengthen democratic norms and foster public debate. This is the kind of public service that the various journalism organizations might undertake, perhaps in cooperation with Elections Canada and journalism schools.

The effectiveness of the workshops could be enhanced by developing a program of constituency internships. Information on local issues or the local implications of national issues is often lacking. A program to hire university students to prepare research studies to be distributed free of charge to local media and candidates would provide a better information base for local campaigns and, incidentally, promote youth involvement in the electoral process.

There are several areas in the electoral regulations themselves that could be reformed to improve local campaign communication. For example, more citizen involvement in the electoral process could be achieved by developing guidelines or regulations respecting the nomination process. Reforms would focus on timing, possible limits to spending and/or tax-credit allowances for campaign contributions for aspiring candidates. The underlying objective is to encourage effective representation and to establish fairness among parties and candidates. This objective relates directly to women, ethnic minorities, Aboriginal people and persons with disabilities who wish to seek the nomination but are discouraged because of existing systemic barriers.

Wider public involvement in the political process would also be encouraged by simplifying the language of election financing regulations while tightening up some provisions. For example, in the 1988 election, some parties benefited from "free" workers who were paid by their employer to work on the campaign. There are several areas where incumbents are believed to have an unfair advantage. For example, the existing regulations permit mailing of constituency newsletters to new constituents in a redrawn electoral district immediately before the election is called. It is important that challengers feel that they are competing on a level playing field and that the barriers to entry for candidates running as Independents or representing smaller parties not be excessive.

While the reforms suggested here are not major, they do confront directly the issue of linkage between citizens and their representatives in the House of Commons. It is important that our electoral regulations and practices strike an appropriate balance between party government and community representation. If the balance is tilted too far in either direction, the legitimacy of the system is threatened.

NOTES

1. *Constituency Party Association Organization and Activity: A Survey on Practice and Reform*. Under the direction of Professor R. Kenneth Carty of the University of British Columbia, a questionnaire was mailed to all constituencies in Canada and achieved a response rate of 53 percent. The data reported here are from a preliminary analysis; final figures may vary slightly. See Carty (1991).

2. These sentiments can be seen as progressive harbingers of a more active and involved citizenry or as atavistic relics of the kind of localistic orientations referred to two centuries ago by Edmund Burke in his "speech to the Bristol electors." A more plausible interpretation of why this development has emerged would link its appearance to the general Americanization of the Canadian political culture.

REFERENCES

Beh, Andrew, and Roger Gibbins. 1991. "The Campaign–Media Interface in Local Constituencies: Two Alberta Case Studies from the 1988 Federal Election Campaign." In *Reaching the Voter: Constituency Campaigning in Canada*, ed. David V.J. Bell and Frederick J. Fletcher. Vol. 20 of the research studies of the Royal Commission on Electoral Reform and Party Financing. Ottawa and Toronto: RCERPF/Dundurn.

Bell, David V.J., and Catherine M. Bolan. 1991. "The Mass Media and Federal Election Campaigning at the Local Level: A Case Study of Two Ontario Constituencies." In *Reaching the Voter: Constituency Campaigning in Canada.*, ed. David V.J. Bell and Frederick J. Fletcher. Vol. 20 of the research studies of the Royal Commission on Electoral Reform and Party Financing. Ottawa and Toronto: RCERPF/Dundurn.

Bernier, Luc. 1991. "Media Coverage of Local Campaigns: The 1988 Election in Outremont and Frontenac." In *Reaching the Voter: Constituency Campaigning in Canada*, ed. David V.J. Bell and Frederick J. Fletcher. Vol. 20 of the research studies of the Royal Commission on Electoral Reform and Party Financing. Ottawa and Toronto: RCERPF/Dundurn.

Carty, R.K. 1991. *Constituency Party Association Organization and Activity: A Survey on Practice and Reform*. Vancouver: University of British Columbia.

Desbarats, Peter. 1991. "Cable Television and Federal Election Campaigns in Canada." In *Election Broadcasting in Canada*, ed. Frederick J. Fletcher. Vol. 21 of the research studies of the Royal Commission on Electoral Reform and Party Financing. Ottawa and Toronto: RCERPF/Dundurn.

Fletcher, Frederick J. 1987. "Mass Media and Parliamentary Elections in Canada." *Legislative Studies Quarterly* 12 (3): 341–72.

Hackett, Robert A. 1991. "Smaller Voices: Minor Parties, Campaign Communication and the News Media." In *Reporting the Campaign: Election Coverage in Canada*, ed. Frederick J. Fletcher. Vol. 22 of the research studies of the Royal Commission on Electoral Reform and Party Financing. Ottawa and Toronto: RCERPF/Dundurn.

Irvine, William P. 1981. "The Canadian Voter." In *Canada at the Polls, 1979 and 1980: A Study of the General Elections*, ed. Howard R. Penniman. Washington, DC: American Enterprise Institute for Public Policy Research.

Kettering Foundation. 1991. *Citizens and Politics: A View from Main Street America*. Dayton: Kettering Foundation.

Lee, Robert Mason. 1989. *One Hundred Monkeys – The Triumph of Popular Wisdom in Canadian Politics*. Toronto: Macfarlane Walter and Ross.

Preyra, Leonard. 1991. "Riding the Waves: Parties, the Media and the 1988 Federal Election in Nova Scotia." In *Reaching the Voter: Constituency Campaigning in Canada*, ed. David V.J. Bell and Frederick J. Fletcher. Vol. 20 of the research studies of the Royal Commission on Electoral Reform and Party Financing. Ottawa and Toronto: RCERPF/Dundurn.

Price, Richard G., and Maureen Mancuso. 1991. "Ties That Bind: Parliamentary Members and Their Constituencies." In *Introductory Reading in Canadian Government and Politics*, ed. Robert M. Krause and R.H. Wagenberg. Toronto: Copp Clark Pitman.

Sayers, Anthony. 1991. "Local Issue Space in National Elections: Kootenay West–Revelstoke and Vancouver Centre." In *Reaching the Voter: Constituency Campaigning in Canada*, ed. David V.J. Bell and Frederick J. Fletcher. Vol. 20 of the research studies of the Royal Commission on Electoral Reform and Party Financing. Ottawa and Toronto: RCERPF/Dundurn.

Taras, David. 1990. *The Newsmakers: The Media's Influence on Canadian Politics*. Scarborough: Nelson Canada.

CONTRIBUTORS TO VOLUME 20

Andrew Beh — University of Calgary

David V.J. Bell — York University and Research Coordinator, RCERPF

Luc Bernier — École nationale d'administration publique

Catherine M. Bolan — York University

Frederick J. Fletcher — York University and Research Coordinator, RCERPF

Roger Gibbins — University of Calgary

Leonard Preyra — St. Mary's University

Anthony M. Sayers — University of British Columbia

ACKNOWLEDGEMENTS

The Royal Commission on Electoral Reform and Party Financing and the publishers wish to acknowledge with gratitude the permission of the following to reprint and translate material:

Gage Educational Publishing Company; *The Liberal* (Thornhill); *Pincher Creek Echo*.

Care has been taken to trace the ownership of copyright material used in the text, including the tables and figures. The authors and publishers welcome any information enabling them to rectify any reference or credit in subsequent editions.

Consistent with the Commission's objective of promoting full participation in the electoral system by all segments of Canadian society, gender neutrality has been used wherever possible in the editing of the research studies.

THE COLLECTED RESEARCH STUDIES*

* The titles of studies may not be final in all cases.

SYLVIA BASHEVKIN   Women's Participation in Political Parties

LISA YOUNG   Legislative Turnover and the Election of Women to the Canadian House of Commons

LYNDA ERICKSON   Women and Candidacies for the House of Commons

GERTRUDE J. ROBINSON AND ARMANDE SAINT-JEAN, WITH THE ASSISTANCE OF CHRISTINE RIOUX   Women Politicians and Their Media Coverage: A Generational Analysis

VOLUME 7
Ethno-cultural Groups and Visible Minorities in Canadian Politics: The Question of Access
Kathy Megyery, Editor

DAIVA K. STASIULIS AND YASMEEN ABU-LABAN   The House the Parties Built: (Re)constructing Ethnic Representation in Canadian Politics

ALAIN PELLETIER   Politics and Ethnicity: Representation of Ethnic and Visible-Minority Groups in the House of Commons

CAROLLE SIMARD, WITH THE ASSISTANCE OF SYLVIE BÉLANGER, NATHALIE LAVOIE, ANNE-LISE POLO AND SERGE TURMEL   Visible Minorities and the Canadian Political System

VOLUME 8
Youth in Canadian Politics: Participation and Involvement
Kathy Megyery, Editor

RAYMOND HUDON, BERNARD FOURNIER AND LOUIS MÉTIVIER, WITH THE ASSISTANCE OF BENOÎT-PAUL HÉBERT   To What Extent Are Today's Young People Interested in Politics? Inquiries among 16- to 24-Year-Olds

PATRICE GARANT   Revisiting the Voting Age Issue under the *Canadian Charter of Rights and Freedoms*

KATHY L. BROCK   Fairness, Equity and Rights

JANET HIEBERT   A Code of Ethics for Political Parties

VOLUME 13
Canadian Political Parties: Leaders, Candidates and Organization
Herman Bakvis, Editor

KEITH ARCHER   Leadership Selection in the New
                                 Democratic Party

GEORGE PERLIN   Attitudes of Liberal Convention
                                 Delegates toward Proposals for Reform
                                 of the Process of Leadership Selection

R.K. CARTY AND   Candidate Nomination in Canada's
LYNDA ERICKSON   National Political Parties

WILLIAM M. CHANDLER   Parties and Party Government in
AND ALAN SIAROFF   Advanced Democracies

RÉJEAN PELLETIER, WITH THE   The Structures of Canadian
COLLABORATION OF   Political Parties: How They Operate
FRANÇOIS BUNDOCK AND
MICHEL SARRA-BOURNET

KEITH ARCHER   The New Democrats, Organized
                                 Labour and the Prospects of Electoral
                                 Reform

VOLUME 14
Representation, Integration and Political Parties in Canada
Herman Bakvis, Editor

DAVID J. ELKINS   Parties as National Institutions:
                                 A Comparative Study

MAUREEN COVELL   Parties as Institutions of National
                                 Governance

RAND DYCK   Links between Federal and Provincial
                                 Parties and Party Systems

PAUL G. THOMAS   Parties and Regional Representation

DONALD E. BLAKE   Party Competition and Electoral
                                 Volatility: Canada in Comparative
                                 Perspective

JOHN FEREJOHN AND   The Personal Vote in Canada
BRIAN GAINES

ROBERT A. HACKETT,
WITH THE ASSISTANCE OF
JAMES MACKINTOSH,
DAVID ROBINSON AND
ARLENE SHWETZ

Smaller Voices: Minor Parties,
Campaign Communication and
the News Media

EILEEN SAUNDERS

Mass Media and the Reproduction
of Marginalization

VOLUME 23
*Canadian Political Parties in the Constituencies:
A Local Perspective*

R.K. CARTY

Canadian Political Parties in the
Constituencies: A Local Perspective

COMMISSION ORGANIZATION

CHAIRMAN
Pierre Lortie

COMMISSIONERS
Pierre Fortier
Robert Gabor
William Knight
Lucie Pépin

SENIOR OFFICERS

Executive Director
Guy Goulard

Director of Research
Peter Aucoin

Special Adviser to the Chairman
Jean-Marc Hamel

Research
F. Leslie Seidle,
　Senior Research Coordinator

Legislation
Jules Brière, Senior Adviser
Gérard Bertrand
Patrick Orr

Coordinators
Herman Bakvis
Michael Cassidy
Frederick J. Fletcher
Janet Hiebert
Kathy Megyery
Robert A. Milen
David Small

Communications and Publishing
Richard Rochefort, Director
Hélène Papineau, Assistant
　Director
Paul Morisset, Editor
Kathryn Randle, Editor

Assistant Coordinators
David Mac Donald
Cheryl D. Mitchell

Finance and Administration
Maurice R. Lacasse, Director

Contracts and Personnel
Thérèse Lacasse, Chief

Editorial, Design and Production Services

Royal Commission on Electoral Reform and Party Financing

Editors   Denis Bastien, Susan Becker Davidson, Ginette Bertrand, Louis Bilodeau, Claude Brabant, Louis Chabot, Danielle Chaput, Norman Dahl, Carlos del Burgo, Julie Desgagners, Chantal Granger, Volker Junginger, Denis Landry, André LaRose, Paul Morisset, Christine O'Meara, Mario Pelletier, Marie-Noël Pichelin, Kathryn Randle, Georges Royer, Eve Valiquette, Dominique Vincent.

Le Centre de Documentation Juridique du Québec Inc.

Hubert Reid, *President*

Claire Grégoire, *Comptroller*

Lucie Poirier, *Production Manager*
Gisèle Gingras, *Special Project Assistant*

Translators   Pierre-Yves de la Garde, Richard Lapointe, Marie-Josée Turcotte.

Technical Editors   Stéphane Côté Coulombe, *Coordinator*;
Josée Chabot, Danielle Morin.

Copy Editors   Martine Germain, Lise Larochelle, Elisabeth Reid, Carole St-Louis, Isabelle Tousignant, Charles Tremblay, Sébastien Viau.

Word Processing   André Vallée.

Formatting   Typoform, Claude Audet; Linda Goudreau, *Formatting Coordinator*.

Wilson & Lafleur Ltée

Claude Wilson, *President*

Printed and bound in Canada by
Best Gagné Book Manufacturers